The Law and Social Work

D0238035

Gower College Swansea
Library
Coleg Gŵyr Abertawe
Llyrfgell

Open University course:
The law and social work in England and Wales

This reader forms part of an Open University course The law and social work in England and Wales (K270), a 60 points second level undergraduate course. The course aims to develop skills, values and knowledge for those working in the social care, social work field.

Opinions expressed in the reader are not necessarily those of the Course Team or of The Open University.

Details of this and other Open University courses can be obtained from the Student Registration and Enquiry Service, The Open University, PO Box 197, Milton Keynes MK7 6BJ, United Kingdom: tel. +44 (0) 845 300 6090, email general-enquiries@open.ac.uk.

Alternatively, you may wish to visit The Open University website at http://www.open.ac.uk, where you can learn more about the wide range of courses and packs offered at all levels by The Open University.

TYR

The Law and Social Work

Contemporary Issues for Practice

2nd Edition

Edited by

Lesley-Anne Long

Jeremy Roche

Debbie Stringer

ACC. No: GCS 022406

GOWER COLLEGE SWANSEA
LEARNING RESOURCE CENTRE
361. 3
CLASS No. 344.033 LON

Compilation, original and editorial material © The Open University 2001, 2010

The Open University, Walton Hall, Milton Keynes MK7 6AA, United Kingdom

All rights reserved. No reproduction, copy or transmission of this publication may be made without written permission.

No portion of this publication may be reproduced, copied or transmitted save with written permission or in accordance with the provisions of the Copyright, Designs and Patents Act 1988, or under the terms of any licence permitting limited copying issued by the Copyright Licensing Agency, Saffron House, 6–10 Kirby Street, London EC1N 8TS.

Any person who does any unauthorized act in relation to this publication may be liable to criminal prosecution and civil claims for damages.

First edition published 2001
Reprinted nine times
Second edition published 2010 by
PALGRAVE

Palgrave in the UK is an imprint of Macmillan Publishers Limited, registered in England, company number 785998, of 4 Crinan Street, London, N1 9XW.

Palgrave Macmillan in the US is a division of St Martin's Press LLC, 175 Fifth Avenue, New York, NY 10010.

Palgrave is a global imprint of the above companies and is represented throughout the world.

Palgrave® and Macmillan® are registered trademarks in the United States, the United Kingdom, Europe and other countries.

ISBN: 978–0–230–54303–4

This book is printed on paper suitable for recycling and made from fully managed and sustained forest sources. Logging, pulping and manufacturing processes are expected to conform to the environmental regulations of the country of origin.

A catalogue record for this book is available from the British Library.

A catalog record for this book is available from the Library of Congress.

Typeset by Aardvark Editorial Limited, Metfield, Suffolk.

Contents

Notes on Contributors

Jane Aldgate OBE is Professor of Social Care at The Open University, Honorary Professor at Queen's University Belfast and Visiting Professor at Strathclyde University. Jane is a social worker by background, trained at the University of Edinburgh. She has undertaken research, written extensively on various topics in child welfare, including children's well-being, family support, children looked after by the local authority, kinship care, child development and child protection. She was involved in the initial development of the *Framework for the Assessment of Children in Need and their Families* in England in the late 1990s. Jane is currently seconded part time to the Scottish Government helping to develop and implement the *Getting it right for every child* programme.

Alison Brammer is a Solicitor and Senior Lecturer in the Department of Law, Keele University. Her specialist interests are Family and Child Law, Social Work Law, Law and Vulnerable Adults, and Adult Protection. Alison has spoken at national and international conferences, is heavily involved in training work with Social Service Departments, and is Legal Editor of the *Journal of Adult Protection*.

Stephen Gilmore is a Senior Lecturer in Law at King's College London, specialising in Family Law. He has written widely on child law issues and is the Case Law Editor of *Child and Family Law Quarterly*. He recently co-edited (with R. Probert and J. Herring) *Responsible Parents and Parental Responsibility* (Oxford: Hart Publishing, 2009).

Robert Johns is Head of Social Work at the University of East London and is also an Honorary Senior Visiting Fellow at City University London. A registered social worker, he has over 25 years' experience of statutory social work across the full range: youth justice, child care, mental health and vulnerable adults. He has published widely in the area of social work law, and besides teaching undergraduate and post graduate social work students, specialises at post qualifying level in mental capacity and deprivation of liberty issues. He has a long association with The Open University, having been an Associate Lecturer since 1982 and more recently being external examiner for the social work law course.

Heather Keating is Senior Lecturer in Law at the Sussex Law School, University of Sussex. She is a founder member of the child and family research group and the Centre for Responsibilities, Rights and the Law.

She is co-author (with Chris Clarkson and Sally Cunningham) of *Criminal Law: Text and Materials* (6th edn, 2007). She has also written widely on issues relating to criminal law and child law and her work now focuses upon children and the criminal law. She was co-editor (with Craig Lind) of a special issue of the *Journal of Law and Society, Children, Responsibilities and the State*, published in 2008 which was simultaneously published by Blackwell as a book. She was co-editor of (with Jo Bridgeman and Craig Lind) and contributor to *Responsibility, Law and the Family* (2008). She was co-editor (with Jennifer Temkin) of a special issue of *Contemporary Issues in Law, Strangers in a Strange Land: the Plight of Foreign Prisoners in British Jails* published in 2009. She is currently editing and contributing to two edited collections arising from an international, interdisciplinary conference on *Gender, Family Responsibility and Legal Change* held at Sussex in 2008. Her current research project is a monograph on children and the criminal law.

Lesley-Anne Long is an experienced family law barrister, now working as a Senior Lecturer in Law at The Open University. Previously Dean of the Faculty of Health and Social Care at The Open University, Lesley-Anne is now Director of an OU international development programme in sub-Saharan Africa.

Joan Loughrey graduated from the University of Oxford with a BA in jurisprudence, then qualified and practised as a solicitor in England and Wales and Hong Kong before becoming an academic. She was a lecturer then senior lecturer at the University of Central Lancashire, Preston and is now a Senior Lecturer in the School of Law, University of Leeds. She has published on a broad range of topics but is particularly interested in ethics and the law and has produced a number of articles in refereed journals on privacy and confidentiality in the medical and legal practice contexts.

Nigel Parton is NSPCC Professor in Applied Childhood Studies at the University of Huddersfield and Honorary Visiting Professor to the Centre for Learning in Child Protection at Edinburgh University. A qualified and Registered Social Worker with the GSCC he has been writing and researching about child welfare and child protection for over 30 years. His most recent books include: *Safeguarding Childhood: Early Intervention and Surveillance in a Late Modern Society* (2006, Basingstoke, Palgrave Macmillan); (with Bob Lonne, Jane Thomson and Maria Harries) *Reforming Child Protection* (2009, London, Routledge); and (with Nick Frost) *Understanding Children's Social Care: Politics, Policy and Practice* (2009, London, Sage). He is also chair of the editorial board of the journal *Children and Society*, published by Wiley-Blackwell in association with the National Children's Bureau, and a member of the editorial board of eleven other national and international journals in the broad areas of social work and child welfare.

Michael Preston-Shoot is Professor of Social Work and Dean of the Faculty of Health and Social Sciences at the University of Bedfordshire, England. He has held posts in universities since 1988 following a career in local authorities and voluntary organisations as a social worker, group worker and team leader. He has also practised as a family therapist and psychotherapist. He was Chair of the Joint University Council Social Work Education, which represents the perspectives of United Kingdom social work education in higher education institutions, between 2005 and 2009. He was editor of *Social Work Education: The International Journal* between 1993 and 2006 and was managing editor of the *European Journal of Social Work* between 2003 and 2007. He is one of the founding editors of the journal *Ethics and Social Welfare*. He was awarded a National Teaching Fellowship by the Higher Education Academy in 2005. His research and writing has concentrated on the interface between law and social work practice, on which in 2005 he co-authored a systematic review on teaching, learning and assessment of law in social work education for the Social Care Institute for Excellence (SCIE). He has subsequently co-authored a resource guide and ten e-learning objects on the subject of law and social work, also published by SCIE. He has also undertaken research and published in the areas of social work education, group work, the involvement of service users in social work education and research, and on the needs and service outcomes for young people in public care and older people requiring care in the community.

Lucy Rai is a qualified social worker and practised in Bristol and Somerset working in statutory contexts with children and families. She has been lecturing in social work and social care since 1995 and has worked for The Open University since 1997. Lucy was the lead author on *Understanding Children*, which was awarded The Commonwealth of Learning award for Distance Learning Materials in 2003, and also on *Foundations for Social Work Practice* which won a CETL Teaching and Learning award in 2006. Lucy has also acted as academic advisor with the BBC programmes *Child of Our Time* and *Someone to Watch Over You*. Lucy has written and presented at conferences internationally on writing in social work, which is the focus of her current research. Lucy is a senior lecturer at The Open University and is the lead academic developing continuing professional development in social work.

Jeremy Roche is Associate Dean (Curriculum and Awards) in the Faculty of Health and Social Care and Senior Lecturer in Law at The Open University. He has written extensively on children and the law and children's rights and is co-editor of *Youth in Society* (1997), *Children in Society* (2001) and *Social Work and the Law in Scotland* (2003).

Debbie Stringer is a solicitor, who continues to practise in the child law arena, and Senior Lecturer in Law in the Faculty of Health and Social Care at The Open University. Her research interests include the relationship between the law and the family, child law and social work law.

Penelope Welbourne is a senior lecturer in social work at the University of Plymouth. Before that she spent 15 years as a residential social worker, then a social worker, then a front-line manager of social workers in local authority child care teams, mainly in North and East London. Her main teaching and research interests are in childcare practice, policy and law, and the development of professional social work practice.

Jane Williams is a senior lecturer at the School of Law, Swansea University. Formerly a practising barrister and government lawyer for the UK and Welsh Assembly governments, her research interests span law-making in the context of multi-level governance and human rights implementation, especially children's rights. She is a member of the Wales NGO monitoring group for the UN Convention on the Rights of the Child. She teaches public law and legal issues in social work and social care. Her publications include *Child Law for Social Work* (Sage, 2008) and, with Antonella Invernizzi (co-editor), *Children and Citizenship* (Sage, 2008).

List of Abbreviations

ACA	Adoption and Children Act
ASBO	Antisocial Behaviour Order
BASW	British Association of Social Workers
BCS	British Crime Survey
CAF	Common Assessment Framework
CAO	Child Assessment Order
CCETSW	Central Council for Education and Training of Social Workers
CCW	Care Council for Wales
CQC	Care Quality Commission
CSCI	Commission for Social Care Inspection
CSDPA	Chronically Sick and Disabled Persons Act
CSSIW	Care and Social Services Inspectorate for Wales
CWDC	Children's Workforce Development Council
CYPA	Children and Young Persons Act
DCSF	Department for Children, Schools and Families
DDA	Disability Discrimination Act
DfES	Department for Education and Skills
DH	Department of Health
EA	Equality Act
ECHR	European Convention on Human Rights
ECM	*Every Child Matters*
EPO	Emergency Protection Order
FGC	Family Group Conference
GLS	Government Legal Service
GSCC	General Social Care Council
HMI	Her Majesty's Inspectors
HRA	Human Rights Act
HSCA	Health and Social Care Act
IASSW	International Association of Schools of Social Work
ICS	Integrated Children's System
ICT	Information, communication and technology
IFSW	International Federation of Social Workers
LGO	Local Government Ombudsman
LPA	Lasting Power of Attorney
MCA	Mental Capacity Act
MHA	Mental Health Act
MOJ	Ministry of Justice
MPS	Metropolitan Police Service

NCH	National Children's Home (now Action for Children)
NHSCCA	National Health Service and Community Care Act
PLO	Public Law Outline
RCPCH	Royal College of Paediatrics and Child Health
RRA	Race Relations Act
RR(A)A	Race Relations (Amendment) Act
SCIE	Social Care Institute for Excellence
SCRs	Serious Case Reviews
SCT	Supervised Community Treatment
SDA	Sex Discrimination Act
SEN	Special Education Needs
TOPPS	Training Organisation for the Personal Social Services
UNCRC	United Nations Convention on the Rights of the Child
YOP	Young Offender Panel

Introduction

LESLEY-ANNE LONG, JEREMY ROCHE AND DEBBIE STRINGER

Law, like social work, is a dynamic and human process constantly changing and impacting on the lives of the service user and professional in different ways. In editing this second collection we have been aware of the significant changes in both law and practice since the first edition of this reader in 2001. It is likely that the pace of change will continue, for example in key areas such as youth justice and safeguarding vulnerable groups of people, and there are areas where the impact of new legislation is yet to be fully played out, such as in relation to mental capacity. Some of these changes have their origins in forces external to the world of social work while others are internal. Demographic changes, whereby more people are living longer and are in need of care and medical services, have given rise to debates about the proper balance to be struck between private responsibility and public welfare. Shifts in the public debate on crime, especially youth crime, have focused on competing and conflicting agendas, values and interests in a way that is highly politicised and has impacted on government policy towards offending by children. In addition, voluntary sector organisations and service users express their political demands for improvements in services in the language of rights rather than needs; there are demands not only for procedural and substantive rights but also for fair and respectful treatment. Such demands for clearer and effective rights can be seen as a direct result of service users' disenchantment with the quality of professional service provided by social workers. At the same time this connects with the language of rights articulated in the European Convention on Human Rights via the Human Rights Act 1998 and increasingly, in the context of family law, the language of children's rights as set out in the United Nations Convention on the Rights of the Child.

Social work continues therefore to be at the centre of much debate and practitioners are still faced on a daily basis with dilemmas over what they can and should be doing. Although the law that frames and regulates social work practice provides social workers with the powers and duties they need to do their job properly, it cannot provide answers to the complex questions that lie at the centre of the social work task. What the law does is provide authority and a structure for decision making; it provides the framework within which individual social workers have to act. In other words, while social workers have discretion in the action they decide to take, this is not an unconstrained discretion. Social workers have to act within the law and in the light of their contractual obligations as employees and undertake their responsibilities within the Codes of Practice set out by the Care Councils. They should also work within a framework that is committed to treating all service users with an equality of concern and respect. It is not simply a matter of deciding whether a certain action is lawful (at the very least one should expect that) and that the social worker was acting within their duties and powers; it also entails a commitment to fairness, a concern with the process whereby decisions are made and how action is taken.

Effective and ethical practice relies upon a commitment to understand, develop and consolidate legal knowledge. One of the challenges facing practitioners, as well as any student of law, is the need to keep up to date with changes in the law. It can make a crucial difference to decision-making processes and the provision of services when social workers are confident in their knowledge of the law and the choices, within the legal framework, available to them as professionals. As well as being clear about legal principles, duties and powers, social workers can also look to regulations and guidance for advice regarding practice; furthermore, the courts from time to time provide guidance on how local authorities should proceed in certain situations. The relationship between law, regulations and guidance and social work practice is therefore characterised by change and development at different levels. This book takes a thematic approach and aims to capture and interrogate some of those changes across a range of law and practice. The contributions cover a wide range of issues, including the changing and contingent character of the idea of welfare, emerging accounts of accountability, the concepts of risk and vulnerability and debates around State intervention in relation to the protection of children.

In the first chapter, 'Social Work Values and the Law', Roche considers the centrality of values and ethics in social work practice. He explores the impact of law and the legal process on the professional commitment to social work values, including the commitment to upholding public trust and confidence in social care services and protecting the rights and promoting the interests of service users and carers. Roche examines the ways in which the law does and does not support social work professionals in such practice. On the one hand the social work profession's commitment to social justice appears consistent with the law's commitment to human rights however imperfectly these might be realised in a specific instance. On the other hand, the fact that the law provides the mandate for social work practice underscores the potentially controlling aspect to practice. Social work professionals have been given a range of duties and powers by statute so that they can take action, including triggering coercive interventions, in order to protect and promote the well-being of those who are vulnerable. Roche looks at the obstacles to value-based practice, how social workers can realise their commitment to social justice and considers the importance of social workers maintaining a 'critical awareness' in their engagements with both service users and their carers and other fellow professionals.

In Chapter 2 'State Intervention in Family Life', Gilmore considers the concept of privacy and private family life and some of the debates surrounding State intervention to protect children. He explores how the law 'regulates' intervention via the articulation of powers and duties on professionals in given situations and the notion of parental responsibility. The chapter begins by outlining the historical context to provide an understanding of how and why current legal provisions emerged as they did, and goes on to assess critically the legislation framing social work practice in England and Wales in relation to child protection, in particular the provisions of the Children Acts 1989 and 2004, and the Human Rights Act 1998. Gilmore highlights concerns regarding a blurring of the boundaries between voluntary and compulsory intervention, pointing to the dominant message that intervention must be proportionate, that is, protecting children but respecting the rights of parents. The chapter refers to the limitations of thinking simply in terms of explicit intervention versus non-intervention, warning that in such an approach possibilities in the middle ground can be overlooked. Gilmore suggests that intervention should have a much broader and proactive meaning.

In the third chapter, on partnership, Rai and Stringer explore the meaning of working in partnership in the context of social work with children and families and consider whether partnership in this area of social work practice is achievable. They discuss why working in partnership is considered to be essential for best practice and consider how professionals strive to achieve partnership. The chapter looks at whether working in partnership is a valid value base, what partnership actually means in practice and whether it is ever achievable, in particular in situations of conflict. Rai and Stringer ask whether it is necessary to accept that partnership is in fact an unattainable goal and question whether professionals in practice truly strive for partnership or are in fact striving for compliance with their accepted value base. They consider the concept of meaningful participation in the social work context and whether this better describes the relationship that exists within the current framework.

In 'The More Things Change, the More They Remain the Same?', Preston-Shoot looks at ways in which the law in relation to discrimination has developed over time and how the legislation reflects social concepts that are contested, evolve and become part of the practice framework within social work and social care. He explores how diversity influences practice and considers how social workers can manage challenges to personal values and avoid discrimination in their practice. The chapter looks at the ways in which people might be denied access to services, information and support, explores the obligations and limitations of the legislation and considers how anti-discriminatory practice goes beyond the limits of the legislation, emphasising ways in which social workers can challenge oppression, discrimination and exclusion.

Parton, in Chapter 5 'Risk, Social Work and Social Care', considers how risk is the focal rationale for policy and practice in the social work field. He looks at the way that risk insurance and risk taking have become key issues for both practitioners and managers, and ways in which notions of risk are embedded in organisational rationales and procedures for the delivery of services and in the relationships with service users and other agencies. The chapter explores how estimations of risk are critical in identifying priorities and making judgements about the quality of performance, and it looks at the concept of risk in modern social work and social care in the context of the legislation in relation to children and vulnerable adults. It acknowledges that much practice operates on the basis of making situated professional judgements based on hunch, experience and 'making sense' of what is going on.

In Chapter 6 on accountability, Welbourne considers what it means to be accountable as a professional to oneself, to one's employer and regulatory body and to society more generally. The chapter looks at the way in which the law defines accountability and outlines the role of the regulatory bodies such as the Care Councils and the Commission for Social Care Inspection. Welbourne also looks at how the law, together with the Codes of Practice, creates responsibilities, imposes duties on social workers and can call social workers to account for breaches of the codes. She explores ways in which accountability can lead to defensive practice and create conflict between professionals, for example where there are tensions between personal and employer accountability. The chapter addresses the link between accountability and the responsibility of professionals for advocating best practice and challenging poor practice and suggests how embracing accountability and responsibility can lead to improvements in the provision of services.

The range of remedies available to empower service users and provide them with autonomy in decision making is examined in Williams' chapter. She reflects upon remedies as an effective tool in ensuring the social work values of empowerment, autonomy and partnership are achieved. Outlining the remedies available to service users in all aspects of social work, Williams explores why there is a need for remedies when working with service users and considers the distinctions between judicial and administrative formal and informal complaints procedures and their use in helping to form effective partnerships with service users. She describes some of the key remedies including complaints procedures and judicial review, and the legal frameworks within which each of these remedies sits, and demonstrates how the use of remedies creates an environment where service users can work in partnership with professionals through empowerment.

Chapter 8 on assessment considers the use of assessments in relation to children and families, whether 'one size' can fit all and whether such assessments are fit for the purpose for which they were designed. Aldgate discusses the historical development of assessments, the policy and legislation which has helped shape them and considers whether they have been developed in order to suit the typical person or the typical service user and whether there is a difference. She considers whether a common approach to assessment leads to discriminatory practice and whether such assessments concentrate on the negative and therefore present a distorted perspective of the service user and his or her needs.

In 'Youth Justice', Keating introduces the competing and conflicting agendas and interests inherent in the youth justice arena and the role of the professional in assisting young people to navigate their way through this system whether as a victim, offender or both. The chapter reflects upon the usefulness of such labels when working with young people particularly when there is duality between victim and offender. The chapter examines the origins of youth justice, considering the 1969 Act and its challenges, the welfare versus justice models employed by successive governments and considers how this led to the formation of policy in the 1990s and more recently. Keating outlines the places where young people encounter justice issues, including the criminal justice arena and Family Proceedings Court. She goes on to consider who justice is for and examines the different approaches to justice of young people, the police, the media and the public, and whether the criminal court is the appropriate forum to resolve children's criminal and antisocial behaviour.

In Chapter 10 Joan Loughrey explores children's and young people's rights in relation to medical confidentiality and what approach the courts take when there is conflict between children's rights and their best interests. Her chapter provides a brief overview of the law relating to privacy and confidentiality and goes on to consider *Gillick, Axon* and other relevant case law where issues of young people's competence and capacity to make decisions are under scrutiny. Loughrey suggests that *Axon* marked a renewed emphasis on teenage autonomy, even for serious medical matters, although she adds the caveat that where there is conflict between a competent child's rights and her welfare, welfare is likely to prevail and the child's or young person's wishes be overridden. The chapter considers confidentiality rights of both children and parents under article 8, respect for family life, and provides examples from case law to illustrate the courts' approach to decision making where there is conflict between a child and her parents. Loughrey concludes by saying that each case is fact specific, but it should not be assumed that even 'non-competent' or very young children can never have the right to confidentiality, or that parents' rights should be respected over their children's.

The different concepts of vulnerability, autonomy, capacity and consent are reviewed in Johns' chapter. He situates these concepts within the legal framework impacting on service users and their carers and examines the ways in which the law can either empower or constrain the provision of services. Johns considers the main themes and trends in the reform of the law relating to capacity and an assessment of the remedies if there are concerns regarding a person's capacity to make a decision: declarations, advance health care decisions, litigation friends, Lasting Power of Attorney and the Court of Protection.

In 'Community Care and the Promotion of Independence', Brammer provides a history of the development of contemporary community care policy, tracing the trajectory of community care from the late 1980s and the passing of the NHS and Community Care Act 1990 to the present day. She charts the growing emphasis on service users' and carers' rights, choice and the promotion of independent living as evidenced by direct payments legislation and specific duties imposed on local authorities in the context of people living with disability. The chapter considers the reality of financial constraints operating on local authorities (the use of 'eligibility criteria'), charging and care planning and research findings on the actual experience of service users. Brammer emphasises the centrality of the duty to assess to social work practice in this field and the distinction between assessment and 'entitlement' to services. She looks at how social work professionals can support people in their own communities (for example via respecting service users' and carers' rights), the importance of being alive to cultural geography and what the emerging personalisation agenda means for social work practice.

Our overall aim in bringing together the contributions in the reader has been to enrich the debate surrounding the role of law in modern social work practice and to highlight the often contested and complex arena within which social work decision making and action are enacted.

Chapter 1

Social Work Values and the Law

JEREMY ROCHE

Introduction

This chapter explores the relationship between social work values and the law. I argue that there is significant common ground between social work values and legal values. This includes a respect for the individual, a commitment to formal equality, the ending of prejudice and discrimination, and a concern with procedural fairness. There is much in the law, in terms of its rules and procedures, including the law's insistence on certain forms of accountability, that can be supportive of social work and issues of social justice and human rights are increasingly significant in contemporary social work discourse and the law.

In this chapter, I consider the recent history of the relationship between the law and social work before moving on to explore social work values and images of law. I then consider the importance of the language of rights and conclude with a consideration of why law and the language of rights are important to social workers and service users alike.

Social work and the law

There are three aspects of the social work and law relationship that require some comment. First, the law provided the mandate for social work practice in the sense that it accorded the local authority wide-ranging discretionary powers to intervene and regulate family life, for example to protect children. At the same time, in cases involving children in care, the courts refused on public policy grounds to be drawn into reviewing local authority decision making: statute having given the local authority powers and duties, it was not for the courts to intervene and usurp the functions of the local authority (*A* v. *Liverpool* C.C. (1982)).[1] The law was not seen as being particularly important in social work education (Vernon et al., 1990), and 'good practice' did not see the law as a key reference point. In other words, the law provided the authority upon which professional social work activity took place, and within which professional discretion could be exercised, but the law itself and a knowledge of the law were not seen as being integral to social work practice on a day-to-day basis. This situation has changed radically over the past two decades. In the 1980s and 1990s, in part as a result of a series of scandals about the ways in which local authorities discharged their social service functions, the relationship between social work and the law was redrawn. The law has an ever-increasing importance in social work education as well as day-to-day professional practice.

Now not only is an understanding of the law seen as essential to professional social work practice but service users and carers are better informed about their rights, and social workers are specifically charged with promoting 'the independence of service users and assisting them to understand and exercise their rights' (GSCC, 2002, para. 3.1). The effective discharge of this professional responsibility requires social workers to know the extent of their powers and duties in a given situation and the range of entitlements that service users and carers can claim.

Second, despite the fact today that the law is an integral part of social work education and frames practice decision making, as Braye and Preston-Shoot observe 'deciding when to invoke the law is not a simple matter' (1997, p. 343). They go on to argue that competence in practice requires both knowledge of the law and assessment skills 'inspired by social work values, theoretical knowledge and practice wisdom' (ibid.). Knowledge of the law by itself is not enough – it needs to be situated within contemporary social work practice and incorporate 'social work values relating to oppression, service users' rights and discrimination' (Brammer, 2007, p. 4).

Third, the way in which professional social workers see and understand the law is important to their practice. Many social workers and academic commentators see the law as complicated, lawyers as unsympathetic if not hostile and the courts as an unwelcoming and inappropriate environment for dealing with the complex human problems that lie at the centre of social work practice (King and Trowell, 1992). Furthermore, the courts are in the position of standing in judgement on social work decision making. It is important to acknowledge that the calling of social work practice to account, which is integral to many cases, can be very unsettling and uncomfortable for the social work professionals involved. From the service user perspective, however, legal accountability might bring some benefits, for example as a result of making a complaint, having a decision reversed and receiving services that the service user believed he or she was entitled to in the first place.

So the law has come to assume a significance to social work practice that would have been hard to predict in the 1980s. Today, social work students are required to demonstrate their competence in applying the law. The argument of this chapter is that this is not merely a technical activity but an ethical one, an ethical activity framed by disagreements over values both within social work and the law.

Social work values

There are a number of different ways in which social work values are discussed in the social work literature. In the Central Council for Education and Training of Social Workers (CCETSW) Revised Rules and Requirements (1995), the section on 'Values of Social Work' makes it clear that meeting the core competences can only be achieved through the satisfaction of the value requirements. The position is that 'values are integral to rather than separate from competent practice' and that 'practice must be founded on, informed by and capable of being judged against a clear value base'. The 'Values Requirements' include the need for students to 'identify and question their own values and prejudices and their implications for practice' and 'promote people's rights to choice, privacy, confidentiality and protection, while recognising and addressing the complexities of competing rights and demands'. These are self-evidently complex and contradictory tasks; the promotion of the client's right to privacy may, for example, conflict with another client's right to protection, and both may be shaped by the social worker's own values. National Occupational Standards for Social Work (2002) identify key roles for social workers, for example preparing for and working with individuals and managing risk, and in relation to each of these there is a requirement to understand, critically analyse, evaluate and apply knowledge of the legal, social, economic and ecological context of social work. Social work practice is thus not simply a technical or administrative enterprise.

In 2002 the British Association of Social Workers (BASW) published its *Code of Ethics for Social Work* which it described as binding on all BASW members. It has strong persuasive power, even though a minority of social workers are BASW members. It makes links between global and social interests and professionalism. It is essentially an aspirational document for guidance of practitioners that sets out what the members of the profession themselves expect of their peers.

BASW has adopted the 2001 International Federation of Social Workers (IFSW) and the International Association of Schools of Social Work (IASSW) definition of social work, which should be used as a reference point for considering the *Code of Ethics*: it is included in the preamble to the *Code of Ethics*. This states that:

The social work profession promotes social change, problem solving in human relationships and the empowerment and liberation of people to enhance well-being. Utilising theories of human behaviour and social systems, social work intervenes at the points where people interact with their environments. Principles of human rights and social justice are fundamental to social work. (BASW, 2002)

Thus the BASW *Code of Ethics* is centrally concerned with the values and principles underlying ethical practice. The *Code of Ethics* asserts that:

Social work is a professional activity. Social workers have obligations to service users, to their employers, to one another, to colleagues in other disciplines and to society. In order to discharge these obligations they should be afforded certain complementary rights.

The BASW Code focuses on the protection of individuals, including protection from State and institutional abuses. It asserts a reciprocal duty on the State and employers to support social workers in the exercise of their professional functions.

The issue of social work values links with the question of professional competence and accountability. As professionals, social workers in England and Wales are now accountable to the General Social Care Council (GSCC) in England and in Wales the Care Council for Wales (CCW). No one is allowed to call themselves a social worker in a professional capacity or practice as a social worker unless they are registered. Personal accountability for professional conduct in social work is regulated by the Codes of Practice for Social Care Workers (CCW 2002; GSCC, 2002).

Braye and Preston-Shoot (1997) see the value base as being central to social work but also see its definition as open. It might refer to 'a commitment to respect for persons, equal opportunity and meeting needs' or, more radically, to a 'concern with social rights, equality and citizenship'. They are not the only commentators who have identified an uncertainty in the meaning of social work's value base. Banks (1995) has observed that 'values' is 'one of those words that tends to be used rather vaguely and has a variety of different meanings'.

Shardlow (1998), however, takes the argument further. It is not just a question of the openness or vagueness of the word 'values', he argues, but that 'no consensus exists about value questions in social work'. He refers to debates within social work over whether the contract culture empowers clients, the extent to which social work is predicated on a respect for the individual person, the significance of ideology in social work (for example the impact of feminism on social work knowledge and practice in the

1980s and 1990s) and the extent to which social workers should be held responsible when something goes wrong. Shardlow writes (1998):

> These debates are inevitably open-ended where social work itself is intrinsically political, controversial and contested, and where the nature of practice is subject to constant change.

The argument about the controversial and changing nature of social work's value base is taken up by Smith (1997), who argues that the application of values is not without difficulty and notes the change in 'values talk' that has taken place, for example the reference to service users rather than clients. Nonetheless, whatever the significance of such shifts in language, Smith argues that it is still the case that a respect for persons and self-determination remain central to social work practice. The complexity of the social work task relates in part to how the professional social worker negotiates the tension between these values and the decision-making dilemmas that are integral to social work. Smith's concern is that 'rights are in danger of becoming dislocated from values' such that values become invisible; what is required is a confirmation of the relationship in particular terms. While Smith sees values and rights as conceptually distinct, she also sees in the idea of fundamental human need, itself predicated upon a respect for the person, a positive link in the values–rights relationship. She argues that a renewed commitment to values does not entail ignoring rights and that values and rights are proper partners in the social work project.

So it is possible to identify agreement on three issues. First, there is no dispute that values are central to social work practice. Second, these values are at times contradictory, and in themselves do not resolve the dilemmas inherent in the social work task. Third, there have been significant changes over the past few years, one of which is the increasing importance accorded to law within the education and practice of social workers.

This said, there is almost a note of regret in the writing, as if social work has taken a wrong turning. As the law has come to assume a greater importance in both social work education and practice, with increasing accountability to the courts, some would argue that it is this trend which threatens to undermine good practice. How can social workers get on with their job if they are always having to look over their shoulders? The complaint is that 'defensive practice' is the result of law's new prominence, of the new relationship between the social work profession and the courts. This is, however, only one dimension of the law–social work relationship, one that is constantly subject to change. Before exploring this further, I want to consider some key images of law and the significance of the language of rights.

Images of law

Just as I have argued that there are competing images of social work practice, the same can be argued about the law. There is a debate about the values underpinning social work and how these find expression (or otherwise) in everyday practice; similarly, the law is properly character-ised by contest and change. In other words, law is, like social work, a dynamic and contested set of discourses.

There are a number of ways of seeing the law. The law can be viewed as a means by which the socio-economic status quo is maintained and guaranteed. The machinery of justice can be viewed as a charade or a genuine attempt to grapple with complex issues and arrive, however imperfectly, at a reasoned decision. Judges can be seen as disinterested adjudicators of disputes whose only allegiance is to the law or as biased individuals whose decisions reflect their class interests and preferences. The law can also be seen as a champion of the unprivileged and dispos-sessed. Within this tradition, contests around the law are part of the struggle for social justice, for example for equal treatment. Williams sees law and the language of rights as playing a part in the fight against discrimination (1991):

> For the historically disempowered, the conferring of rights is symbolic of all the denied aspects of their humanity: rights imply a respect that places one in the referential range of self and others, that elevates one's status from human body to social being.

This progressive imagery of the law is strangely absent from social work. So the law is not just about, for example, the right to property: it also concerns human rights such as the right to liberty and the right to a fair trial. In this sense, the law concerns us all, irrespective of our social identity and location.

When it comes to discussing the meaning of rights, there is no less debate. Positivists argue that the law is simply those rules laid down by the proper law-making procedures. There is thus no necessary moral content to the law – in the past, some legal regimes have sanctioned slavery, others the 'rights of man'. For utilitarian thinkers like Bentham, the question of 'what the law is' is distinct from the question of 'what the law ought to be'. A critique of the law was not to be confused with an accurate account of what was the law. Events in the twentieth century, however, rendered this neat distinction problematic. The State in Nazi Germany had all the trappings of the rule of law (referred to as the 'tinsel of legality'), yet unimaginable horrors were committed.

Natural law thinkers such as Fuller and Dworkin argued that unless the law satisfied certain criteria in terms of its content and procedures, it could not properly be called law. While Fuller (1969) was mainly concerned with procedural questions, for example whether the rules of law were known to those who were required to obey them, whether they were comprehensible and whether obedience to them was possible, Dworkin addressed the issues of law's content. Dworkin (1980) argued that, in a democracy, individuals require rights and that the interests of the minority cannot be sacrificed to those of the majority. He then argued that such a belief in the importance of rights requires a respect for persons and a commitment to political equality. It is this commitment to an equality of concern and respect that makes rights so important. While Dworkin does concede there are circumstances in which rights can be overridden, for example because it is necessary in order to uphold another's rights or because the cost of not doing so is excessive, it is only if rights are seen as special that there can be said to be any real constraint on the power of government.

This argument is important because it opens up a number of issues, two of which concern us here. First, it alerts us to debates surrounding State power. When the State proposes new legislation in the field of social care, it often raises controversial issues concerning, for example, a redistribution of resources or new powers to intervene into the private sphere. Second, it serves as a reminder that when we are talking about social work and the law, we are also talking about human relationships in which a commitment to an equality of concern and respect is important. However, what also needs to be made explicit is the idea that the public power of the State may be needed in order to correct a past injustice, to prevent discriminatory and oppressive behaviour in the 'here and now' and, practically and symbolically, to signal that certain forms of behaviour are not acceptable.

All legal systems have a value base. The important question about the law is what are the values upon which the laws are built. Some legal regimes have been built on values that have been explicitly discriminatory, for example the law in Apartheid South Africa or the legal regime in Nazi Germany. In the UK, the law with the passing of the Human Rights Act 1998 has embraced more directly the fundamental freedoms in the European Convention on Human Rights (ECHR). The freedoms contained in the ECHR are those commonly associated with Parliamentary democracies, for example the right to a fair trial and the right to family life, both of which are issues central to social work practice.

The question of rights

According to some, however, talk of rights does not progress the interests of the disadvantaged in our society. The Critical Legal Studies movement argued that rights talk is unable to address structural oppression and often serves to depoliticise social issues, while some feminist critiques of rights include the charge that they are abstract, impersonal, atomistic and induce conflict. Others suggest that rights talk 'obscures male dominance' while its strategic implementation 'reinforces a patriarchal status quo and, in effect, abandons women to their rights' (Kiss, 1997).

Perhaps the most sustained arguments against the language of rights come from those who embrace an ethic of care, influenced by the work of Gilligan (1982), with which they seek to supplement or even supplant the ethic of rights. The ethic of care is based on the idea of connectedness and thus focuses on caring as moral action (see Tronto, 1993; Heckman, 1995). As such, an ethic of care is as concerned with welfare as it is with justice – what is important is the ambiguity and context of the action in question rather than simply the application of abstract legal principles. Thus the proper response to dependency and vulnerability is a rethinking of caring relationships. Sevenhuijsen argues for the recognition of vulnerability to be 'incorporated into the concept of a "normal" subject in politics'. She observes, however, that:

> Clearer ideas about what constitutes necessary care can be gained by granting those who are the 'object' of care cognitive authority over their needs and giving them the opportunity to express these in a heterogeneous public sphere which allows open and honest debate. (Sevenhuijsen, 1998)

Minow and Shanley (1997) agree with feminist critics of rights theory 'that a political theory inattentive to relationships of care and connection between and among people cannot adequately address many themes and issues facing families'. However, they go on to observe that rights-based views require 'public articulation of the kinds of freedoms that deserve protection and the qualities of human dignity that warrant societal support' and that 'rights articulate relationships among people'.

There are a number of important distinctions to be made about the different ways in which rights are considered. First, at a theoretical level, rights can be a source of protection, allowing one to make claims on others, for example for services, and allowing people to change relationships, via, for example, divorce law. Kiss argues that rights can also be seen as being concerned with mutual obligations:

There is nothing isolating about a right to vote, to form associations, or to receive free childhood immunisations. And while many rights, like political rights and rights to free expression, do enable people to express conflicts, they also create a framework for social co-operation ... Rights define a moral community; having rights means that my interests, aspirations and vulnerabilities matter enough to impose duties on others. (Kiss, 1997)

Kiss (1997) argues that the problem is not so much with rights but with 'the tendency to cast the State in the role of exclusive rights violator': employers, service users and colleagues can all threaten one's rights. What we need to consider is the effect of rights – whether or not they make a practical and valuable difference to people's lives and the quality of their relationships. It is in the political aspects of rights that the link with social work values becomes most clear-cut. How, for example, are we to understand the failure of social work to engage with service users in the sense of showing respect for them and their choices? The example of social work and confidentiality is revealing here.

The traditional argument for respecting confidentiality is that without such an assurance people would not seek help, they would be reluctant to make any significant disclosures and hence there would not be a relationship of trust: this would undermine the professional–service-user relationship. There is a critical professional interest in working in partnership and building a positive relationship with the service user. Where the service user is a child there is also the issue of ensuring that working in partnership with parents and carers does not deflect attention from the needs and rights of the child and there is evidence that some social welfare professionals find it hard to work with children in a way that takes their rights seriously (Roche and Tucker, 2003).

Swain (2006) in his analysis of confidentiality[2] in contemporary social work practice reminds us that the right to confidentiality is an integral part of one's privacy rights. He argues that while a commitment to respecting client confidentiality is central to effective social work practice, as allowing a trusting and helping relationship to develop between professional and service user, in reality the commitment to confidentiality is misleading. Swain questions whether practitioners are confident that clients expect confidentiality to be respected and cites Ormrod and Ambrose's research (1999) which found that the profession with 'the greatest discrepancy between what should happen in respect of confidentiality and what actually happened was social work'. He asks what the promise of confidentiality actually means in the context of working with children and families and concludes that social work needs to come clean and recognise that the 'commitment' is so qualified that instead the social work professional should simply commit to respectful and open dealings with the client. It is clear that absolute confidentiality is not sustainable and that 'the protection afforded by an ethical commitment to confidentiality is arguably diminished by the increasing community demands for professional accountability, by legislative obligations across various practice areas, by the mandated duties to protect and warn ...' (2006, p. 99). This echoes in some ways the work of McLaren (2007) in her analysis of 'forewarning' in the context of Australian social work practice. McLaren observes that 'many human service associations require their members to inform clients of the parameters of confidentiality, including their child abuse reporting obligations, at the onset of worker–client relationships' (2007, p. 23). However her research found that workers avoided forewarning because they believed that clients would feel threatened and that to do so would put obstacles in the way of relationship building.[3] She observed that most social workers in her study thought that 'forewarning clients may be received by clients as an authoritarian act, thus creating suspicion and mistrust' (2007, p. 30). This research captures the complexity of the social work task, the different ways in which social workers negotiate the professional–service-user relationship and charts how difficult it can be to work according to the ethical ideals of the profession. It is, however, not just a matter of individual social work professionals experiencing difficulty in working with service users and carers in particular circumstances. At times the accepted practices of their agency can give rise to problems.

Braye and Preston-Shoot (1998), in their discussion of social work and the law, provide the following instance in which it is social work and its organisational and managerial context, rather than the law, that is undermining of social work values:

> Social Workers attending law workshops have recounted experiences of being instructed not to inform service users of their rights, and of users being charged for services which fall outside the legal mandate to charge.

More recently Braye and Preston-Shoot (SCIE, 2006) have noted that managers can provide misleading advice and that agencies can refuse to listen to another agency's concern about risks to children and adults (2006, p. 19). Recognising that there are few absolute duties in social work law, that social work professionals do have discretion, they argue that the:

> key task is to ensure that students and social workers know how that discretion should be exercised, drawing on values, knowledge and

statutory guidance and are skilled in its use to support sensitive, innovative and informed practice. (ibid.)

It is clear from their discussion that they see part of the social work task as having the skill to challenge unfair or illegal policies and procedures. When faced with unlawful action on the part, for example, of their employer, the social work professional might feel they have no choice but to blow the whistle. 'Whistle-blowing' can be seen as a way of enabling an organisation to take responsibility for poor practice and to be more accountable for the actions of its employees. To be a whistle-blower involves individuals taking responsibility for highlighting problems within an organisation that they are not in a position to rectify by themselves. In 2009, in the wake of the death of Baby P, a confidential 'whistle-blowing hotline' was set up so that employees and former employees of local authorities could contact Ofsted to raise concerns about practice in relation to safeguarding children.

The GSCC *Code of Practice for Social Care Workers* specifies that the requirements of a professional social care worker include:

> Bringing to the attention of your employer or the appropriate authority resource or operational difficulties that might get in the way of the delivery of safe care; [and] Informing your employer or an appropriate authority where the practice of colleagues may be unsafe or adversely affecting standards of care. (paras. 3.4 and 3.5)

This is reflected in a requirement that employers are prepared to address any such issues brought to their attention: the *Code of Practice for Employers of Social Care Workers* states they must:

> Hav[e] systems in place to enable social care workers to report inadequate resources or operational difficulties which might impede the delivery of safe care and [work] with them and relevant authorities to address those issues. (para. 2.3)

Social workers should uphold the ethical principles and responsibilities of this Code, even though employers' policies or instructions may not be compatible with its provisions and familiarise themselves with the complaints and whistle-blowing procedures of their workplace, and with the relevant provisions of the Public Interest Disclosure Act 1998. (BASW, 2002)

Conclusion

Social work and law are properly characterised as contested and multiple discourses. The value of law and rights resides not in the idea that the law has the answer or that the language of rights makes social conflict disappear – on the contrary, the latter is a key part of making it visible. Rights talk is the language in which differently positioned people can articulate their own definitions of their needs and interests. I would thus argue that law and the language of rights is a necessary but not sufficient condition for good practice. As Banks argues (1995):

> The law does not tell us what we ought to do, just what we can do ... most decisions in social work involve a complex interaction of ethical, political, technical and legal issues which are all interconnected.

The law by itself cannot and does not provide a clear guide to action in a whole host of complex circumstances. To argue that it did would be to misrepresent the importance of law. The law is open textured and contested, and when this is considered, alongside the detail of social work decision making, it is clear that the law cannot and does not provide the answer. Instead, it provides the framework within which social work knowledge is applied.

Nor, it must be conceded, does the law always provide an immediate practical remedy – often, some would say too often, the law lags behind, failing to support anti-oppressive practice. Thus the law might at times deny the legitimacy of a claim, for example proscribing discrimination on the basis of age. At other times, however, it is not the law that fails to provide a remedy, but the actions of officials working within the authority of the law that deny the remedy, as in, for example, police inaction over instances of domestic violence. However, because the law can be seen as, among other things, an expression of the power of the State to meet certain outcomes, and one which can be mobilised to secure a wide range of objectives, it is important not to underestimate its power. Individual decisions of the courts, some existing practices of the legal system and indeed some statutory provision might all be vulnerable to criticism when considered in the context of social work's commitment to respect for persons and self-determination. Yet, like social work itself, the law is the site of contest and debate, and one must not lose sight of the fact that one of the distinctive aspects of modern developments is the deployment of the language of rights by service users and service-user organisations.

Braye et al. point out that social workers have to engage with the law, recognising its potential to oppress and often seek to minimise 'the negative constraints it might place upon people'. They argue that the concept of proportionality is important in this context, that law might be used to challenge oppression and that it is important to develop a perspective on law 'that is not confined to coercive intervention'. (2005, p. 183)

For social work today, the relation between social work values and rights need not be seen in exclusively negative terms. This is not to deny that there are court decisions that disadvantage the socially marginal or to claim that recourse should always be had to the courts and lawyers. It is instead to recognise that, for some service users and professionals, the language of rights is the only means by which their perspective can be heard. The language of care might not allow the object of care to break free of their dependent, being-cared-for status. The language of rights is also about values – not necessarily in the form of a preferred list of 'correct' values but through the recognition of different viewpoints and through the hearing of different and perhaps unfamiliar voices on questions of need and respect.

References

Banks, S. (1995) *Ethics and Values in Social Work,* Basingstoke, Macmillan – now Palgrave Macmillan.

BASW (British Association of Social Workers) (2002) *The Code of Ethics for Social Work,* London, Venture Press.

Brammer, A. (2007) *Social Work Law* (2nd edn), Harlow, Pearson.

Braye, S. and Preston-Shoot, M. (1997) *Practising Social Work Law,* Basingstoke, Macmillan – now Palgrave Macmillan.

Braye, S. and Preston-Shoot, M. (1998) 'Social work and the law' in Adams, R., Dominelli, L. and Payne, M. (eds) *Social Work Themes, Issues and Critical Debates,* Basingstoke, Macmillan – now Palgrave Macmillan.

Braye, S., Preston-Shoot, M. with Cull, L., Johns, R. and Roche, J. (2005) 'Teaching learning and assessment of law in social work education' *Social Work Education Knowledge Review,* Bristol, SCIE.

Care Council for Wales (CCW) (2002) *Code of Practice for Social Care Workers,* Cardiff, CCW.

Central Council for Education and Training of Social Workers (CCETSW) Revised Rules and Requirements (1995) *Assuring Quality in the Diploma in Social Work I – Rules and Requirements for the Dip.SW,* London, CCETSW.

Dworkin, R. (1980) *Taking Rights Seriously,* London, Duckworth.

Fuller, L. (1969) *The Morality of Law,* New Haven, CT, Yale University Press.

Gilligan, C. (1982) *In a Different Voice,* Cambridge, MA, Harvard University Press.

GSCC (General Social Care Council) (2002) *Code of Practice for Social Care Workers,* London, GSCC.

Heckman, S. (1995) *Moral Voices, Moral Selves,* Cambridge, Polity.

King, M. and Trowell, J. (1992) *Children's Welfare and the Law: The Limits of Legal Intervention,* London, Sage.

Kiss, E. (1997) 'Alchemy of fool's gold? Assessing feminist doubts about rights' in M. Shanley and U. Narayan (eds) *Reconstructing Political Theory: Feminist Perspectives,* Cambridge, Polity Press.

McLaren, H. (2007) 'Exploring the ethics of forewarning: Social workers, confidentiality and potential child abuse disclosures', *Ethics and Social Welfare,* 1(1): 22–40.

Minow, M. and Shanley, M. (1997) 'Revisioning the family: relational rights and responsibilities' in M. Shanley and U. Narayan (eds) *Reconstructing Political Theory: Feminist Perspectives,* Cambridge, Polity Press.

National Occupational Standards for Social Work (2002), Leeds, Skills for Care.

Ormrod, J. and Ambrose, L. (1999) 'Public perceptions about confidentiality in mental health services', *Journal of Mental Health,* 8(4): 413–21.

Roche, J. and Tucker, S. (2003) 'Extending the social inclusion debate: an exploration of the family lives of young carers and young people with ME', *Childhood – A Global Journal of Child Research,* 10(4): 439–56.

SCIE (Social Care Institute for Excellence) (2006) Teaching, Learning and Assessment of Law in Social Work Education, *Social Work Education Resource Guide* 06, SCIE, Bristol.

Sevenhuijsen, S. (1998) *Citizenship and the Ethics of Care: Feminist Considerations on Justice, Morality and Politics,* London, Routledge.

Shardlow, S. (1998) 'Values, ethics and social work' in Adams, R., Dominelli, L. and Payne, M. (eds) *Social Work Themes, Issues and Critical Debates,* Basingstoke, Macmillan – now Palgrave Macmillan.

Smith, C. (1997) 'Children's rights: have carers abandoned values?', *Children and Society,* 11: 3–15.

Swain, P. A. (2006) 'A camel's nose under the tent? Some Australian perspectives on confidentiality and social work practice', *British Journal of Social Work,* 36(1): 91–107.

Tronto, J. (1993) *Moral Boundaries,* London, Routledge.

Vernon, S., Harris, R. and Ball, C. (1990) *Towards Social Work Law: Legally Competent Professional Practice Paper 4.2,* London, CCETSW.

Williams, P. (1991) *The Alchemy of Race and Rights,* Cambridge, MA, Harvard University Press.

Notes

1. *A* v. *Liverpool C.C.* (1982) AC363.
2. Swain describes this as 'a core practice dimension for social workers' (2006, p. 91).
3. Although she points out that this is not respectful of the rights of service users: by not forewarning the social worker 'retains knowledge and retains power to be used against clients' when necessary.

Chapter 2

State Intervention in Family Life

STEPHEN GILMORE

Introduction

This chapter critically examines the issue of State intervention in family life to protect children in the context of a discussion of English law. The topic is controversial on many levels. The very idea of talking in terms of State intervention in family life has been challenged. One view is that the notion that there is a private sphere of family life into which the State intervenes is a myth (Olsen, 1985). As Olsen observes:

> The state is responsible for the background rules that affect people's domestic behaviors. Because the state is deeply implicated in the formation and functioning of families, it is nonsense to talk about whether the state does or does not intervene in the family.[1]

There is also a sense in which the State subtly governs families (Donzelot, 1980). As Archard explains, a 'therapeutic medical model stipulates a norm of familial "health" which, by means of professionals, insinuates into the "private" life of families' (Archard, 2004, p. 155).

While acknowledging the pervasiveness of State involvement in families, it is, however, still possible to talk meaningfully about 'State intervention in family life' provided there is clarity about the sense in which the term is used. In this chapter the concern is not with background rules defining the family, but with the explicit legal basis for *particular* State involvements in family life to protect and care for children.[2] Where the law defines whether particular involvement is permitted or not, there seems nothing strange about describing the actions of State actors as 'intervention' or 'non-intervention' as the case may be.

The chapter begins by exploring at a general level the different methods which a society might adopt to protect children, highlighting some of the broad issues which arise. It then moves on to examine how the law has engaged with the issue. First, the relevant legislation, the Children Act (CA) 1989, is set briefly in a historical context, demonstrating some of the tensions with which such legislation must engage and providing some understanding of how and why the current legal provisions emerged as they did. There follows an account of the current law, with reference to academic commentary and research evidence. The chapter closes with a brief critical assessment of the law and some concluding thoughts.

The State as family or a more liberal approach?

A society's duty to protect children probably derives from a general moral duty to promote human flourishing (Eekelaar, 1991), and also reflects a widely held ethic of respect for the interests of other human beings. How those ideals are achieved, however, is a matter for the particular society, including the allocation of the task of parenting children. The task might be left entirely in the hands of natural parents, but experience tells us that some children will suffer. At the other extreme, a society might opt for a collectivist approach with the State directly concerned in all children's upbringing. While this might achieve a measure of social justice for children who might otherwise find themselves within a family less fortunate than others, there are many good reasons why a society might not wish to nationalise children's upbringing completely (for a detailed account of the arguments, see Archard, 2004). It would be rightly cautious of adopting such a system because of the difficulty of finding some basis for deciding upon a preference for one vision of children's upbringing over another.

An intermediate position might be to introduce a form of licensed parenthood (LaFollette, 1980; Mangel, 1988; Westman, 1994) to secure what might be described as the child's right to responsible parents (Freeman, 2008). Such an approach has been advocated by Dwyer (2006),[3] focusing on children's relationship rights, who suggests that parenthood could be attributed following consideration by the State of whether in each case a proposed parent/child relationship will promote the child's welfare. However, implementing a system of scrutinising 'would be' parents (other than perhaps in a very limited way to question the initial parenthood of those who had previously harmed a child) encounters the considerable problem of predicting parenting abilities and attracts similar criticisms to those in relation to the wholesale nationalisation of child upbringing. One of the most important features of family life is the diversity it brings to a society. Children are brought up within different cultures and religions, among parents of differing backgrounds, personalities, attitudes and talents, enriching society and providing a 'natural' barrier to the imposition of a State view on matters of children's upbringing. A system which imposes a State view about who is an appropriate parent risks stifling that diversity.

So within liberal democracies, like England and Wales, a path is negotiated between the extremes of entire deferral to the family and the State as parent, adopting instead what has been termed a 'liberal standard' (Archard, 2004). On this view, it is presumed that the upbringing of children within families is desirable and that the State should not be the child's parent in the first instance. Parents are entitled to bring up their child as they wish, free from State intrusion, unless they consent to State intervention or certain stated conditions for State intervention are fulfilled.

The adoption of this liberal approach, however, requires a particular society to address several difficult questions. First, where and how the line regarding State intervention is to be drawn and how the interests of children and parents are to be protected. Given the liberal standard's recognition of the primary importance of children's upbringing within their families, the question immediately arises as to how a general criterion for intervention is to be reconciled with the family context and a recognition of pluralism. The tension arises not only from the perspective of those who would seek to limit State intervention into family life, but also those who might see the family as a threat to respect for fundamental values and to the child's right to an open future rather than one closed off by particular family values. Secondly, there is a need to consider the nature of any State intervention and how in practice the system of intervention is to be organised and to operate. How the law has addressed these issues is tackled in the rest of the chapter.

Childcare and protection: background to the current law

The inadequacies of the previous law

The law on childcare and protection prior to the CA 1989 was unsatisfactory in several respects (see Hayes, 2009). A local authority could obtain a 'place of safety order'[4] to remove a child immediately to its care for 28 days and parents had no right to challenge the order or the local authority's decisions regarding access to the child. A child could enter the (longer term) care of a local authority via several routes, in each case according to different, yet problematic criteria. A care order could be made[5] on various grounds in respect of a child who was in need of care and control, for example, in respect of a child who was ill-treated or neglected, or one who had committed an offence. This merging of children who were both victims and offenders (Eekelaar et al., 1982) meant that there was no explicit reference to a lack of reasonable parental care because it was not relevant in the case of the juvenile offender where the focus was on commission of an offence; and consequently parents were not parties in care proceedings.

Perhaps of greater concern was the fact that a local authority could assume parental rights and duties in respect of a child in its care administratively, simply by passing a Council resolution.[6]

A child could also be placed in care by a judge exercising his or her inherent jurisdiction to protect children, where the sole consideration was the child's welfare. Thus a child could be placed in care simply on the basis that the child would fare better with substitute carers than with his or her parents; there was no threshold barrier to State intervention and care proceedings could be bypassed; and as Hayes explains, parental access to the child in care was in the complete control of the local authority (Hayes, 2009, pp. 99–101).

The route to change

The political impetus for change came with an investigation and report of the House of Commons Social Services Committee in 1984 (Short Report, 1984), which recommended that the law be rationalised. In consequence an Interdepartmental Working Group was set up to review the law, the recommendations of which in its report, the *Review of Child Care Law* (DHSS, 1985), formed the core of the new philosophy and framework for State intervention in family life within the public law provisions of the CA 1989 (see Parton, 1991 for a full account of the influences on the Act). The aim was to create a clearer distinction between voluntary and compulsory intervention in family life, to establish clear and uniform criteria for intervention, and to ensure greater protection of parents' interests.

Several other factors, however, were influential in shaping particular features of the legislation. Inquiry reports into the deaths of children highlighted deficiencies in practice (see Parton and Martin, 1989). Of particular influence on the law was the inquiry into the death of Kimberley Carlile, aged four, at the hands of her stepfather, Nigel Hall (London Borough of Greenwich, 1987). A visiting social worker failed to examine the child when Hall refused to allow him into the home. This highlighted the need for clearer legal provisions on gaining access to children in cases of suspected abuse, and the law now places a clear duty on social workers to act where access to a child is frustrated.

While these high profile inquiry cases showed failures to intervene, research evidence at the time (Packman, 1986) painted a rather different picture. If anything, in general there was precipitate intervention and overuse of place of safety orders. Not surprisingly, therefore, there soon emerged another scandal, revealed by the Cleveland Child Abuse Inquiry (Secretary of State for Social Services, 1988), which graphically demonstrated this picture. Over 200 children had been taken into care under Place of Safety Orders in the north-east of England over a short period, following suspicion of sexual abuse by their parents. The basis of the suspicion in each case was a medical diagnosis by two paediatricians. The inquiry found that social workers had simply deferred to the medical diagnosis rather than placing this finding within the context of a family assessment, and that magistrates had rubber-stamped the applications. It highlighted the need for greater protection of parents' and children's rights in the context of emergency protection.

A new vision

The CA 1989 sought to remedy the major defects of the previous law with a new vision, neatly conveyed in the Government's White Paper (Secretary of State for Social Services, 1987) which preceded the Act:

(1) The prime responsibility for the upbringing of children rests with parents; the state should be ready to help parents to discharge that responsibility especially where doing so lessens the risk of family breakdown.
(2) Services to families in need should be arranged in voluntary partnership with parents.
(3) Transfer to local authority of parents' legal powers and responsibilities for caring for a child ... by a full court hearing ... must rest on establishing that there is harm or risk of harm to a child who is not receiving adequate parental care or is beyond control.
(4) Application for emergency powers should be of short duration and subject to challenge by parents.

The relevant legislation is in Parts III, IV and V of the CA 1989 and associated schedules. Part III contains various provisions which facilitate local authorities' working with parents to safeguard and promote the welfare of children in their area; Part IV provides the legal framework for compulsory intervention by way of care or supervision of children; and Part V deals with emergency protection.

Guidance on practice and procedure

The legislation is supplemented by guidance on how assessments are to be carried out (*Framework for the Assessment of Children in Need and Their Families* (Department of Health, 2000)) and on inter-agency cooperation, (*Working Together to Safeguard Children* (Department of Health, the Home Office and DfES, 2006)).[7] The guidance on inter-agency cooperation was updated in 2006 following changes in practice in the light of the findings of Lord Laming's inquiry into the death of Victoria Climbié (Laming, 2003). Victoria Climbié suffered appalling abuse at the hands of her great-aunt and her partner and remained unprotected despite the fact that she was known to 'four social services departments, two child protection teams of the Metropolitan Police Service (MPS), a specialist centre managed by the NSPCC, and was admitted to two different hospitals because of suspected deliberate harm' (Summary Report of an Inquiry by Lord Laming, p. 3). The report recommended structural changes to the child protection system, leading to enactment of the Children Act 2004, which seeks clearer accountability for children's services and enhanced integration of services (see Conway, 2002). The 2004 Act places a duty on a local authority to promote cooperation between it and its relevant partners (see s.10 and s.25), and requires the setting up of Local Safeguarding Children Boards (see ss.13–16 and ss.31–34) whose role it is to ensure cooperative and coordinated responses to the goal of safeguarding and promoting children's welfare. Concerns about delays in care proceedings led to the Public Law Outline (1 April 2008), which streamlines and seeks a more efficient procedure for bringing care proceedings (for criticism, see Masson, 2008).

The human rights dimension

The Human Rights Act (HRA) 1998 made more explicit another important dimension to professional work in this area. The Act requires that so far as it is possible to do so legislation must be interpreted in a way which is consistent with the various human rights under the European Convention for the Protection of Human Rights and Fundamental Freedoms (the ECHR) 1950, as scheduled to the 1998 Act (see HRA 1998, s.3). Furthermore, public authorities must not act in ways which are inconsistent with those rights (HRA 1998, s.6). These provisions mean that practitioners should always have in mind the *rights* of children and their families.

The most relevant under the ECHR in this context are arts.3, 6 and 8: art.3 prohibits inhuman or degrading treatment; art.6 protects a right to a fair trial; and art.8 provides a right to respect for private and family life. In compliance with art.3, therefore, a local authority has a duty to prevent inhuman and degrading treatment of which it has knowledge or ought to have knowledge. In *Z and Others* v. *United Kingdom* (2000)[8] a violation was found where a local authority took little action for several years in respect of children about whom there were serious concerns. The children had suffered psychological damage and neglect which should have been prevented. The roles of arts.6 and 8 of the Convention may be illustrated by reference to the case of *P, C and S* v. *United Kingdom* (2002).[9] In that case, a child was the victim of alleged Munchausen's syndrome by proxy,[10] and the child's mother had been convicted in the US of an offence related to those concerns. She came to the UK in breach of her probation and became pregnant. The local authority sought emergency protection of the baby at birth and eventually a care order was made in proceedings at which the mother was unrepresented. The European Court of Human Rights held that there had been breaches of arts.6 and 8 of the Convention. There had been a breach of art.6 as representation was indispensable to fair access to a court. There was also a violation of art.8: the State had to show that a careful assessment of the impact of the proposed care measure on the parents and child, as well as possible alternatives to care, was carried out. The removal at birth was disproportionate, not supported by relevant and sufficient reasons, and the mother had been prevented from being involved in the decision-making process to a sufficient degree.[11] It has also been held that there is a positive duty under art.8 to seek to facilitate reunion between a child and his or her parents. While this duty is not absolute, all reasonable steps must be taken to do so (see for example *Hokkanen* v. *Finland* (1996)).[12]

An outline of the law

Working with children and families

One way that the CA 1989 seeks to avoid a disproportionate response is with the message that compulsory intervention should be a last resort (provided that a child's welfare can be satisfactorily safeguarded otherwise). This is reflected in the idea that local authorities should, where possible, work with children and their families. Part III and Schedule 2 to the CA 1989 set out a range of powers and duties within which such work is intended to operate. Section 17(1) provides a general duty of every local authority:

(a) to safeguard and promote the welfare of children within their area who are in need;[13] and
(b) so far as it is consistent with that duty, to promote the upbringing of such children by their families, by providing a range and level of services appropriate to those children's needs.

This is supplemented by specific duties which arise in particular circumstances, for example the duty to provide accommodation (s.20(1)).

A local authority cannot accommodate a child if a parent with parental responsibility objects, and the child can be removed from accommodation at any time. Accommodation is an entirely voluntary arrangement, in which the child's parents are in control, and the local authority's duty to safeguard the child's welfare does not entitle it to override the wishes of a parent with parental responsibility.[14]

A child who is accommodated or in the care of the local authority is known as a 'looked after' child, to whom duties in ss.22 and 23 of the CA 1989 are owed. The local authority must consult with, and give due consideration to the wishes and feelings of the child and parents before making decisions, and to the child's religious persuasion, racial origin and cultural and linguistic background. Where possible the child should be placed with a family member or relative.

There are also various duties to provide ongoing assistance to children who are leaving or have left the care of the local authority (ss.23A–24). Schedule 2 sets out further specific duties, including, in para. 4(1), the duty to take steps to provide services to prevent children from suffering ill treatment and neglect.

Significant harm: the threshold for compulsory intervention

The CA 1989 establishes a threshold for compulsory intervention in family life based on the concept of 'significant harm'. 'Harm' is defined in s.31(9) as meaning:

ill-treatment or the impairment of health or development including, for example, impairment suffered from seeing or hearing the ill-treatment of another;

And s.31(10) explains:

Where the question of whether harm suffered by a child is significant turns on the child's health or development, his health or development shall be compared with that which could reasonably be expected of a similar child.

The courts are given some scope in deciding whether harm is significant, but it has been said that harm is significant if it is 'considerable, noteworthy or important'.[15] As we shall see below, the extent to which the existence, or risk, of 'significant harm' must be established varies according to the nature of the intervention.

The duty to investigate and emergency protection

Where child protection concerns come to the attention of a local authority, it has a duty to investigate. The duty is set out in s.47 of the CA 1989, which provides:

(1) Where a local authority –
   (a) are informed that a child who lives, or is found, in their area –
      (i) is the subject of an emergency protection order; or
      (ii) is in police protection; or
      (iii) has contravened a ban imposed by a curfew notice within the meaning of Chapter I of Part I of the Crime and Disorder Act 1998; or
   (b) have reasonable cause to suspect that a child who lives, or is found, in their area is suffering, or is likely to suffer, significant harm, the authority shall make, or cause to be made, such enquiries as they consider necessary to enable them to decide whether they should take any action to safeguard or promote the child's welfare.

The section goes on to provide that reasonable steps must be taken to gain access to the child (s.47(4)). Where access is refused the local authority must apply for an emergency protection order (EPO), child assessment order, or care/supervision order unless the child's welfare can be satisfactorily safeguarded without doing so (s.47(6)). An EPO can be obtained by an application to court under s.44(1) of the CA 1989, which provides that a court may make the order, if, but only if, it is satisfied that otherwise 'there is reasonable cause to believe that the child is likely to suffer significant harm' or s.47 enquiries are:

being frustrated by access to the child being unreasonably refused to a person authorised to seek access and that the applicant has reasonable cause to believe that access to the child is required as a matter of urgency.[16]

An EPO authorises the child's removal or prevents removal and gives the applicant parental responsibility, which may be exercised so far as reasonably required to safeguard or promote the child's welfare (s.44(5)). The court can give directions for contact and medical examination, although a child of sufficient understanding can refuse such examination. Once it becomes safe the child must be returned (s.44(10)), although the applicant may again exercise powers if the circumstances make it necessary (s.44(12)). Reasonable contact must be allowed with parents and others closely associated with the child (see s.44(13)). Section 44A enables the court to include an exclusion provision in the EPO to exclude a person from a dwelling-house if the child would thereby cease to suffer or be likely to suffer significant harm.

An EPO can be made for up to 8 days, as specified in the order (s.45(1)), and can be extended for up to 7 days if the court has reasonable cause to believe the child is likely to suffer significant harm if the order is not extended (s.45(5) and (6)). The child, parents and others connected with the child may apply to discharge the order; however the order cannot be discharged if the applicant was informed of the initial hearing and attended, or the order has been extended (s.45(11)).

An EPO is reserved for emergency situations, and the courts have emphasised the draconian nature, and human rights implications, of the EPO. In *X Council* v. *B (Emergency Protection Orders)* (2004)[17] Munby J drew attention to some unsatisfactory features of the EPO: that there is no appeal; an application for discharge can only be made after 72 hours; and there is no appeal against a refusal to discharge the order. He observed that rulings of the European Court of Human Rights require that intervention be proportionate and the least interventionist and thus there is a requirement of necessity, of imminent danger, before an EPO could be made. Several points were made by way of guidance (at para. [64]), including that: (1) consideration should be given to whether a Child Assessment Order would suffice; (2) applications should be on notice save in wholly exceptional cases, with detailed precise evidence; (3) no EPO should be made for longer than necessary; (4) contact should be driven by the family's needs *not* resources; (5) parents must be sufficiently involved; (6) if the application is made without notice, a record of the proceedings and evidence must be kept and supplied to the parents on request.

The onerous requirement regarding evidence has been criticised by Masson as unrealistic in the context of the nature of this order (Masson,

2004). However, the guidance was endorsed by McFarlane J in *Re X* (*Emergency Protection Orders*) (2006),[18] who suggested that it be put before every court hearing an EPO application. He was critical of a local authority's 'without notice'[19] application, made within two hours of a case conference at which there was no suggestion that the child should be removed. The local authority was concerned, however, that the mother suffered from Munchausen's syndrome by proxy and reacted when the mother presented at hospital asking that the child be examined. The judge was critical of the use of an EPO in this situation, where there was no emergency, of the 'without notice' application, and of the social worker's evidence, which erroneously claimed (among other things) that the mother suffered from Munchausen's syndrome by proxy, when there was no medical evidence to that effect. Similarly, in *Haringey LPC* v. *C E and Anor* (2005),[20] Ryder J was critical of the use of a 'without notice' EPO where the allegation was that the child had been trafficked into the parents' care, but was otherwise well cared for.

Where time does not permit an application for an EPO, the police power under s.46 (police protection) may assist 'where a constable has reasonable cause to believe that a child would otherwise be likely to suffer significant harm'. The child cannot be kept in police protection for more than 72 hours. A designated officer can, however, apply on behalf of the authority in whose area the child lives for an EPO.

If the child's situation does not disclose an emergency, but compulsory intervention is required to obtain assessment of the child's health or development to ascertain whether the threshold criteria are fulfilled, a child assessment order (CAO) can be sought under s.43(1). This imposes a duty to produce the child to a person named in the order and to comply with directions relating to assessment of the child (s.43(6)). The child may refuse a medical examination if of sufficient understanding (s.43(8)). The court can treat this application as an application for an EPO and the court cannot make a CAO if there are any grounds for making an EPO and it ought to make an EPO instead.

The discussion above suggests a neat demarcation between voluntary and compulsory intervention. Empirical research by Judith Masson on the use of EPOs and police protection, however, indicates that in practice the boundary between voluntariness and coercion may be much more blurred. (Masson, 2002, 2005). Masson found evidence (reflecting an obvious tension between risk assessment and working in partnership), that agreements between parents and the local authority were not always freely negotiated:

Rather, they were conditions imposed on parents, which allowed the social services department to conclude that the issue of the children's care could remain a matter determined by the department and need not be brought before a court. (Masson, 2005, p. 82)

As she points out, this form of de facto compulsion does not carry with it the safeguards of formal compulsory intervention. Furthermore, the failure to comply with an agreement was then sometimes seen as a reason, and further ground, for compulsory intervention. Masson's study of police protection (Masson, 2002) found that one of the main categories of use was in response to requests by social workers out of hours, for example in the case of emergency duty teams lacking court work experience. Her study of the use of EPOs (reported in Masson, 2005) found variations in the use of 'without notice' applications within different areas. In some areas there were quite high proportions (for example in one area just under 50% of applications), and in areas where the courts were more reluctant to hear applications without notice, 'on notice' applications were much more likely to be preceded by police protection (in one area, in 53% of cases). The prior existence of police protection then tended to reinforce the local authority's case. In the light of her findings, Masson rightly questions whether these practices surrounding emergency intervention adequately secure accountability and protect parents' rights (Masson, 2005, pp. 94–6).

Longer term intervention: care and supervision

If a local authority (or the NSPCC) is to secure, by compulsory intervention, a child's longer term protection it is necessary to apply for a care order or supervision order[21] pursuant to s.31 of the CA 1989. Section 31(2) provides:

> A court may only make a care or supervision order if it is satisfied –
> (a) that the child concerned is suffering, or is likely to suffer, significant harm; and
> (b) that the harm or likelihood of harm, is attributable to:
>   (i) the care given to the child, or likely to be given to him if the order were not made, not being what it would be reasonable to expect a parent to give to him; or
>   (ii) the child's being beyond parental control.

Pending the final outcome of proceedings, an interim care or supervision order can be made under s.38[22] (initially for eight weeks, renewable thereafter for periods of up to four weeks) where the court is satisfied that there are reasonable grounds for believing the circumstances are as in s. 31(2).

To obtain a final order, however, the threshold criteria must first be proved.

It is necessary to show that the child 'is suffering or is likely to suffer significant harm'. This refers to present or future harm, not past harm.[23] The courts have interpreted the word 'likely' to mean that there must simply be a real possibility of harm.[24] This is a very pro-child-protection interpretation. However, it is balanced by the requirement that an inference of future harm must be based upon facts which are themselves proved on the balance of probabilities.[25] In *Re H and R (Child Sexual Abuse: Standard of Proof)* (1996)[26] a local authority was concerned that the eldest of four siblings had been sexually abused by her stepfather and wished to obtain a care order to protect her younger siblings. The House of Lords held that it was necessary to show that it was more probably true than not that the eldest girl had been abused before an inference could be drawn that the younger children were likely to suffer such harm. The House also held that the more serious an allegation the less likely it was to have occurred and therefore the more cogent the evidence would need to be to prove it. This approach was heavily criticised as illogical, and for making the obtaining of a care order more difficult the more serious the allegations were (see for example Keating, 1996). While endorsing the rest of the reasoning in *Re H and R* the House of Lords in *Re B (Children)* (2008)[27] has now rejected this 'cogent evidence test', clarifying that the standard of proof is the simple balance of probabilities. This is a move which will be welcomed by many commentators (see for example, Hayes, 2008; Keating, 2009).

The second limb of the threshold test requires a link between the harm suffered and lack of reasonable parental care. Thus it is not possible to obtain a care order simply because a child is orphaned,[28] unless there are already protective measures in place at the time of the parents' death[29] or the child has suffered harm through abandonment.[30] In *Lancashire CC v. A* (2000)[31] the House of Lords held that where it is unclear whether harm to a child has been caused by a parent or a third party (for example a child minder), the threshold criteria can still be fulfilled even though there may be no positive evidence that the parent is the perpetrator (see Hall, 2000; Hayes, 2000).

Even though the threshold criteria may be fulfilled, it does not follow that a care or supervision order will be made. The court must apply the child's welfare as its paramount consideration and consider the checklist of factors in s.1(3) in deciding whether to make an order. The House of Lords has held in *Re O & N; Re B* (2003)[32] (see Hayes, 2004) that in unknown perpetrator cases the court should proceed at the welfare stage on the basis that the child's parent is a possible perpetrator.

The court must consider which, if any, of a care or supervision order is proportionate and necessary in the circumstances.[33] The local authority must present a care plan to the court for the child's future care,[34] and the public law outline requires the local authority to consider convening a family group conference and to demonstrate that it has considered members of the child's wider family and friends as potential carers.

The effect of a care order is to give the local authority parental responsibility and the power to determine the extent to which a parent may meet his or her parental responsibility.[35] But even that power must be exercised insofar as it is necessary to safeguard and promote the child's welfare, and with due regard for the parents' right to respect for family life in art.8 of the ECHR.[36] The court must consider contact before making a care order[37] and a local authority is to allow reasonable contact with specified persons unless the court has authorised refusal.[38]

There is some evidence of judicial sensitivity to cultural factors and to the need for acceptance of pluralism in the context of care proceedings. Hedley J has commented:

> Society must be willing to tolerate very diverse standards of parenting, including the eccentric, the barely adequate and the inconsistent. It follows too that children will inevitably have both very different experiences of parenting and very unequal consequences flowing from it. It means that some children will experience disadvantage and harm, while others flourish in atmospheres of loving security and emotional stability. These are the consequences of our fallible humanity and it is not the provenance of the state to spare children all the consequences of defective parenting. In any event, it simply could not be done.[39]

There is, however, rather limited research evidence on the role which information on ethnic, cultural and religious diversity plays in care proceedings. A study of 100 cases by Brophy et al. (2003a), while cautioning that there is no room for complacency, found that in most cases the court had access to some such information although, worryingly, some expert reports were completely blind to diversity issues. However, research evidence suggests that there is no evidence that care proceedings are brought without good reason (Masson et al., 2008), and there is evidence that most cases contain multiple allegations of parenting failures, in respect of parents who have multiple vulnerability factors (for example alcohol/drug abuse, mental health problems, chaotic lifestyles) (Brophy, 2006). Indeed Brophy et al.'s study (2003a) did not recommend any change to the threshold criteria, having found that:

there were no 'single issue' cases where allegations of significant harm to a child rested unequivocally on behaviours/attitudes defended as culturally acceptable by a parent but that professionals argued were unacceptable within western European assessments of ill-treatment. (Brophy et al., 2003b)

Summary and concluding thoughts

English and Welsh law adopts a liberal standard in child protection, seeking to reconcile the child's interests with a society's interest in protecting pluralism in parenting. The dominant messages are that intervention must be proportionate, protecting children while also respecting the interests of parents. The law seeks to ensure the involvement of parents and children in decision making, that children are placed, where possible, within their families, and that account is taken of the child's cultural background. An examination of the law and of research evidence suggests that on the whole the law and legal process provide robust protection of parents' interests while seeking to protect children.

There are concerns, however, at the level of practice, where there is a blurring of the boundary between voluntary and compulsory intervention, and evidence that sometimes legal safeguards are bypassed in the context of emergency intervention. In addition there are ongoing concerns about inter-agency cooperation and sharing of information, the efficiency of which is crucial to a system which adopts a 'liberal standard'. If the system cannot efficiently highlight cases of suspected child abuse, then there may be a case for a more modest collectivist proposal (as advocated by Archard (2004)), for example introducing random checks on children's well-being.

This discussion of risk management brings this chapter back full circle to Olsen's work (1985), with which it opened. One of her reasons for seeking to disclose the myth of State intervention was to draw attention to the limitations of thinking simply in terms of explicit intervention versus non-intervention; in such an approach possibilities in the middle ground can be overlooked. It is interesting that this view resonates with a recent critique of child protection policies across jurisdictions by child protection experts, who advocate a new ethical framework for social work practice and that child protection should be placed in a 'broader context of effective and comprehensive support for children, young people and families' (Lonne et al., 2009). In other words, 'intervention' should have a much broader and proactive meaning.

References

Archard, D. (2004) *Children: Rights and Childhood* (2nd edn), London, Routledge.

Brophy, J. (2006) *Research Review: Child Care Proceedings Under the Children Act 1989*, DCA Research Series 5/06, May, 2006.

Brophy, J., Jhutti-Johal, J. and Owen, C. (2003a) *Significant Harm: Child Protection Litigation in a Multi-cultural Setting*, Department of Constitutional Affairs.

Brophy, J., Jhutti-Johal, J. and Owen, C. (2003b) 'Assessing and documenting child ill-treatment in ethnic minority households', *Family Law*, 756.

Conway, H. (2002) 'The Laming Inquiry – Victoria Climbié's Legacy' *Family Law*, 755.

Department of Health (2000) *Framework for the Assessment of Children in Need and Their Families*.

Department of Health, the Home Office and DfES (2006) *Working Together to Safeguard Children*.

DHSS (Department of Health and Social Security) (1985) *Review of Child Care Law: Report to Ministers of an Inter-departmental Working Party*, London, HMSO.

Donzelot, J. (1980) *The Policing of Families: Welfare versus the State,* London, Hutchinson.

Dwyer, J. G. (2006) *The Relationship Rights of Children*, New York, Cambridge University Press.

Eekelaar, J. (1991) 'Are parents morally obliged to care for their children?', *Oxford Journal of Legal Studies*, 11(3): 340.

Eekelaar, J., Dingwall, L. R., Murray, T. (1982) 'Victims or threats? Children in care proceedings', *Journal of Social Welfare and Family Law*, 4(2): 68–82.

Freeman, M. (2008) 'The right to responsible parents', in J. Bridgeman, H. Keating and C. Lind (eds) *Responsibility, Law and the Family*, Aldershot, Ashgate.

Gilmore, S. (2008) Book Review: *The Relationship Rights of Children*, James G. Dwyer, New York, Cambridge University Press, 2006 (2008) *International Journal of Law, Policy and the Family*, 22(2): 273.

Hall, S. J. (2000) 'What price the logic of evidence?', *Family Law* 260.

Hayes, J. (2000) 'The threshold test and the unknown perpetrator', *Family Law* 260.

Hayes, J. (2008) 'Farewell to the cogent evidence test: *Re B*', *Family Law*, 859.

Hayes, M. (2004) '*Re O & N; Re B* – Uncertain evidence and risk-taking in child protection cases', *Child and Family Law Quarterly*, 63.

Hayes, M. (2009) 'Removing children from their families – law and policy before the Children Act 1989', in G. Douglas and N. Lowe, *The Continuing Evolution of Family Law,* Bristol, Jordan Publishing Limited.

Herring, J. (2009) 'Protecting vulnerable adults: a critical review of recent case law', *Child and Family Law Quarterly* (forthcoming).

Houlgate, L. D. (1998) 'What is legal intervention in the family? Family law and family privacy', *Law and Philosophy*, 17: 141–58.

Keating, H. (1996) 'Shifting standards in the House of Lords', *Child and Family Law Quarterly,* 157.

Keating, H. (2009) 'Suspicions, sitting on the fence and standards of proof', *Child and Family Law Quarterly,* 230.

LaFollette, H. (1980) 'Licensing parents' 9 *Philosophy and Public Affairs,* 182.

London Borough of Greenwich (1987) *A Child in Mind: Protection of Children in a Responsible Society: Report of the Commission of Inquiry into the Circumstances Surrounding the Death of Kimberley Carlile.*

Lonne, B., Parton, N., Thomson, J. and Harries, M. (2009) *Reforming Child Protection,* Oxford, Routledge.

Laming, Lord (2003) *The Victoria Climbié Inquiry: Report of an Inquiry by Lord Laming,* (CM 5730, January, 2003).

Mangel, C. P. (1988) 'Licensing parents: how feasible?' 22 *Family Law Quarterly* 17.

Masson, J. (2002) 'Police protection – protecting whom?', *Journal of Social Welfare and Family Law* 157.

Masson, J. (2004) 'Emergency protection, good practice and human rights', *Family Law* 882.

Masson, J. (2005) 'Emergency intervention to protect children: using and avoiding legal controls', *Child and Family Law Quarterly* 75.

Masson, J. (2008) 'Improving care proceedings: can the PLO resolve the problem of delay?' Parts I and II at *Family Law* 1019 and 1029 respectively.

Masson, J., Pearce, J., Bader, K., with Joyner, O., Marsden, J. and Westlake, D. (2008) *Care Profiling Study,* Ministry of Justice, March, 2008.

Olsen, F. E. (1985) 'The myth of state intervention in the family' (1984–85) *University of Michigan Journal of Law Reform,* 18, pp. 835–64.

Packman, J. (1986) *Who Needs Care? Social Work Decisions about Children,* Chichester, Blackwell Publishing.

Parton, N. (1991) *Governing the Family: Child Care, Child Protection and the State,* Basingstoke, Macmillan – now Palgrave Macmillan.

Parton, N. and Martin, N. (1989) 'Public inquiries, legalism and child care in England and Wales' 3 *International Journal of Law and the Family,* pp. 21–39.

Secretary of State for Social Services (1987) *The Law on Child Care and Family Services,* (Cm 62), London, HMSO.

Secretary of State for Social Services (1988) *Report of the Inquiry into Child Abuse in Cleveland,* Cmnd 412, London, HMSO.

Short Report, Social Services Committee (1984) London, HMSO (HC 360).

Westman, J. C. (1994) *Licensing Parents: Can We Prevent Child Abuse and Neglect?,* Cambridge, MA, Perseus Books.

Williams, J. (2008) 'State responsibility and the abuse of vulnerable older people: is there a case for a public law to protect vulnerable older people from abuse?', in J. Bridgeman, H. Keating and C. Lind (eds) *Responsibility, Law and the Family,* Aldershot, Ashgate.

Notes

1. At p. 837. This position has been criticised by Houlgate (1998) who argues that because nothing can count as non-intervention the conclusion that there is no such thing as non-intervention is logically empty.
2. Space precludes any consideration of State intervention to protect vulnerable adults, on which see Williams (2008) and Herring (2009).
3. For an account of Dwyer's arguments, and criticism, see Gilmore (2008).
4. Children and Young Persons Act 1969, s.28.
5. Ibid., s.1.
6. Child Care Act 1980, s.3.
7. Issued pursuant to s.7 of the Local Authority Social Services Act 1970, and with which local authorities must therefore comply in carrying out their social services functions.
8. (*Z and Others v. United Kingdom* [2000] FLR 603.
9. *P, C and S v. United Kingdom* [2002] 2 FLR 631.
10. Now known as fabricated or induced illness by carers: see RCPCH. *Fabricated or Induced Illness by Carers; Report of Paediatrics and Child Health* (2002).
11. See also *K and T v. Finland* [2000] 2 FLR 79 where there was a breach of article 8 in removing a baby at birth from his mother who had a history of schizophrenia. Removal of the child from the mother, whose mental health was good at the time, without consultation, was arbitrary and unjustified, and constituted a disproportionate interference with the mother's rights.
12. *Hokkanen v. Finland* [1996] FLR 289.
13. A child is 'in need' if : '(a) he is unlikely to achieve or maintain, or to have the opportunity of achieving or maintaining, a reasonable standard of health or development without the provision for him of services by a local authority under this Part; (b) his health or development is likely to be significantly impaired, or further impaired, without the provision for him of such services; or (c) he is disabled, and 'family', in relation to such a child, includes any person who has parental responsibility for the child and any other person with whom he has been living [CA 1989, s.17(10)].
14. *R v. Tameside Metropolitan Borough Council ex parte J* [2000] FLR 442.
15. *Humberside CC v. B* [1993] 1 FLR 257.
16. There is also a similar frustrated access ground in the case of enquiries by the NSPCC.
17. [2004] EWHC 2015, [2005] 1 FLR 341.
18. [2006] EWHC 510 (Fam), [2006] 2 FLR 701.
19. An application made without giving notice of it in advance to the child's family.
20. *Haringey LPC v. C E and Anor* [2005] 2 FLR 47.
21. See CA 1989, s.35 and Sch 3.
22. An exclusion requirement similar to that under s.44A can be attached to an interim care order (see s.38A). The court may give directions for medical, psychiatric or other assessment of the child although a child of sufficient understanding has a right to refuse such assessment.

23. See *Re M (A Minor) (Care Order: Threshold Conditions)* [1994] 3 WLR 558, HL. See for example, *Re L (Children) (Care Proceedings)* [2006] 3 FCR 301.
24. *Re H and R (Child Sexual Abuse: Standard of Proof)* [1996] 1FLR 80, HL.
25. Ibid.
26. Ibid.
27. [2008] UKHL 35.
28. *Birmingham CC* v. *D*; *Birmingham CC* v. *M* [1994] 2 FLR 502.
29. *Re SH (Care Order: Orphan)* [1993] 1 FLR 746, FD.
30. *Re M (Care Order: Parental Responsibility)* [1996] 2 FLR 84.
31. [2000] 1 FLR 583.
32. [2003] UKHL 18, [2003] 1 FLR 1169.
33. *Re O (Supervision Order)* [2001] 1 FLR 923, CA.
34. CA 1989, s.31A.
35. Ibid., s.33(3)(a) and (b).
36. *Re G (Care: Challenge to Local Authority's Decision)* [2003] 2 FLR 42, FD.
37. Ibid. s.34(11).
38. s.34(4). Under s.34(6) the local authority may deny contact for a period of no more than 7 days where refusal is decided on as a matter of urgency, and the local authority is satisfied that it is necessary to safeguard or promote the child's welfare.
39. *Re L (Care: Threshold Criteria)* [2007] 1 FLR 20, at para [50].

Chapter 3

Partnership or Participation?

LUCY RAI AND DEBBIE STRINGER

Introduction

This chapter considers the concept of working in partnership with parents in the context of social work practice with children and families. It considers the origins and development of partnership working with parents through an exploration of relevant research, policy and legislation and examines what practitioners understand working in partnership to mean. The chapter concludes with consideration of the practice issues related to involving parents in decision making when children are in need or at risk and explores the possibility that participation, rather than partnership might better define the relationship between social workers and parents.

The origins of partnership working with families

Developments in childcare legislation, policy and practice over the past three decades have been driven by both high profile investigations into child deaths or abuse and research. The childcare system and professionals who work within it have constantly been accused of a failure to protect children from harm or abuse despite a number of significant changes in legislation and practice. Anxieties about the effectiveness of the childcare system were deepened during the 1980s by the tragic deaths of Jasmine Beckford (1984), Tyra Henry (1984), Heidi Koseda (1984), Kimberly Carlile (1986) and Doreen Mason (1987). All of these children died despite having been brought to the attention of local authority social workers (or in the case of Heidi an NSPCC social worker). While the competence of social workers was brought into question, so was the effectiveness of the legislation available to them to protect children in an emergency. While the deaths of these children had a great influence on the policy that led to the enactment of the Children Act 1989 (for a fuller discussion on the influences see Parton, 1991), concerns about the ability of the legislative framework and the professionals who work within it have remained. The tragic death of Victoria Climbié, at the hands of her great-aunt and partner in 2000, in circumstances which mirrored the death of Maria Colwell in 1973 (DHSS, 1974), and the subsequent report of Lord Laming, detailing the inquiry into her death (DH and the Home Office, 2003) led directly to the enactment of the Children Act 2004. This Act altered the structure of local authority provision of services to children and families and sought to increase accountability by the introduction, for example, of the role of Director of Children's Services. It also introduced the role of the Children's Commissioner (for a detailed account of this role see Williams, 2005). Despite the introduction of such radical changes, the death of Baby P in 2008 while in the care of his mother and her partner and known to social services, police and health service professionals caused further public concern that both the childcare system and professionals working within it were ineffective in protecting children (Laming, 2009).

While public and professional concern about the ability of professionals, within the current childcare system, to protect children have remained a constant, prior to the introduction of the Children Act 1989 there was also widespread public and professional concern relating to parental rights. Concerns first arose in the early 1980s about the limited rights of parents and the fact that the law did not recognise the importance of parental involvement in the lives of children who had entered the public care system. Legislation in place prior to 1989 enabled children to be removed from the care of their parents under a place of safety order for a month without the matter being taken before a court and with no guarantee of the parents being represented when the case did eventually come before the magistrates. When the matter did come before the court the magistrates often appeared to rubber stamp decisions and not really hold social workers or doctors to account for their actions. (DHSS, 1988). Concerns were twofold, firstly that a parent ought to be consulted and have their views considered and secondly, concern over the harm that could be caused to a child by having their links with a parent severed or severely curtailed. Research into the experiences of parents of children in the public care system was reported in *Social Work Decisions in Childcare* (DH, 1985) and suggested that parents' links with their children were intentionally or otherwise being lost and that outcomes for children were better where greater involvement with parents could be maintained. As early as 1983 it was recognised that parental involvement in the lives of children living away from home was crucial and practice guidance was issued to assist social workers with implementing systems which encouraged greater involvement of parents (DHSS, 1983).

Alongside the drive for parental involvement in order to improve outcomes for children in the public care system, the work of the Family

Rights Group drew to the attention of policymakers the importance of parental involvement and rights of access to children where intervention was voluntary, that is where parents had agreed to place their children in care. It was recognised that the loss of contact for children, many of whom were in 'voluntary' care, was detrimental to the child even where there were concerns about the safety of the child. Policy was influenced by the lobbying of the Family Rights Group and the decision of the European Court of Human Rights in *B* v. *UK* 8th July 1987 which stated that *'the mutual enjoyment by parent and child of each other's company constitutes a fundamental element of family life'*.

Further research conducted during the 1980s suggested that parents' experiences of compulsory intervention were diverse. Findings from these studies indicated that while parents appreciated an approach which encouraged their involvement (Fisher et al., 1986) they also expressed fear and suspicion about social work intervention (Rees and Wallace, 1982). These findings illustrated the perennial tension in child protection between care and control, empowerment and anti-discriminatory practice (DHSS, 1985). Even where efforts were being made by social workers to involve them, the relationships between social workers and parents were strained by the imbalance of power and consequent lack of trust. These difficult relationships were further hampered by the unhelpful complexity and adversarial nature of protective legislation prior to the Children Act 1989 (Dale et al., 1986, p. 73).

Although public and professional concern had been expressed about the childcare system generally throughout the 1980s, it was events in Cleveland that focused attention on parents' rights to be consulted. The Cleveland Inquiry (Butler-Sloss, 1987) was instigated as a result of a large number of children (over 100) being taken into care against the wishes of parents on the grounds that they had possibly been sexually abused. The social services department was guided by local consultant paediatricians who identified what they thought were cases of serious abuse,[1] but at that time the law afforded only limited provision for oversight of such decisions to take children away from their parents. It was difficult for parents to challenge both the diagnosis itself and the professional practice of the social workers. Many parents were given either little or no information about their children and were denied access to them, in some instances for a month or more. Extracts from the Cleveland report indicate the situation parents found themselves in:

> 2.34 The parents of three children aged 9, 7 and just under 2 years, described the total denial of access to their children both while in hospital and in foster care ...

2.36 Many parents felt strongly that they should be heard at case conferences. A number told the inquiry that they were informed that case conferences were to be held. Some said they were told they could not attend. Others said they were informed they could attend but would not be admitted or would not be heard while the meeting was in progress. Some said they were told the results of case conferences. Others complained they were told neither of case conferences nor of decisions reached there.

The Cleveland Inquiry occupied headlines for over a year, raising questions not only about the reliability of the medical 'diagnosis' of abuse but also the lack of procedural rights afforded to parents and the detrimental impact on the children resulting from removal and subsequent loss of contact with their parents.

In summary, therefore, over the 1980s concerns were expressed about the ineffectiveness of the childcare system to protect children in an emergency while at the same time allowing children to be removed from their parents based upon limited evidence with little or no opportunity to effectively challenge such a decision:

There were concerns that social workers did not have the appropriate power to act swiftly to protect children in emergencies. On the other hand, the law had allowed social workers to be heavy-handed and remove children on flimsy evidence for unwarranted periods. Either way, assessment of the impact of abuse on children's development was faulty. (DH, 2001, p. 6)

In addition, there was concern about the harmful outcomes for children resulting from losing parental involvement in their lives and the inability of the legislation of the day to enable and encourage parents to be involved in decision making about their children in both voluntary and emergency intervention. This was recognised and attributed in part to the inherently adversarial system which hindered any attempts made to develop collaborative working relationships with parents based on trust.

The introduction of partnership to legislation

Although the events in Cleveland raised the issue of the lack of parental involvement in decisions to remove children from their care in a very public way, the government of the day had been aware some time before Cleveland that parents' rights were limited and that this had implications for children's welfare. Michael Meacher, at the time MP for

Oldham West, when informed by the then health minister that there would be a public enquiry into events at Cleveland, asked in the House of Commons:

> Why is there nothing in this statement about implementing last year's proposals for reform of the law on childcare and family services, which command all-party agreement and are tailor-made for strengthening parental rights, which have been such an issue in Cleveland? The Government produced a White Paper on these agreed proposals in January this year. Why was there no Bill to implement them set out in the Queen's Speech? (Commons Debate, 9th July 1987, Vol. 119, cc. 528–38)

The White Paper referred to by Michael Meacher (DHSS, 1987) recommended that, in order to protect parents' rights in future legislation the distinction between compulsory and voluntary intervention should be clearer. The White Paper which provided the foundations for the Children Act 1989, referred directly to partnership stating that:

> (2) Services to families in need should be arranged in voluntary partnership with parents. (DHSS, 1987, para. 5)

This is perhaps the first time that the term 'partnership' appears in relation to work with children and families; the term is however qualified by the word 'voluntary' and arguably refers to the situation where a local authority is providing support for a family where there is a child 'in need' (s.17). It does not provide assistance when discussing intervention that is compulsory, nor does it provide any guidance as to what is meant by 'partnership'.

The introduction of the concept of parental responsibility in s.2 of the Children Act 1989 signified an important change in the role of parents, bestowing on parents enduring rights and responsibilities even where the state intervened in the lives of their children. It is a concept as much about parents' duties towards their children as it is about their rights but the introduction of such a concept does provide acknowledgement of the importance of parents to the welfare of children. Parental responsibility is defined as:

> all the rights, duties, powers, responsibilities and authority which by law a parent of a child has in relation to the child and his property. (S.3 Children Act 1989)

With the introduction of the concept of parental responsibility, recognising the rights of parents to make important decisions about their child, such as the right to consent to medical treatment on the child's behalf or the right to decide the child's religious and cultural upbringing, the law created a framework whereby the rights of parents could no longer be ignored particularly as parents retain responsibility for their children unless and until the children are adopted even when compulsory orders are made by the court, such as a care order (s.31). While a child is subject to a care order the local authority also has parental responsibility for the child and can to a certain extent limit the exercise of parental responsibility by the parents, arguably eroding but never extinguishing the parental responsibility of the parents. This is referred to as the '49%/51% partnership balance' (Cocker and Allain, 2008), with the local authority having at least 51% of the decision-making authority in the partnership. The law however limits the local authority's power, in that a local authority cannot change the child's name or religion, appoint a guardian or consent to an adoption order (s.33(6)). Recognition of parents' rights did not exist in this form prior to the introduction of the Children Act 1989. It is arguable that as parents retain rights in respect of their children, even when they are deemed unable to care for them, that a partnership was envisaged by the legislators. Unfortunately, as the term did not appear in the legislation, neither professionals nor service users have had the benefit of the courts' interpretation. Perhaps, had the courts been asked to interpret the term they would have made use of extrinsic aids such as the research which informed the legislation of the time (DHSS 1985; Thoburn et al., 1986). This research recommended a more participatory approach to parents where they were to be actively involved in the decision-making process; the importance of the parents' role was as that of participant rather than partner. Despite this, the process of involving parents in the decision-making process became known as working 'in partnership'.

Although the term 'partnership' did not make its way into the Act itself, it does appear in the guidance which was published by the Department of Health alongside the Act. This overarching guidance provided a coherent framework for the detail of the collected volumes of Guidance and Regulations that followed. The operational principles were intended 'to assist practitioners and supervisors to relate law to practice and to understand the context in which Regulations and Guidance were issued'. One of the key operational principles was as follows:

> The development of a working partnership with parents is usually the most effective route to providing supplementary or substitute care for their children. (Home Office, 1989)

A further nine volumes of Guidance and Regulations were published in 1991; Volume 2, *Family Support, Day Care and Educational Provision for Young Children*, (DH, 1991) refers directly to partnership working. It reinforces the duty of the social workers to attempt to reach voluntary arrangements with families in order to meet the needs of their children, particularly where it is thought appropriate to offer accommodation:

> Work with parents to achieve an initial agreement to the accommodation of the child by the local authority will usually ensure that the ongoing plan for the child can be operated in partnership with his parents. (DH, 1991, p. 12)

Guidance to the Children Act 1989 therefore identified working in partnership with children and families as an important aspect of achieving best outcomes for children where the cooperation of parents could be sustained in order to involve them in meeting their children's needs. Even within this initial guidance, however, there was recognition that the primary role of partnership working was prior to compulsory intervention and the guidance offers little advice on how such a partnership would manifest itself or how it could be maintained where protective measures were imposed.

Partnership in practice

Following the enactment of the Children Act 1989, the Department of Health commissioned a number of studies intended to review the effectiveness of the Act. Thoburn et al. (1995) focused specifically on the effectiveness of partnership working in work with children and families after the introduction of the Act. Thoburn et al. concluded that social workers in their study were inconsistent in their use of partnership working or their understanding of it. The confusion about the interpretation of the term 'partnership' remains today. Taylor and Le Riche (2006, p. 215) in their review of partnership working, note that 'there are a plethora of terms to be grappled with, including "participation and partnership", "involvement" and "collaboration"'. Given the Family Rights Group campaigned for a recognition of parents' rights and defined partnership in the early 1990s, it seems surprising that such uncertainty remained:

> Partnership is about a redistribution of power from the very powerful (professionals) to the powerless (families and children). Partnership means respect for one another, rights to information, accountability,

competence and value accorded to each individual input. In short, each partner is seen as having something to contribute, power is shared, decisions are made jointly, roles are not only represented but backed by legal and moral rights. (Family Rights Group, 1991)

Despite such a clear steer from the Family Rights Group, Thoburn et al. (1995) found that the confusion about what partnership actually meant remained but that where there was a commitment to some form of participation by parents in relation to decisions and planning about their children, the outcomes for children were better. Of those parents questioned in the study however, only 35% said that they considered that they had taken part in decision making. The study recognised that the degree of involvement was significantly attributable to the nature of the family circumstances or problems but also suggested that a failure to involve parents could 'almost always be traced to aspects of agency procedures' (DH, 1995a, p. 86). Thoburn et al. also suggested that a degree of working in partnership with parents was possible even where there were suspicions of child abuse. They acknowledged, however, that there was a difference between a parent seeking assistance from the local authority, for example short-term respite care where there would be little evidence of tension, compared with the situation where a parent is suspected of mistreating their child. Inevitably, in such a situation there will at least be tension and almost inevitably conflict. The vision of partnership extolled by the Family Rights Group did not manifest itself in practice according to the research conducted by Thoburn et al.

There were, therefore, genuine tensions that arose in the decade following 1989 when social workers were attempting to put the principle of partnership working into practice, although there is little discussion of such tensions in the social work literature (Taylor and Le Riche, 2006, p. 15). While the Guidance to the 1989 Act suggests that partnership most naturally arises where social workers are intervening on a voluntary basis, the research supporting the benefits of partnership resulted in a strong moral imperative to maximise partnership working in all interventions. Partnership working was, however, always recognised as a challenge for practitioners but the view that partnership working was of benefit to children and families remained:

The fact that [parents] can take part in decision making helps build up their self-esteem and encourages adults to feel more in control of their lives. Professional practice which reduces a family's sense of powerlessness, and helps them feel and function more competently, is likely to improve the well-being of both parents and children. (DH, 1995b)

In 1995 the Department of Health published *The Challenge of Partnership in Child Protection: Practice Guide* (DH, 1995b). This guidance explored the benefits of partnership working, such as greater effectiveness, the value of families as a source of information, parents' and children's rights and also the emerging agenda of service-user empowerment. In addition, the guide introduced the concept of 'participatory practice' as a component of partnership. It was suggested that partnership is the ultimate goal which lies along a sequential path:

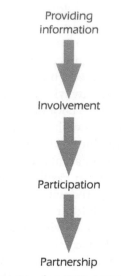

Source: Based on DH, 1995b, p. 10.

The guidance advises social workers that although partnership is always the goal, it may only be a reality at certain points in the working relationship due to changes in circumstances and levels of trust (DH, 1995b, p. 11). One important barrier to effective partnership working arises from the inevitable imbalance of power between service users and professionals. A true partnership relies on equality of power and shared aims, neither of which may be in place where social workers use statutory powers to intervene in family life. Marsh and Fisher (1992), argue however that partnership can still exist even with the imposition of intervention, as intervention can only be imposed with the authority of an external mandate, for example the court. They suggest that in such circumstances the social worker and the parents have equal power and authority and therefore remain partners while the court acts as arbitrator. This view does not acknowledge the fact that only the local authority or an authorised person can bring matters to the attention of the court nor the manner in which the court views the evidence, giving more weight to the evidence of the social work professional who is usually seen as having greater knowledge of what is in a child's 'best interests'. It is arguable therefore that partnership cannot be achieved where there is such an imbalance of power; indeed a small number of studies suggest that partnership working in some circumstances had become a 'sham' (DH, 2001, p. 51). Hunt et al. (1999) highlight the inherent conflict created by an attempt to work in partnership with parents in what might be described as a situation in which the commitment to partnership leads to coercion:

> The fact that we have to go for accommodation with a threat of an application if parents don't agree, that's a much more subtle use of power than actually putting it before the court. I would have thought it felt more oppressive. Best practice would ensure you use accommodation wherever possible but this is forcing accommodation. (Hunt et al., 1999)

In April 2008 the government introduced the Public Law Outline (PLO) (MOJ, 2008) in England and Wales. The PLO is a case management system for all court cases involving public law proceedings relating to children. While seeking to manage cases that are already before the court the PLO also sets out steps that should be taken by the local authority where an application to the court for a care or supervision order is contemplated. The steps to be taken are designed to prevent the necessity of court proceedings and include a duty upon the local authority to facilitate a Family Group Conference (FGC). An FGC allows the family an opportunity to find their own solutions to difficulties that they are facing. This model of working evolved in New Zealand. It is not a single event but a process whereby the family can share information and resources in order to address the issues the local authority have. The social worker does not participate in the conference itself but provides information to the family such as the nature of the local authority's concerns and the range of support that might be available to the family in addressing these concerns. The impact of the PLO and Family Group Conferences, in particular their success in averting care proceedings, is not known at the time of writing but it is arguable that such a process represents a redistribution of power away from the local authority to the family, perhaps allowing the type of partnership originally envisaged by the Family Rights Group. The local authority, however, must approve and monitor the family's plan for change suggesting that power remains firmly with them; given the PLO aspires to avoid court proceedings, the opportunity to challenge the local authority's decision is limited.

Genuine partnerships?

There has been criticism over the past two decades that the optimism around partnership working with parents is unfounded and that, although procedures for information sharing may have improved, the degree of genuine involvement by parents in decision making remains very limited (Corby, 1996). The challenge of working in partnership with parents when there are differences of view between professionals and parents are numerous (Clifford and Burke, 2004); Aldgate (2001) acknowledges that although the concept of 'partnership' became one of the key principles of the Children Act 1989, the term is not helpful in conveying the reality of working with parents. She suggests that the term 'participation' might have been more helpful:

> With hindsight, the term 'partnership' was perhaps unfortunate, subject to much variation in interpretation and unable to convey the tension that surrounds social work intervention in cases of maltreatment ... 'Participation' might have had a more precise and measurable meaning. However, the intention was clear; to include parents in decision-making concerning their children who were in receipt of child welfare services. (Aldgate, 2001)

Despite the inherent challenges of maintaining a partnership approach, however, the concept of partnership working has remained a credible one with the outcomes of working in a participatory manner being justification for the effort needed to make it work, especially where compulsory action is warranted (Aldgate, 2001). As a result the concept of working in partnership has been further embedded into best practice through guidance provided in the *Framework for the Assessment of Children in Need and their Families* (DH, 2000):

> The importance of partnership has been further reinforced ... In the process of finding out what is happening to a child, it will be critical to develop a co-operative working relationship, so that parents or caregivers feel respected and informed, that staff are being open and honest with them, and that they in turn are confident about providing vital information about their child, themselves and their circumstances. (DH, 2000, pp. 12–13)

The Framework very clearly repositions partnership working as a vital component of *safeguarding* children. Although genuine 'partnership' remains difficult to achieve in the context of unequal power, the reality remains that it is in children's interests for their parents to be consulted and involved in assessments, decision making and planning as well as, where safe to do so, to maintain contact with them:

> It was never the intention of the Act that partnership should be an end in itself, but rather that the participation of parents in decisions should be part of the process of promoting children's welfare at all levels, from participation in family centres to participation in the courts. (DH, 2001, p. 57)

Clearly therefore, it is intended that partnership should be applied to compulsory as well as voluntary contexts and that social workers should be working towards partnership in order to improve outcomes for children. Recognising both the challenges as well as the importance of involving parents, Stratham and Aldgate (2003) offer the following features of successful participatory practice with parents:

- services that are targeted at the whole family, not just the child;
- inter-agency services that are well coordinated;
- services that offer a combination of practical and emotional help;
- services that are offered in a welcoming, non-stigmatising manner;
- family centres that combine referred and non-referred cases and offer open access to a range of services or activities;
- transparency about the purpose and expected outcomes of services; and
- social workers who are approachable, honest, understanding, reliable, helpful and have time to listen.

(Stratham and Aldgate, 2003, p. 152)

These seven aspects of effective participatory practice broaden out the concept of partnership. Stratham and Aldgate recognise the importance of providing non-stigmatising services for the wider family in order to support the child at risk or in need and providing services that meet emotional as well as practical needs. They also highlight the importance of developing relationships based on openness and honesty. Sharing information in an honest and straightforward manner could be argued to be the baseline of participatory practice. Even in situations where statutory intervention results in parents having very little power or influence on decision making, social workers who are demonstrably reliable, treat parents with respect and empathy and share information honestly can create an environment where cooperation can be fostered.

Conclusion

Building partnership working with parents into the childcare system has been a challenging task for social work professionals. While there are those who remain of the view that a genuine and equal partnership can be maintained even where there is compulsory intervention (Jordan, 2001) there is little strong evidence of the survival of 'partnership' other than in facilitating participation. However, the substantial body of research which accrued in support of partnership working prior to 2001 has left a mark on professional practice. Despite initial public concern being for parental rights in a highly adversarial legal context, it has in fact been children's welfare that has provided the enduring argument for involving parents. Not only does contact with parents continue to be important for children's welfare but there is information that only parents can contribute in important ways to assessing and meeting the needs of children. Engaging in the challenges of partnership working has also provided some important lessons about best practice with families. For example, it is rarely helpful to try and meet the needs of a child in isolation from the needs of the wider family, although social workers must be alive to the risks of concentrating on the needs of the family as a whole to the detriment of the child. Partnership working has also confronted social workers directly with the impact of the imbalance of power between social workers and families and demanded that they develop ways of working which build constructive relationships within the context of inequality. Through facing head-on the accusation that partnership working is a sham, social work has been challenged to develop skills in empathic, open communication within a context of hostility and mistrust. Maybe most importantly, the challenge of facilitating participatory working has re-focused assessments onto the strengths and resources that families can offer in meeting the needs of their children. Identifying such strengths can only be achieved through open communication and valuing diverse families honestly. In maintaining such a dialogue, then, social workers might be better served by abandoning the term 'partnership', and the false premise of equal power that the term implies, and instead embrace the term 'participation', which more accurately describes the complex relationship between the social worker and the family.

References

Aldgate, J. (2001) 'Safeguarding and promoting the welfare of children in need living with their families' in Cull, L-A. and Roche, J. (eds) *The Law and*

Social Work: Contemporary Issues for Practice, Basingstoke, Palgrave Macmillan, 2001.

Butler-Sloss, E. (1987) *Report of the Inquiry into Child Abuse in Cleveland*, CM 413, London, HMSO.

Clifford, D. and Burke, B. (2004) 'Moral and professional dilemmas in long-term assessment of children and families', *Journal of Social Work*, 4(3): 305–21.

Cocker, C. and Allain, L. (2008) *Social Work with Looked After Children*, Exeter, Learning Matters.

Corby, B. (1996) 'Risk assessment in child protection', in Kemshall, H. and Pritchard, J. (eds), *Good Practice in Risk Assessment and Risk Management*, London, Jessica Kingsley.

Dale, P., Davies, M., Morrison, T. and Waters, J. (1986) *Dangerous Families: Assessment and Treatment of Child Abuse*, Tavistock.

DH (Department of Health) (1985) *Social Work Decisions in Childcare*, London, HMSO.

DH (Department of Health) (1991) *The Children Act 1989 Guidance and Regulations Vol. 2.* London, HMSO.

DH (Department of Health) (1995a) *Child Protection: Messages from Research*, London, HMSO.

DH (Department of Health) (1995b) *The Challenge of Partnership in Child Protection: Practice Guide*, London, HMSO.

DH (Department of Health) (2000) *Framework for the Assessment of Children in Need and their Families*, London, HMSO.

DH (Department of Health) (2001) *The Children Act Now: Messages from Research* London, HMSO.

DH (Department of Health) and the Home Office (2003) *The Victoria Climbié Inquiry: Report of an Inquiry by Lord Laming*, London, HMSO.

DHSS (Department of Health and Social Security) (1974) *The Report of the Committee of Inquiry into the Care and Supervision Provided in Relation to Maria Colwell.* London, HMSO.

DHSS (Department of Health and Social Security) (1983) *Access to Children in Care: Code of Practice*, London, Butterworths.

DHSS (Department of Health and Social Security) (1985) *Review of Child Care Law: Report to Ministers of an Interdepartmental Working Party*, London, HMSO.

DHSS (1987) *The Law on Child Care and Family Services*, CM 62, London, HMSO.

DHSS (Department of Health and Social Security) (1988) *The Report of the Inquiry into Child Abuse in Cleveland* (Butler-Sloss inquiry), London, HMSO.

Family Rights Group (1991) *The Children Act 1989: Working in Partnership with Families*, Reader, A five-day training programme for social workers, their managers and allied professionals, London, Family Rights Group.

Fisher, M., Marsh, P., Phillips, D. and Sainsbury, E. (1986) *In and Out of Care: The Experiences of Children, Parents and Social Workers*, London, B.T. Batsford.

Home Office (1989) *An Introduction to the Children Act,* London, HMSO.

Hunt, J., Macleod, A. and Thomas, C. (1999) *The Last Resort: Child Protection, the Courts and the 1989 Children Act*, London, The Stationery Office.

Jordan, L. (2001) 'Practising Partnership', in Cull, L.-A. and Roche, J. (eds) *The Law and Social Work: Contemporary Issues for Practice*, Basingstoke, Palgrave Macmillan.

Laming, Lord (2009) *The Protection of Children in England: A Progress Report*, London, HMSO.

Marsh, P. and Fisher, M. (1992) *Good Intentions: Developing Partnership in Social Services*, York, Joseph Rowntree Foundation.

MOJ (Ministry of Justice) (2008) *The Public Law Outline: Guide to Case Management in Public Law Proceedings*, London, HMSO.

Parton, N. (1991) *Governing the Family: Child Care, Child Protection and the State*, Basingstoke, Macmillan Press – now Palgrave Macmillan.

Rees, S. and Wallace, A. (1982) *Verdicts on Social Work*, London, Edward Arnold.

Stratham, J. and Aldgate, J. (2003) 'From legislation to practice: learning from the Children Act 1989 research programme', *Children & Society*, 17: 149–56.

Taylor, I. and Le Riche, P. (2006) 'What do we know about partnership with service users and carers in social work education and how robust is the evidence base?', *Health and Social Care in the Community*, 14(5): 418–25.

Thoburn, J., Lewis, A. and Shemmings, D. (1995) *Paternalism or Partnership?: Family Involvement in the Child Protection Process*, London, HMSO.

Thoburn, J., Murdoch, A. and O'Brien, A. (1986) *Permanence in Child Care*, Oxford, Blackwell.

Williams, J. (2005) 'Effective government structures for children? The UK's four children's commissioners', *Child and Family Law Quarterly*, 17: 37–53.

Cases

B v. UK 1987

Note

1. In Cleveland the local authority was guided by two consultant paediatricians regarding whether or not the children had in fact suffered abuse. Cleveland therefore also highlights the issues inherent in partnership working between professionals.

Chapter 4

The More Things Change, the More They Remain the Same?
Law, Social Work and Counteracting Discrimination

MICHAEL PRESTON-SHOOT

Introduction

One purpose of this chapter is to outline the law on discrimination and to illustrate how it has developed and continues to evolve through time. From hesitant beginnings with race relations legislation in 1965, the pace has quickened, especially in the twenty-first century. This particularly reflects the United Kingdom's obligations arising from membership of the European Union and the incorporation into domestic law via the Human Rights Act 1998 of the European Convention on Human Rights (ECHR). Another purpose is to explore the reasons underpinning this legislative trajectory, in essence addressing the question of why particular legal rules are (not) enacted. The advent of legal rules to counteract discrimination and to promote equality of opportunity has been marked by struggle. The enactment in 1995 of the first legal rules concerning disability discrimination followed numerous failed attempts. Debates surrounding equality legislation continually reveal the extent to which this is a site of social, moral and religious contest, with, for example, advocating and dissenting voices in respect of enabling gay men and lesbians to adopt, equalising the age of consent, or allowing young people to wear faith-based dress in school.

A third purpose is to reflect on the interface between these legal rules and social work with its espousal of anti-discriminatory practice. With social work sometimes sceptical of the degree to which the legal rules endorse and support social work's value commitments (Preston-Shoot et al., 2001), this chapter provides an opportunity to investigate the degree to which the legal rules on counteracting discrimination have become part of social work's practice framework and constrain or promote its ethical commitments. For balanced interpretation, light can also be shone on how practice interprets and responds to legal obligations, adheres to codified ethical principles, and manages the dilemmas that have their roots in diversity. That social work practice must rest and draw upon a legal, rights and values literacy (Braye and Preston-Shoot, 2006; Braye et al., 2007) will be highlighted as this chapter unfolds.

Counteracting discrimination: social work practice frameworks

Social workers must not discriminate either unlawfully or unjustifiably (GSCC, 2002). They must promote social justice, challenge individual, institutional and structural discrimination, uphold legal rules on equality, and combat processes that lead to marginalisation and social exclusion (QAA, 2008). They must respect people's human rights, value their diversity, and enable them to maintain independence and develop their potential. This involves drawing on principles of equality and diversity to dismantle barriers and to resist stereotyping (GSCC, 2008). National occupational standards (TOPSS, 2002) require social workers to be competent in managing complex ethical issues and dilemmas, in explaining clearly their legal powers and duties, and in challenging injustice and lack of access to services. Their critical gaze should be cast upon their employing organisations as well as upon the legislative process itself as part of demonstrating respect for individuals, families, groups and communities regardless of age, ethnicity and culture, and challenging discriminatory practices affecting them.

A code of ethics (BASW, 2002) provides another benchmark. Practice should emphasise human dignity and worth, enhance people's well-being, ensure their protection, promote their rights and offer respect. The codes (BASW, 2002; GSCC, 2002), however, anticipate that practitioners and managers will sometimes find the requirements of their employers diverge from these core principles. On these occasions social workers are exhorted to challenge and work to improve agency policies, procedures and service provision.

Immediately, then, anti-discriminatory practice is foregrounded in official documents which seek to shape social work's practice and education. This builds on a substantial social work tradition. Anti-discriminatory practice is good practice. A failure to meet an individual's needs and to alleviate disadvantage is, arguably, an act of injustice, an abuse of power and indicative of an absence of care. Organisations should provide a satisfactory and appropriate service for all communities. Practice to counteract discrimination and promote equality of opportunity should feature centrally to ensure that services are appropriate and accessible to each community. To what degree, however, do social work services counteract discrimination, promote equality of opportunity and enhance people's well-being? To what extent do agencies meet their legal as well as ethical obligations here? How do social workers and their managers foreground these codified values, especially when they are opposed by other imperatives that impact on and drive welfare organisations, such as the drive to reduce public expenditure?

Counteracting discrimination: the equality legislation framework

Social work's key commitment to anti-discriminatory practice finds increasing support in the legal rules, including the ECHR, article 14 of which provides that Convention rights themselves must be enjoyed without discrimination on grounds such as sex, race, language, religion, political opinion or birth status.

Section 71 of the Race Relations Act (RRA) 1976 imposed a duty on local authorities to ensure that their functions were performed with due regard for the need to eliminate unlawful racial discrimination, and to promote equality of opportunity and good relations between people of different racial groups. The Race Relations (Amendment) Act (RR(A)A) 2000 extends this original duty by requiring that all public authorities work towards the elimination of unlawful discrimination and promote equality of opportunity and good race relations. They must have strategies to prevent, investigate and record racist incidents. Exemptions are allowed for certain immigration and nationality functions, and judicial proceedings, including decisions not to prosecute. This trend is continued by the Disability Discrimination Act 2005 and the Equality Act 2006. Thus in respect of race, disability and gender, public authorities must now consider the equality implications of what they do, prepare impact statements and adopt schemes for equality in employment and service provision. The duties on public authorities thereby shift the focus beyond preventing or remedying individual acts of discrimination to taking positive action to address institutional processes and practices, attitudes and structural relationships that might otherwise perpetuate inequality.

Section 20 (RRA 1976) makes it unlawful for anyone providing goods, facilities or services to the public to discriminate by refusing or deliberately omitting to provide them or by the quality, manner or terms in which they are provided. Section 35 allows the special education, training and welfare needs of particular racial groups to be met by preferential allocation or restriction of access to such groups. The Race Relations Act (Amendment) Regulations 2003 implement the European Union article 13 Race Directive (2000/43/EC) into United Kingdom law, outlawing discrimination on grounds of racial or ethnic origin in employment, vocational training, goods and services, social protection, education and housing. The regulations allow any job to be subject to a genuine occupational requirement for a person of a particular race. There is a statutory prohibition of harassment, being when someone's actions or words are unwelcome and violate another person's dignity or create an environment that is intimidating, hostile, degrading, humiliating or offensive. The burden of proof is revised so that where a claimant has established a prima facie case of discrimination or harassment, the complaint will be upheld unless respondents provide evidence to prove the contrary. Business partnerships, charities, landlord/tenant relationships and employment in private homes are now covered.

The Sex Discrimination Act (SDA) 1975 (amended 1986) parallels the RRA 1976 in making it unlawful to discriminate on grounds of sex and marital status in employment, education and provision of goods, facilities and services. The Employment Equality (Sex Discrimination) Regulations 2005 bring the European Union Equal Treatment Directive (2002/73/EC) into United Kingdom law, requiring equal treatment for men and women in access to employment, vocational training and promotion, and working conditions. A further European Union Directive (2006/54/EC) reinforces the prohibition on sexual harassment, defined as a form of sex discrimination and a violation of dignity in the workplace. The Gender Recognition Act 2004 enables people who have decided to live permanently and fully in their chosen gender to apply for legal recognition of that change. Moreover, following the Equality Act (EA) 2006, public authorities must now promote equality of opportunity to counter sex discrimination, thereby mirroring the positive organisational duty demanded in respect of racial equality (RR(A)A 2000).

The Disability Discrimination Act (DDA) 1995 makes it unlawful to discriminate in connection with employment, access to buildings, and the provision of goods, facilities and services. Discrimination is defined as the refusal of a service or less favourable treatment that cannot be justified for reasons relating to disability. Disability is defined as a physical or mental impairment which has substantial and long-term adverse effects on an individual's ability to carry out normal daily activities. Employers and service providers must make reasonable adjustments, changing practice, policy and procedures that make it unreasonably difficult for disabled people to access jobs and services, and giving extra help or providing aids and other facilities to promote inclusion (*Roads* v. *Central Trains* (2004); *Ross* v. *Ryanair and Stansted*

Airport (2004)). What is reasonable depends on the resources available and the practicality of the adjustments, and should be based on a proper assessment of what is required to eliminate any substantial disadvantage (*Southampton City Council* v. *Randall* (2006)).

Partial reinforcement of the 1995 Act followed as a result of criticisms of vague drafting and weak provisions. The Disability Rights Commission Act 1999 created a commission with powers to prepare and enforce statutory codes of practice, provide advice and assistance to disabled people to secure their rights, and conduct formal investigations. Exemptions for small employers, originally contained in the 1995 Act, were removed in 2004. The Special Educational Needs and Disability Act 2001 extended the DDA 1995 to cover education, training and any services provided wholly or mainly for students. It is unlawful for those providing such services to treat a disabled person less favourably than a non-disabled person for a reason that relates to the person's disability. If a disabled person is at a substantial disadvantage, those providing services must take reasonable steps to prevent it, such as changes to policy and practice, course requirements and timetables, physical features of a building, provision of interpreters, and alternative forms of delivery materials.

The Disability Discrimination Act 2005 (s.2) amends and extends the DDA 1995. It is now unlawful for a public authority to discriminate against a disabled person in carrying out its functions unless this would endanger the health or safety of others, or substantial extra costs are involved and having regard to resources these would be too great, or non-compliance is necessary to protect the rights and freedoms of others, or to achieve a legitimate aim.

Public authorities must make reasonable adjustments to practice, policy and procedures which make it unreasonably difficult for a disabled person to access or use a service. Section 3 requires public authorities to perform their functions with due regard to the need to eliminate unlawful discrimination or harassment of disabled people, to promote equality of opportunity, to take account of disabled people's disabilities (even where this involves treating disabled people more favourably than others) and to encourage participation by disabled people in public life. The Disability Discrimination (Public Authorities) (Statutory Duties) Regulations 2005 specify that, to comply with the s.3 requirements, organisations must design and publish disability equality schemes in order to demonstrate how they will meet their new obligations. Section 18 extends the definition of disability to include people with some cancers, HIV infection and multiple sclerosis. Protection is extended for people with mental health difficulties by removing the requirement that the condition is clinically recognised.

The Employment Equality (Sexual Orientation) Regulations 2003, Employment Equality (Religion or Belief) Regulations 2003 and Employment Equality (Age) Regulations 2006 outlaw discrimination in employment and vocational training. They have been introduced to comply with European Union Employment Directive (2000/78/EC), demonstrating the influence of European Community membership on the development of United Kingdom law, which prohibited discrimination on grounds of sexuality, religion or belief, disability and age in employment and vocational training. The regulations outlaw direct and indirect discrimination, harassment and victimisation. They apply throughout the employment relationship and to all employers/businesses, qualification bodies and further and higher education institutions.

The sexual orientation regulations cover people whatever their sexuality and discrimination on grounds of perceived and actual sexual orientation. The religion or belief regulations cover actual or perceived religion, religious belief or similar philosophical belief, but not other kinds of belief. However, the right to manifest a religious belief (art.9, ECHR) may be qualified by public authorities providing that this was proportionate and in pursuit of a legitimate purpose (*R (Begum)* v. *Headteacher and Governors of Denbigh High School* (2006)). Under the age regulations, employers must consider requests to continue working beyond retirement age. However, employers can still, with six months notice, retire people over 65 and refuse applications for employment from people within six months of 65. Thus, the regulations do not tackle institutionalised ageism comprehensively.

In respect of service provision, the Equality Act 2006 prohibits discrimination in the provision of goods, facilities and services on the grounds of religion or belief and sexuality, with further guidance in the Equality Act (Sexual Orientation) Regulations 2007. The 2006 Act also dissolves the Commission for Racial Equality, the Equal Opportunity Commission and the Disability Rights Commission, each established under single anti-discriminatory legislation, and creates a single Equality and Human Rights Commission, with investigation and enforcement powers, to disseminate awareness of human rights and secure equality and good relations between diverse groups. It may intervene in court cases covering equality and human rights issues. However, its responsibilities are extensive, embracing disability, age, gender, sexuality, race, and religion or belief. Its resources may be stretched to give each aspect, as well as their interlocking features, the same focused attention as previously available for sex, disability and race through their separate commissions.

Convergence or divergence? The interface of welfare law and equality legislation

Parallel with the developing emphasis within equality legislation on counteracting discrimination in the provision of goods and services, charted above, powers and duties given to Councils with Social Services Responsibilities and other organisations concerned broadly with social welfare have also featured anti-discriminatory measures. Thus, the Mental Health Act (MHA) 2007 lists principles later developed in the *Code of Practice* (DH, 2008), which include respect for diversity, including religion, culture and sexual orientation, and avoidance of unlawful discrimination. However, these principles must compete against those concerned with public safety and the effectiveness of treatment. Moreover, this juxtaposition, combined with the absence of overt reference to human rights in the principles, reinforces long-standing concerns (reviewed in Braye and Preston-Shoot, 2009) about institutional racism, cultural relevance of assessments and services, and marginalisation of the ethnicity agenda within mental health provision.

Section 95 of the Criminal Justice Act 1991 requires those administering justice to avoid discrimination, for example on grounds of race and gender. The Crime and Disorder Act (CDA) 1998 (s.28) permits tougher sentences for racially aggravated offences, crimes rendered more serious by racial motivation (*R* v. *Saunders* (2000)). More recently, incitement to hatred on grounds of sexual orientation has been made a criminal offence (s.74, Criminal Justice and Immigration Act 2008).

The Children Act (CA) 1989 and the regulatory guidance issued subsequently, affirm anti-discriminatory practice. The CA 1989 includes:

(1) race, culture and religion as characteristics which courts should consider in determining children's welfare (s.1(3)(d));
(2) religious persuasion, racial origin, cultural and linguistic background as features to which local authorities must give due consideration in making decisions about looked after children (s.22(5));
(3) a duty to consider racial groups to which children in need belong and, in respect of day and foster care, to have regard to different racial groups (Schedule 2(11)).

The Adoption and Children Act (ACA) 2002 mirrors these requirements concerning racial background and religion (s.1(5)). Regulatory guidance reinforces, for instance, the importance of valuing children's religious, cultural, racial and linguistic identity (DH, 1991a) and assessing young people's needs arising from their ethnic origins, religion and special need (DH, 1991b). Inter-agency arrangements for working

together to safeguard children must promote their best possible development regardless of gender, ability, race and age, and take into consideration the effects of racial discrimination and institutional racism, and
the influence of religious beliefs and cultural traditions, when families
respond to assessment and enquiry procedures, without condoning
abuse and neglect (DfES, 2006). Assessing children in need and their
families should respect differences of religion, culture and ethnic origins,
work knowledgeably with diversity, and neither reflect nor reinforce
people's experiences of discrimination (DH, 2000). Standards for
fostering services (DH, 2002a) require that placements take account of,
and address needs relating to, ethnic origin, religion, gender, disability
and sexuality. Advocacy services for children and young people can
promote equality issues and monitor discrimination (DH, 2002b).

Equality concerns have been less prominently highlighted in community care. The NHS and Community Care Act 1990 does not contain
anti-discriminatory provisions. Policy guidance issued immediately
afterwards (DH, 1990) does refer to equal opportunities in assessment
procedures, especially in relation to their accessibility for disabled people
and those from minority ethnic groups. It is silent in respect of promoting
equality for women. Practice guidance (DH, 1991d), however, does
recognise that community care services have tended to discriminate
against female carers as well as not addressing satisfactorily the needs of
disabled people and those from black and minority ethnic groups.
Subsequently, policy guidance on eligibility has stated that assessments
should not unfairly discriminate in respect of gender (DH, 2002c). It has
also required that eligibility criteria, assessment and care provision
should respect cultural, ethnic and emotional needs, and that information provided takes account of special needs, different languages and
cultural backgrounds. More recently still, gender has been strongly
foregrounded in respect of support for carers (DH, 2005), following the
Carers (Equal Opportunities) Act 2004, within which local authorities
must consider carers' work, education, training and leisure needs.

Change has also reached the legal rules governing sexuality. The ACA
2002 extends adoption to same-gender couples, representing a challenge
to the norm of heterosexual parenthood. Section 28 of the Local Government Act 1988, which viewed homosexual partnerships as 'pretended
family relationships' and prohibited local authorities from promoting
them, was repealed by s.127 of the Local Government Act 2003. The
Civil Partnership Act 2004 has given legal recognition to same-sex partners while, following unsuccessful litigation before the House of Lords
and the European Court of Human Rights, the Gender Recognition Act
2004 has now enabled people who have decided to live permanently and
fully in their chosen gender to apply for legal recognition of this change.

The age of consent for sexual activity has been equalised (Sexual Offences (Amendment) Act 2000). Discrimination against gay and lesbian nearest relatives under the Mental Health Act 1983 (s.26) was successfully challenged (*R (SSG)* v. *Liverpool City Council and Others* (2002)) resulting in amendment to ensure equal treatment. The Human Fertilisation and Embryology Act 1990 (s.13(5)), requiring that deliberations on the welfare of the child must include consideration of their need for a father, has been revoked (Human Fertilisation and Embryology Act 2008). People in same-sex relationships are no longer disqualified from adoption, provided they can demonstrate an 'enduring family relationship'. Civil partners may acquire parental responsibility in a similar way to step-parents (s.144(4), ACA 2002). However, earlier policy on leaving care (DH, 1991c) and foster care (DH, 1991b) has not been updated to reflect changing attitudes. Moreover, guidance on assessment of children in need (DH, 2000) is silent on sexuality.

Crucially, however, legislation can strike a more oppositional tone in respect of social work's commitment to anti-discriminatory practice. The Children and Adoption Act 2006 contains measures to enforce contact between children and non-resident parents, even where this might destabilise the care being given by the resident parent. The Asylum and Immigration (Treatment of Claimants, etc) Act 2004 allows the withdrawal of support from failed asylum-seeking families. Until declared unlawful because it contravened arts.12 and 14 of the ECHR (*R (Baiai and Others)* v. *Secretary of State for the Home Department* (2006)) the 2004 Act also required (s.19) people subject to immigration rules who wished to contract a non-Anglican marriage to seek permission of the authorities first. Despite amendments to the Children Act 1989 by the Adoption and Children Act 2002 in respect of how unmarried birth fathers may obtain parental responsibility, the legal rules still distinguish between married and unmarried fathers since the latter may have parental responsibility removed from them in situations other than adoption.

Navigating dilemmas at the interface between practice and the legal rules

The official recognition of institutional racism (MacPherson, 1999) provided (unrecognised) endorsement for social work's long-standing recognition (CCETSW, 1989) of structural oppression. Social work students express high levels of satisfaction with their education in respect of anti-discriminatory practice, values and ethics, and law (Lyons and Manion, 2004; Evaluation of Social Work Degree Qualification in England Team, 2008). However, the 2008 evaluation found that some social work educators were concerned that qualifying training was paying insufficient attention to anti-discriminatory practice. Equally, students when analysing vignettes presented by the researchers did not consistently reference ethics or anti-discriminatory practice, or pay sufficient attention to people's cultural and ethnic backgrounds. The researchers also concluded that practice learning paid insufficient attention to dealing with ethical concepts and ethical dilemmas. Placed alongside research findings that practice teachers struggle with providing learning and assessment on the legal rules (Braye et al., 2007), foundational experience for ethically and legally literate anti-discriminatory practice is weakened.

This is potentially serious because the structure and content of the legal rules, and the context for practice, will leave practitioners with several dilemmas. What action should they take when they believe agencies are discriminating unlawfully? What should be their response when agency procedures treat service users indifferently or seek to deny them their lawful entitlement to assessment and/or services (Preston-Shoot, 2000)? How should they respond when the legal rules themselves appear to leave people in degrading situations (Humphries, 2004)? The variable outcome of social work's commitment to anti-discriminatory practice and evidence (Braye and Preston-Shoot, 2009) of acquiescence to organisational misuse of power, highlights the importance of exploring how public authorities respond to the intentions expressed in legal rules and how practitioners and managers understand the authority of social worker registration in which they agree to uphold practice standards (GSCC, 2002). Otherwise, legal rules and ethical commitments may remain comfortable rhetoric only.

Achieving equality: social work practice

Judicial decisions have sometimes criticised local authority attitudes. For instance, discriminating against kinship carers when providing financial support has been described as discriminatory, arbitrary, inflexible and irrational (*R (L and Others)* v. *Manchester City Council* (2002)). The importance of human dignity has been emphasised as a core value in respect of promoting the family life of disabled people (*R (A & B and X & Y)* v. *East Sussex County Council and the Disability Rights Commission (Interested Party)* (2003)) and in sharing information (*R (Greenwich LBC)* v. *Secretary of State for Health and Bexley LBC* (2007)). Decision making concerning the transfer of an older person from residential to nursing care, contrary to an assessment and her expressed wishes and those of her daughter, was described as insensitive and unreasonable (*R (Goldsmith)* v. *Wandsworth LBC* (2004)).

Attitudes in child protection have come under the spotlight too. For example, local authorities have been criticised for defensive and obstructive behaviours (*Re J (a child) (care proceedings: disclosure)* (2003)) and for failing to involve parents in investigations and decision making (*TP and KM* v. *UK* (2002)). In one case involving the interface between a housing authority and a children's department, an absence of concern to ensure that a young person's needs were properly identified and met was alleged (*R (M)* v. *Hammersmith and Fulham LBC* (2008)). Local authorities have also been found wanting under equalities legislation. One judgement against a local authority found that it had failed to conduct a race equality impact assessment before changing funding criteria for voluntary organisations (*R (Kaur and Shah)* v. *Ealing LBC* (2008)). In another case the disability equality duty (s.3, DDA 2005) was used successfully to challenge a local authority's amendment to its eligibility criteria for access to community care services (*R (Chavda)* v. *Harrow LBC* (2007)). The local authority had not considered the impact on disabled people of its proposed policy change. Further, in *R (JL)* v. *Islington LBC* (2009) the local authority was found to have unlawfully used eligibility criteria to deny a disabled child and family a core assessment and the possibility of services under both the CA 1989 and the Chronically Sick and Disabled Persons Act 1970. It had, akin to the *Chavda* case, also failed to consider its obligations towards disabled people contained within DDA 2005 (s.3) when creating, implementing or amending procedures.

In three interlinked reports the Commission for Social Care Inspection found that 94% of services were undertaking work around equality and diversity, such as the provision of training for staff. However, only 9% of providers were carrying out specific work to promote equality relating to sexuality (CSCI, 2008a). This work tended to focus on young people rather than older people. The report identifies the need for positive leadership in this area, for a review of organisational policies on assessment and care planning, and for staff training and other initiatives to challenge assumptions about older people, disabled people and sexuality.

Similarly, only 37% of providers could give examples of work specifically relating to race equality, and only 24% of services appeared to have implemented programmes to make their provision more culturally appropriate, while over half of black and minority ethnic people who responded reported feeling that assessments had not adequately considered their needs and around one-quarter had experienced prejudice or discrimination when using services (CSCI, 2008b). The same report identifies that only 8% of providers were offering language support and only 7% were taking steps to enable people to maintain contact with their communities. It advises that services must recognise differences in cultures, challenge assumptions either that race equality work is unnecessary or that communities make their own provision (see also Begum, 2006), and work actively to promote safety and provide accessible information. It recommends that organisations review their policies and practice, especially concerning assessment and the management of complaints.

When focusing on disability (CSCI, 2009), only 33% of providers gave examples of work specifically relating to disability equality. Initiatives were more likely to focus on addressing physical barriers, such as access, than services (such as transport) promoting access to communities or facilitating access to information. The same survey reports that only 38% of disabled people who participated felt that workers communicated well and only 29% believed that services had promoted social inclusion. Disabled people receiving home care and who were under 65 were more likely to feel positive about the degree to which services were addressing barriers relating to exclusion and attitudes. The report recommends that greater attention is paid to developing equality strategies with disabled people, to ensuring that practitioners and managers understand the social model of disability, and to configuring assessments and care plans around the lives that disabled people want to live.

Research also highlights challenges in respect of gender and age. For instance, Cestari et al. (2006) found that women receive poorer access to, or a lower level of, resources when seeking community care provision. Turning the spotlight to ageism, while the national service framework for older people (DH, 2001) sets a standard that services should not discriminate on grounds of age, managers and practitioners struggle to identify and address age discrimination in provision, for instance in the use of direct payments or when disabled people transfer from adult services to specialist services for older people (Clark et al., 2004; Postle et al., 2005).

The three Commission for Social Care Inspection publications reinforce what research studies have been reporting. Braye and Preston-Shoot (2009) detail the research evidence from across the interface between equality legislation, welfare law and social work practice. Headlines from criminal justice include prisoners with learning disabilities experiencing systematic and routine discrimination, with criminal justice services failing to comply with legal duties to promote disability equality (Talbot, 2008). This research study found evidence of maltreatment, inaccessible information, and higher rates of restraint and segregation. Appropriate Adults were not always in attendance when learning disabled people were questioned by the police. Learning disabled people also found it difficult to participate in trials and to understand court decisions. The report recommends that criminal justice, health, education and social services share information, adopt a needs-led approach to prevent (re)offending, and provide awareness training for staff. Perhaps better known is the research evidence that African-Caribbean people are more likely to be stopped or arrested by the police, less likely to receive unconditional bail or to be cautioned, and are over-represented in the prison population (Yarrow, 2005). Black people also remain over-represented in mental health social control measures (Bartlett and Sandland, 2003).

In childcare, black children are over-represented among young people looked after by local authorities (Brophy, 2008). Research also suggests that greater attention still should be paid to assessing children from black and minority ethnic groups to ensure equality of access to services (Cleaver et al., 2004). Who the local authority believes it is relevant to consult, for example before making decisions concerning a child (s.22(4), CA 1989) should be influenced by that young person's cultural background. Ombudsman investigations (LGO, 2002) and case law (for example *R (CD) (a child by her litigation friend VD)* v. *Isle of Anglesey CC* (2004); *R (LH and MH)* v. *Lambeth LBC* (2006); *R (JL)* v. *Islington LBC* (2009)) also find failures to make appropriate provision for disabled children and to follow duties in the Children Act 1989 to minimise the effects of disability and to ascertain the wishes and feelings of young people.

Services for people with physical and sensory disabilities (Clark, 2003) and for black young people caring for disabled family members (Jones et al., 2002) have been found to be insufficiently culturally sensitive. Disturbing evidence has emerged in services for learning disabled people of poor quality care, inadequate performance monitoring, stereotyping, poor communication between NHS Trusts and social services, sidelining of carers and mishandling of complaints (LGO, 2008; Michael, 2008), with continuing barriers relating to social inclusion (choice of residence, employment and community support) (HM Government, 2009). Pejorative attitudes continue towards disabled parents (Wates, 2002) and learning disabled people seeking direct payments (Leece, 2007).

Social workers must demand and protect the reflective spaces, such as continuing professional development and supervision, to focus on the personal, professional and organisational aspects to counteracting discrimination and promoting equality, and the interaction between them. Such spaces are crucial for capturing learning about anti-discriminatory practice as well as navigating through the multiple and sometimes contradictory purposes contained within the legal rules and the ethical challenges of working in and challenging hierarchical and bureaucratic structures. They are essential too for working through when and how to promote people's rights and build on their strengths while also using the legal rules effectively to safeguard and promote their welfare.

Achieving equality: the legal rules

One function of the law is to shape attitudes and behaviour; another is to solve social problems (Braye and Preston-Shoot, 2009). Equality legislation exemplifies both functions. However, the gradual evolution of anti-discriminatory legislation demonstrates that the legal rules do not yet provide a consistent, unambiguous and coherent framework. Moreover, the research evidence presented herein would appear to indicate that the achievements of equality legislation have been limited, at least concerning equality in the provision of welfare services. One reason may reside in the conceptual models underpinning the legislation. Earlier legislation reflected two models (Newman, 1994): a liberal model, promoting fair access for example through recruitment and selection requirements but with a focus on individuals and on access to provision; and a social welfare model, aiming to tackle problems and barriers through special provision but reflecting a tendency to stigmatise people in minority groups and oriented towards bringing people closer to dominant norms. Deeper seams of inequality, the underlying structures that result in racism, sexism and disablism for instance, were left unaddressed.

The RR(A)A 2000 marks a shift towards a more radical model, which focuses on power structures and collective concerns, and seeks transformational change. An outcome from the Stephen Lawrence inquiry report (MacPherson, 1999), which recognised that systematic disadvantage occurs through institutional procedures, policies and practices, including the unequal distribution of power, opportunity and resources, it seeks to address institutional racism by requiring equality duties of public organisations. Schedule 1 of the 2000 Act outlines that public authorities must have race equality schemes or policies that demonstrate how they will review their functions and policies, enhance staff awareness and knowledge, and thereby meet their duties under s.71, RRA 1976. The Race Relations Act 1976 (Statutory Duties) Order 2001 requires through equality impact assessments that public authorities monitor their policies for adverse impact on the promotion of race equality. The Disability Discrimination Act 2005 and the Equality Act 2006 extend this approach to institutional change to disability and gender. However, initial implementation of the requirements regarding race equality schemes was variable across sectors, with only one-third of public authorities responding with highly developed policies and with patchy progress on integration of equality as a mainstream responsibility (CRE, 2003). Subsequent reports by CSCI (2008a; 2008b; 2009) reinforce the picture of patchy progress. The number of cases remains small where people are claiming discrimination in the provision of goods and services.

A second reason lies in how legislation is constructed. It is not always easy to define which groups of people are being protected. Some DDA 1995 provisions, for instance, remain vague and are not comprehensive in terms of groups of disabled people or areas of daily living covered. The scope of the legal rules may be restricted. For example, RRA 1976 permits budgets to be ring-fenced for the development of services appropriate to minority ethnic groups and SDA 1975 allows specific training for women where they are under-represented in a workforce. Neither, however, is founded on the principle of discrimination *for* black people or women. The focus is on remedial action. It may feel daunting for complainants to use available provisions for redress and the available sanctions are mainly remedies for individuals rather than measures that could have an impact on inherited disadvantage or inequality experienced by groups of people. Implementation of the legal rules may be monitored by inspectorates, tribunals, the Ombudsman and the courts. The Equality and Human Rights Commission may assess an organisation's performance of public sector duties required by RR(A)A 2000, DDA 2005 and EA 2006, issue compliance notices and enforce requirements through legal action. However, compelling employers and service providers to combat inequality is unusual even when permitted. It remains questionable whether sanctions are effective and enforcement sufficiently rigorous.

A third reason is rooted in the concept of resistance. Those who shape statute or who must implement the law may be reluctant to cede power and privilege. Both the law-in-theory and the law-in-action (Jenness and Grattet, 2005) will be influenced by dominant cultures and beliefs. For instance, as yet DDA legislation does not provide rights for independent living. Service provision legislation is narrowly focused on particular types of care-based services. The range of services which may be provided under the CA 1989 and the CSDPA 1970 do little to challenge discrimination because they reflect the non-disabled assumptions and orientation of social arrangements. They emphasise individualised needs and resources, rather than rights and inclusion. Equally, debates surrounding the future of equality legislation continue to highlight division within public concern and support, and the influence of other narratives, for instance concerning young offenders, mentally distressed adults or asylum-seekers, when policies and regulations are reviewed. McLaughlin (2005) captures this critique clearly by remarking that what might be considered radical measures, such as the public sector equality duties, themselves become institutionalised and, rather than being a challenge to the State, allow it to reposition itself, enforce moral codes of behaviour on welfare recipients, and uphold existing social relations.

Possible futures

Currently before Parliament is an Equality Bill. If enacted, the government's aim (Government Equalities Office, 2008) is that it will create a single equality duty, thereby harmonising existing public sector equality duties in RR(A)A 2000, DDA 2005 and EA 2006, and extending the duty to embrace gender reassignment, age, sexuality, and religion and belief. It will simplify the definition of disability discrimination, the interpretation of which has proved exceedingly complex and remains contested, for example in housing eviction cases (*Mayor and Burgesses of the London Borough of Lewisham* v. *Malcolm* (2008)). It proposes to outlaw age discrimination in the provision of goods, services and facilities, again harmonising the legal rules in this area across social divisions. The Bill also proposes to outlaw discrimination by association, as highlighted by the European Court of Justice in respect of a parent caring for her disabled child who experienced discrimination at work (*Coleman* v. *Attridge Law* (2008)).

The powers of the Equality and Human Rights Commission may be extended to include inquiring into equality practices in the private sector, perhaps partly in response to investigations which have identified neglect and abuse of vulnerable adults (LGO, 2008; Michael, 2008). Tribunal and court powers may be extended beyond redress for individuals who bring successful applications to other people connected with the agency in question, in order to ensure that organisations do change their policies, procedures and practices.

The proposals in the Equality Bill have reawakened the debate that surrounded the passing of the Equality Act 2006, namely whether consolidating and harmonising the legal rules relating to diverse social divisions will strengthen progress towards counteracting discrimination and promoting equality of opportunity, for example by recognising that individuals may belong to more than one social division and group vulnerable to discrimination, or weaken the effectiveness of provision by diluting the focus on separate areas of discrimination. It may also represent another lost opportunity to reinforce the interface between human rights and anti-discriminatory legislation and to extend the former from the civil and political rights contained in the ECHR to social and economic rights, the lack of which social workers will know daily affect the lives of their clients. It does recognise that socio-economic disadvantage perpetuates discrimination and, therefore, proposes that public organisations should consider this when planning and reviewing services. However, what will prove possible with such target duties in a climate of fiscal restraint remains doubtful.

Conclusion

Since 2000, anti-discrimination legislation has been, and remains, a site of significant change. From an originally reformist ambition it has taken steps to address the structures that can promote inequality. However, the degree to which the legal rules have changed or can transform individual attitudes and organisational practices is more questionable. In parallel, social work narratives strongly foreground a value commitment to counteracting discrimination and promoting equality of opportunity, and knowledge of and skilled responses to diversity. However, the evidence indicates that acknowledgement of people's rights and meeting their needs can prove vulnerable when faced with institutional procedures and available resources.

References

Bartlett, P. and Sandland, R. (2003) *Mental Health Law: Policy and Practice* (2nd edn), Oxford, Oxford University Press.

BASW (2002) *The Code of Ethics for Social Work*, Birmingham, British Association of Social Workers.

Begum, N. (2006) *Doing it for Themselves: Participation and Black and Minority Ethnic Service Users*, London, Race Equality Unit and Social Care Institute for Excellence.

Braye, S. and Preston-Shoot, M. (2006) *Teaching, Learning and Assessment of Law in Social Work Education: Resource Guide*, London, Social Care Institute for Excellence.

Braye, S. and Preston-Shoot, M. (2009) *Practising Social Work Law* (3rd edn), Basingstoke, Palgrave Macmillan.

Braye, S., Preston-Shoot, M. and Thorpe, A. (2007) 'Beyond the classroom: learning social work law in practice', *Journal of Social Work*, 7(3): 322–40.

Brophy, J. (2008) 'Child maltreatment in diverse households: challenges to law, theory, and practice', *Journal of Law and Society*, 35(1): 75–94.

CCETSW (1989) *Requirements and Regulations for the Diploma in Social Work* (Paper 30). London, Central Council for Education and Training in Social Work.

Cestari, L., Munroe, M., Evans, S., Smith, A. and Huxley, P. (2006) 'Fair Access to Care Services (FACS): implementation in the mental health context of the UK', *Health and Social Care in the Community*, 14(6): 474–81.

Clark, H., Gough, H. and Macfarlane, A. (2004) 'It Pays Dividends': Direct Payments and Older People, Bristol, Policy Press.

Clark, J. (2003) Independence Matters: An Overview of the Performance of Social Care Services for Physically and Sensory Disabled People, London, Department of Health.

Cleaver, H., Barnes, J., Bliss, D. and Cleaver, D. (2004) Developing Identification, Referral and Tracking Systems: An Evaluation of the Processes Undertaken by Trailblazer Authorities, London, Department for Education and Skills.

CRE (2003) Towards Racial Equality. An Evaluation of the Public Duty to Promote Race Equality and Good Race Relations in England and Wales, London, Commission for Racial Equality.

CSCI (2008a) Putting People First: Equality and Diversity Matters 1. Providing Appropriate Services for Lesbian, Gay and Bisexual and Transgender People, London, Commission for Social Care Inspection.

CSCI (2008b) Putting People First: Equality and Diversity Matters 2. Providing Appropriate Services for Black and Minority Ethnic People, London, Commission for Social Care Inspection.

CSCI (2009) Putting People First: Equality and Diversity Matters. Achieving Disability Equality in Social Care Services, London, Commission for Social Care Inspection.

DfES (2006) Working Together to Safeguard Children: A Guide to Inter-Agency Working to Safeguard and Promote the Welfare of Children, London, Department for Education and Skills.

DH (1990) Community Care in the Next Decade and Beyond; Policy Guidance, London, HMSO.

DH (1991a) The Children Act 1989 Guidance and Regulations, Volume 2, Family Support, Day Care and Educational Provision, London, HMSO.

DH (1991b) The Children Act 1989 Guidance and Regulations, Volume 3, Family Placements, London, HMSO.

DH (1991c) The Children Act 1989 Guidance and Regulations, Volume 4, Residential Care, London, HMSO.

DH (1991d) Care Management and Assessment: Practitioners' Guide, London, HMSO.

DH (2000) Framework for the Assessment of Children in Need and their Families, London, The Stationery Office.

DH (2001) National Service Framework for Older People, London, Department of Health.

DH (2002a) Fostering Services: National Minimum Standards Fostering Services Regulations, London, The Stationery Office.

DH (2002b) National Standards for the Provision of Children's Advocacy Services, London, The Stationery Office.

DH (2002c) Fair Access to Care Services. Guidance on Eligibility Criteria for Adult Social Care, Issued with LAC (2002) 13, London, Department of Health.

DH (2005) *Carers and Disabled Children Act 2000 & Carers (Equal Opportunities) Act 2004 Combined Policy Guidance,* London, Department of Health.

DH (2008) *Code of Practice: Mental Health Act 1983,* London, The Stationery Office.

Evaluation of Social Work Degree Qualification in England Team (2008) *Evaluation of the New Social Work Degree Qualification in England. Volume 1: Findings,* London, King's College London, Social Care Workforce Research Unit.

Government Equalities Office (2008) *Framework for a Fairer Future: The Equality Bill,* London, The Stationery Office.

GSCC (2002) *Codes of Practice for Social Care Workers and Employers,* London, General Social Care Council.

GSCC (2008) *Social Work at its Best. A Statement of Social Work Roles and Tasks for the 21st Century,* London, General Social Care Council.

HM Government (2009) *Valuing People Now: A New Three Year Strategy for People with Learning Disabilities,* London, Department of Health.

Humphries, B. (2004) 'An unacceptable role for social work: implementing immigration policy', *British Journal of Social Work,* 34(1): 93–107.

Jenness, V. and Grattet, R. (2005) 'The law-in-between: the effects of organizational perviousness on the policing of hate crime', *Social Problems,* 52(3): 337–59.

Jones, A., Dharman, J. and Rajasooriya, S. (2002) *Invisible Families: The Strengths and Needs of Black Families in which Young People have Caring Responsibilities,* Bristol, Policy Press.

Leece, J. (2007) 'Direct payments and user-controlled support: the challenges for social care commissioning', *Practice,* 19(3): 185–98.

LGO (2002) *Report Summaries: Social Services,* London, Local Government Ombudsman.

LGO (2008) *Injustice in Residential Care: A Joint Report by the Local Government Ombudsman and the Health Service Ombudsman for England. Investigations into Complaints against Buckinghamshire County Council and against Oxfordshire and Buckinghamshire Mental Health Partnership,* London, The Stationery Office.

Lyons, K. and Manion, H. (2004) 'Goodbye DipSW: trends in student satisfaction and employment outcomes. Some implications for the new social work award', *Social Work Education,* 23(2): 133–48.

McLaughlin, K. (2005) 'From ridicule to institutionalization: anti-oppression, the state and social work', *Critical Social Policy,* 25(3): 283–305.

MacPherson, W. (1999) *The Stephen Lawrence Enquiry: Report of an Enquiry by Sir William MacPherson of Cluny,* London, The Stationery Office.

Michael, J. (2008) *Healthcare for All. Report of the Independent Inquiry into Access to Healthcare for People with Learning Disabilities,* London, The Stationery Office.

Newman, J. (1994) 'The limits of management: gender and the politics of change', in J. Clarke, A. Cochrane and E. McLaughlin (eds) *Managing Social Policy,* London, Sage.

Postle, K., Wright, P. and Beresford, P. (2005) 'Older people's participation in political activity – making their voice heard: a potential support role for welfare professionals in countering ageism and social exclusion', *Practice*, 17(3): 173–89.

Preston-Shoot, M. (2000) 'What if? Using the law to uphold practice values and standards', *Practice*, 12(4): 49–63.

Preston-Shoot, M., Roberts, G. and Vernon, S. (2001) 'Values in social work law: strained relations or sustaining relationships?' *Journal of Social Welfare and Family Law*, 23(1): 1–22.

QAA (2008) *Subject Benchmark Statements: Social Work*, Gloucester, The Quality Assurance Agency for Higher Education.

Talbot, J. (2008) *No One Knows. Prisoners' Voices. Experiences of the Criminal Justice System by Prisoners with Learning Disabilities and Difficulties*, London, Prison Reform Trust.

TOPSS (2002) *The National Occupational Standards for Social Work*, Leeds, Training Organisation for the Personal Social Services.

Wates, M. (2002) *Supporting Disabled Adults in their Parenting Role*, York, Joseph Rowntree Foundation.

Yarrow, S. (2005) *The Experiences of Young Black Men as Victims of Crime*, London, Criminal System Race Unit/Home Office.

Cases

Coleman v. *Attridge Law* [2008] All ER (EC) 1105.

Mayor and Burgesses of the London Borough of Lewisham v. *Malcolm* [2008] UKHL 43.

R (A & B and X & Y) v. *East Sussex County Council and the Disability Rights Commission (Interested Party)* [2003] 6 CCLR 194.

R (Baiai and Others) v. *Secretary of State for the Home Department* [2006] *The Times*, 14 April.

R (Begum) v. *Headteacher and Governors of Denbigh High School* [2006] UKHL 15.

R (CD) (a child by her litigation friend VD) v. *Isle of Anglesey CC* [2004] 7 CCLR 589.

R (Chavda) v. *Harrow LBC* [2007] 11 CCLR 187.

R (Goldsmith) v. *Wandsworth LBC* [2004] 7 CCLR 472.

R (Greenwich LBC) v. *Secretary of State for Health and Bexley LBC* [2007] 10 CCLR 60.

R (JL) v. *Islington LBC* [2009] EWHC 458 (Admin).

R (Kaur and Shah) v. *Ealing LBC* [2008] EWHC 2062.

R (L and Others) v. *Manchester City Council* [2002] 1 FLR 43.

R (LH and MH) v. *Lambeth LBC* [2006] 9 CCLR 622.

R (M) v. *Hammersmith and Fulham LBC* [2008] UKHL 14.

R (SSG) v. *Liverpool City Council and Others* [2002] 5 CCLR 639.

R v. *Saunders* [2000] 1 CR App Rep 458.

Re J (a child) (care proceedings: disclosure) [2003] *The Times*, 16 May.

Roads v. *Central Trains* [2004] EWCA Civ 1541.

Ross v. *Ryanair and Stansted Airport* [2004] EWCA Civ 1751.

Southampton City Council v. *Randall* [2006] IRLR 18.

TP and KM v. *UK* [2002]) 34 EHRR 42.

Chapter 5

Risk, Social Work and Social Care: The Example of Children's Social Care

NIGEL PARTON

Introduction

An increased awareness about risk seems to constitute one of the key defining dimensions of our contemporary experience, and is present in most areas of our social, economic, political and cultural lives (Mythen and Walklate, 2006; Taylor-Gooby and Zinn, 2006; Petersen and Wilkinson, 2008). Nowhere is this more evident than in the area of social work and social care more generally, where concerns about risk to service users and risk to workers have become a central concern and much of the work is now framed in terms of: risk assessment; risk management; the monitoring of risk; risk insurance; and risk taking.

It is particularly notable that while interest in the concept of risk in the context of social work research, theory, practice and education has grown almost exponentially in recent years (Warner and Sharland, 2010), this is a very recent development (Stalker, 2003; Barry, 2007). Effectively, writing about risk in the social work literature is only really evident from the mid 1990s onwards (see, for example, Parton, 1996; Kemshall and Pritchard, 1996, 1997; Kemshall et al., 1997; Alaszewski et al., 1998). As Brearley, in the only book written on the topic prior to the mid 1990s, commented, 'while social work might have considerable knowledge and ideas about risk ... it might not always be expressed in those terms' (Brearley, 1982, p. 31). Understanding and responding to risk as a central issue for social work and social care policy and practice is thus a recent phenomenon and something of considerable significance; it seems to capture many of the key current tensions and characteristics of the work and how it is carried out. However, and as we will see in the next section, the concept of risk covers numerous themes and ideas and is difficult to pin down.

The concept of risk

It seems that the concept of risk emerged in the seventeenth century in the context of gambling and insurance and was used to refer to the probability of an event occurring and the size of the associated gains and losses (Douglas, 1992). Up until this time both positive and dangerous events were attributed primarily to divine or supernatural intervention; however, with the emergence of the Enlightenment, rational thought and objective knowledge were seen as crucial for bringing about progress and order (Lupton, 1999). Both the natural and social worlds were increasingly seen as subject to laws and regularities which could be identified and measured so that humans could begin to make calculations in order to intervene to improve the world. It was the time when probability and statistics emerged so that predictions could be made (Hacking, 1975). Risk only comes into wide usage in a society that is future oriented and which sees the future as a territory to be conquered or colonised – a society which *actively* tries to bring the future into the present.

Concerns about risk can be seen to characterise societies which aim to determine their own future rather than assuming the future is predetermined or subject to fate or 'God's will'. However, at the outset risk was concerned with calculating both losses and gains – in the sense of gambling – and thus pointed to potential positives as well as negatives. It was a neutral concept in the sense it was associated with the idea of calculating outcomes for the future. Risk understood in this sense is still very important as the primary idea involving a whole variety of different activities including gambling, investing in the stock exchange and so on.

However, as Mary Douglas (1986, 1992) has argued, as the idea of risk became more central to politics and public policy, the connection of risk with technical calculations weakened. While it continued to combine a probabilistic measure of the consequences of events, increasingly the concept of risk in terms of public policy became primarily associated with negative outcomes only. As a result, the idea of risk has become much more associated with hazards, dangers, harms and losses. The risk that has become central for policy has now not got much to do with neutral probability calculations. 'The original connection is only indicated by arm-waving in the direction of possible science: the word *risk* now means danger: *high risk* means a lot of danger' (Douglas, 1992, original emphasis). The *Oxford Dictionary*, for example, defines risk as 'a situation involving exposure to danger', while Alaszewski et al. (1998), who were writing specifically in relation to health and welfare, defined risk as 'the possibility that a given course of action will not achieve its desired and intended outcome but instead some *undesired* and *undesirable* situation will develop' (emphasis added).

Whereas a high risk originally meant a game in which a throw of the die had a strong possibility of bringing about great joy or great pain, the language of risk has become, in public policy, reserved almost exclusively for talk of undesirable outcomes. Discussions about risk have become primarily concerned with levels of danger and our abilities to predict danger and thereby avert it.

Douglas (1992), however, argues that this shift is not the major significance of the contemporary concerns with risk. 'The big difference is not the predictive uses of risk, but in its forensic functions.' The concept of risk emerges as a key idea for contemporary times because of its uses as a forensic resource. The more culturally individualised a society becomes, the more significant is the forensic potential of the idea of risk. Its forensic uses have become particularly important in the development of different types of blaming systems, and 'the one we are now in is almost ready to treat every death as chargeable to someone's account, every accident as caused by someone's criminal negligence, every sickness a threatened prosecution' (Douglas, 1992, pp. 15–16).

However, and as I will argue further in a later section, the situation has been developing in some interesting ways in recent years. For, while the idea of risk is no longer so dominated by notions of danger and avoiding the worst and is increasingly influenced by the idea of well-being and bringing about positive improvements, the forensic emphasis on individualised responsibility and accountability seems to have got stronger.

More than ever risk has become centrally implicated in developments which hold people to account not just for their actions, but also the *consequences* of their (in)actions; for the idiom of risk not only presupposes ideas of choice and calculation, but also responsibility. Whether or not the risk attitude prevails depends on the degree to which areas of social life are assumed to be fixed, inevitable and influenced by fate, or subject to human agency and control, and hence responsibility. The more we have assumed that areas of life have moved from the former category (fixed, inevitable and subject to fate) to the latter (subject to human agency and control), the more we have taken them from the sphere of the natural and God-given and made them the objects of human intervention and responsibility. As I will argue below, the wider the sphere whereby it is assumed that human intervention can have the effect of preventing harm and improving well-being, in an increasingly individualised and forensically driven political and organisational context, the more welfare agencies, managers and practitioners are required to account for their actions when situations or cases in which they might have some involvement are seen to go wrong.

While this is most obvious in the areas of children's social care and child protection, it is also evident in mental health, work with older people, and criminal justice. A 'culture of blame' can be seen to dominate where a whole plethora of policies and procedures have been introduced to make practice transparent so that any negative outcomes can be defended, often in the full glare of the media (Parton, 1996; Franklin, 1999; Franklin and Parton, 2001). The concern thereby shifts from trying to make the *right* decision to making a *defensible* decision. In the process, the concern is not so much 'risk' as 'safety', and a 'precautionary logic' comes to dominate.

Safety and precaution become a fundamental value, such that the passions which might previously have been devoted to the struggle to change the world for the better are now invested in trying to ensure that we are safe (Beck, 1992; Furedi, 2002). Increasingly it seems that concerns about safety have come to characterise our contemporary social and political culture, including the nature of social work and social care policy and practice.

More recently a number of theorists have suggested that in the twenty-first century these concerns with safety are framed within a *logic of precaution* which insists on a politics and practice based on 'strict safety' (Ericson, 2007) and where the dominating concern is the pre-emption of harm. Importantly, under the logic of precaution uncertainty is no longer seen as an excuse and, in fact, provides the driver for ever increased surveillance. Assessed against the 'worst case' scenario, rather than calculative risk probabilities, everyone is required to be responsible for playing their part and thereby preventing future harm (Parton, 2006, 2008; Hebenton and Seddon, 2009).

What I am suggesting, then, is that while risk is a wide-ranging and slippery concept we can identify a number of key elements which have come to characterise it:

- it is future oriented;
- it emphasises calculability, human agency and responsibility;
- it gives the impression of being predictable and scientific and aims to bring the future into the present, so that it can be controlled and modified;
- in public policy and practice, it tends to emphasise the negative consequences and outcomes;
- it fulfils an important series of forensic functions, with their implication for blame allocation and holding people and organisations to account in the context of an increasing 'logic of precaution'.

These elements can be seen to have played an important role in influencing social work and social care policy and practice, particularly over the past 20 years. However, there is also evidence of serious attempts being made to develop the much more positive, creative and empowering dimension to risk which the above characteristics tend to, at best, undervalue, and, at worst, ignore. Recent years have witnessed a growing emphasis on the importance of encouraging independence, empowerment and choice for service users in order to maximise their well-being – particularly in the areas of adult services (DH, 2007). In attempting to give due weight to the positive and creative dimensions of risk which were evident in its original conception, it is recognised that a fine balance has to be struck between trying to ensure that individuals can develop their full humanity and maximise their well-being, while also ensuring that they are safe and protected from harm. Such tensions lie at the heart of social care and social work policy and practice. I am going to illustrate how these different conceptions of and approaches to risk have been addressed and are subject to change by analysing one area of policy and practice in some detail: the approach to child protection and safeguarding in England.

Changing and competing conceptions of risk in child welfare work in England

Following the high profile and very public criticisms of social workers and other health and welfare professionals in cases of child abuse in the 1970s and 1980s (Parton, 1985; Butler and Drakeford, 2005), the long-established State child welfare services in England came under increasing pressure and came to be dominated by narrowly focused, forensically oriented concern with child protection. Similar developments were evident in the other nations in the UK, as well as North America and Australia (Waldfogel, 1998; Lonne et al., 2009).

By the early 1990s, the child protection and child welfare systems in England could be characterised in terms of the need to identify 'high risk', in a context where agencies and professionals 'working together' was set out in increasingly complex and detailed procedural guidelines, and where the work was informed by a narrow and defensive emphasis on legalism and the need for professionals to identify forensic evidence (Parton, 1991). The work had become concerned with trying to identify the 'high risk' or 'dangerous' families and differentiate these from the rest, so that children could be protected, family privacy was not undermined for the vast majority of parents, and scarce resources could be directed to where, in theory, they were most needed (Parton et al., 1997).

This was clearly stated in the title and contents of the official govern-ment guidance at the time, *Working Together Under the Children Act 1989: A Guide to Arrangements for Inter-Agency Cooperation for the Protection of Children from Abuse* (Home Office et al., 1991). While working in partnership with parents and children was seen as impor-tant, the focus was very much upon 'children at risk of significant harm', such that the whole document was framed in terms of when and how to carry out an investigation in terms of s.47 of the Children Act 1989 and to establish whether the key threshold criterion for formal State inter-vention had been met in terms of whether the child was 'suffering or likely to suffer significant harm' (s.31(91)(9)).

However, during the 1990s a major debate opened up about how policies and practices in relation to child protection integrated with and were supported by policies and practices concerned with family support and child welfare more generally (DH, 1995; Parton, 1997). Rather than simply be concerned with a narrow, forensically driven focus on child protection, it was argued there needed to be a 'rebalancing' or 'refocusing' of the work, such that the essential principles of a child welfare approach could dominate. Policy and practice should be driven by an emphasis on partnership, participation, prevention and family support. The priority should be on *helping* parents and children in the community in a supportive way and should keep notions of policing and coercive intervention to a minimum.

This change in thinking was evident in the official guidance published at the end of the decade, *Working Together to Safeguard Children: A Guide to Inter-agency Working to Safeguard and Promote the Welfare of Children* (DH et al., 1999). The words 'protection' and 'abuse' were dropped from the title which was framed in terms of the general duty placed on local authorities by s.17(1) of the Children Act 1989 'to safe-guard and promote the welfare of children in their area who are in need'. The guidance underlined the fact that local authority social services had wider responsibilities than simply responding to concerns about 'signifi-cant harm' and identifying child abuse and was explicitly located in the much wider agenda for Children's Services being promulgated by the New Labour Government, which came into power in 1997, associated with social exclusion (Frost and Parton, 2009). The Assessment Framework (DH et al., 2000) published at the same time as the 1999 *Working Together*, attempted to move the focus from the assessment of risk of child abuse and 'significant harm' (DH, 2001) to one which was concerned with the broader idea of risk of impairment to a child's overall develop-ment in the context of their family and community environment.

We can thus identify an important change in the nature of the risk which policy and practice were expected to respond to. The object of concern was no longer simply children at risk of abuse and 'significant harm'. Effective measures to safeguard children were seen as those which also promoted their welfare, and should not be seen in isolation from the wider range of support and services provided to meet the needs of all children and families.

This is not to say, however, that child protection had disappeared, but that it was being located in the wider concerns about 'safeguarding and promoting the welfare of children'. In the most recent 'Working Together' published in 2006, it was stated that:

> Safeguarding and promoting the welfare of children is defined for the purposes of this guidance as:
>
> 1. protecting children from maltreatment;
> 2. preventing impairment of children's health or development; and
> 3. ensuring that children are growing up in circumstances consistent with the provision of safe and effective care;
>
> and undertaking that role so as to enable those children to have optimum life chances and enter adulthood successfully (HM Government, 2006, para.1.18, original emphasis).

Child protection continued to be specifically concerned with assessment and intervention in situations where children were 'suffering, or likely to suffer, significant harm'. While the focus of both assessment and intervention had thus considerably broadened between 1991 and 2006, the forensic investigation of possible 'significant harm' continued to inhabit the core of the system and it was local authority children's social workers who had the clear statutory responsibility in this regard.

However, what becomes apparent is that we have two conceptions of risk running alongside each other, both in law and in official guidance: the one concerned with the forensic investigation of the risk of significant harm, the other with identifying and responding to risks associated with possible impairments to a child's development and it is to these I now want to give more specific attention.

Risk and *Every Child Matters*

The 2006 *Working Together* guidance (HM Government, 2006) was published at a time of major change in children's services in England. The government had launched its *Every Child Matters: Change for Children (ECM)* programme (DfES, 2004a), where the overriding vision was to bring about 'a shift to prevention while strengthening protection' (DfES,

2004b, p. 3). The consultative Green Paper *Every Child Matters* (Chief Secretary to the Treasury, 2003) had originally been launched as the government's response to a very high profile child abuse public inquiry into the death of Victoria Climbié (Laming, 2003). However, the changes were much broader than simply being concerned with overcoming the problems with responding to cases of child abuse. The priority was to intervene at a much earlier stage in children's lives in order to prevent a range of problems both in childhood and later life, including educational attainment, unemployment, crime and antisocial behaviour. The ambition was to improve the outcomes for all children and to narrow the gap in outcomes between those who do well and those who do not. The outcomes were defined in terms of: being healthy; staying safe; enjoying and achieving; making a *positive contribution*; and achieving economic well-being. Together these five outcomes were seen as key to improving 'well-being in childhood and later life'. It was a very ambitious programme of change and was to include *all children*, as it was felt that any child, at some point in their life, could be seen as vulnerable to some form of risk and therefore might require help. The idea was to identify problems before they became chronic. Two figures included in the Green Paper (Figures 1 and 2) are particularly helpful in understanding how the reform of children's services was conceptualised.

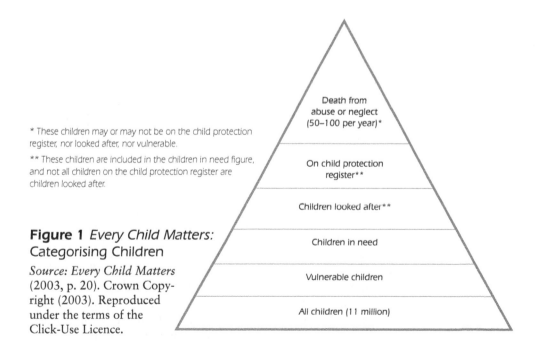

* These children may or may not be on the child protection register, nor looked after, nor vulnerable.

** These children are included in the children in need figure, and not all children on the child protection register are children looked after.

Figure 1 *Every Child Matters:* Categorising Children

Source: Every Child Matters (2003, p. 20). Crown Copyright (2003). Reproduced under the terms of the Click-Use Licence.

Death from abuse or neglect (50–100 per year)*

On child protection register**

Children looked after**

Children in need

Vulnerable children

All children (11 million)

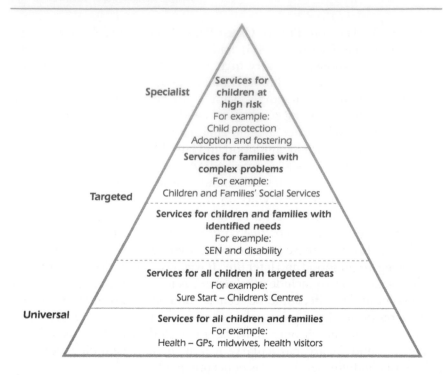

Figure 2 *Every Child Matters:* Targeted services within a universal context

Source: Every Child Matters (2003, p. 26). Crown Copyright (2003). Reproduced under the terms of the Click-Use Licence.

All children in the population are included in the triangle in Figure 1 and categorised according to their level of vulnerability; while in Figure 2 services are organised according to whether they are specialist, targeted or universal. The idea is that problems are identified as quickly as possible to ensure they do not escalate and that services are integrated to ensure that this takes place.

The model informing the changes was very much influenced by a public health approach to prevention and has been characterised as 'the paradigm of risk and protection-focused prevention' (France and Utting, 2005), whereby the knowledge of risk factors derived from prospective longitudinal research is drawn upon to design particular programmes and reorient mainstream services. The work of David Farrington in relation to youth crime prevention has proved particularly influential in identifying a number of 'risk factors' for future criminality (Farrington, 1996, 2000, 2007). What was particularly attractive to policymakers was that a range of overlapping personal and environmental 'risk factors' have been identified not only in relation to future criminal behaviour, violence and drug abuse, but also for educational failure, unsafe sexual behaviour and poor mental health (Dryfoos, 1990; Mrazek and Haggerty, 1994; Goldblatt and Lewis, 1998). The Green Paper stated that:

> we have a good idea what factors shape children's life chances. Research tells us that *the risk of experiencing negative outcomes* is concentrated in children with certain characteristics. (Chief Secretary to the Treasury, 2003, p. 17, emphasis added)

and that these included:

- low income and parental unemployment
- homelessness
- poor parenting
- postnatal depression among mothers
- low birth weight
- substance misuse
- individual characteristics, such as intelligence
- community factors, such as living in a disadvantaged community.

The more risk factors a child had, the more likely it was that they would experience 'negative outcomes' and it was 'poor parenting' which was seen to play the key role. Identifying the risk factors and intervening early provided the major strategy for overcoming the social exclusion of children and avoiding problems in later life.

However, the role of prevention was not only to combat the negatives involved but to enhance the positive opportunities for child development via maximising protective factors and processes. The approach is informed by the work of Michael Rutter (1990) who conceived of risk and protection as processes rather than fixed states and saw protectors as the basis for opening up opportunities. The timing of interventions was crucial, for, if they were to have the most impact, the 'early years' were key and success depended on recruiting parents – usually mothers – to the role of educators. The notion of protection was thus much wider than simply protection from harm or abuse. In trying to maximise childhood 'strengths' and 'resilience' the idea of risk was itself reframed in far more positive ways (Little et al., 2004; Axford and Little, 2006).

To achieve the outcomes, the changes aim to integrate health, social care, education, and criminal justice agencies and thereby overcome traditional organisational and professional 'silos'. Such a development requires agencies and professionals to share information so that risks can be identified early and opportunities maximised. To take this forward, a variety of new systems of information, communication and technology (ICT) are being introduced.

The CAF (Common Assessment Framework) is an electronic assessment form to be completed by any professional when they consider a child to have 'additional needs' that require the involvement of more than one service. It includes a wide-ranging set of data covering most aspects of a child's health and development, including details about parents and siblings. The CAF is designed to identify those children who might not progress towards the five *ECM* outcomes without additional services. It is important 'to identify these children early and help them before things reach crisis point. The CAF is an important tool for intervention' (CWDC, 2007). The *CAF Practitioners' Guide* states that children 'at risk of poor outcomes' are:

> *children with additional needs* and they will require targeted support from education, health, social services and other services. Their needs will in many cases be cross-cutting and might include:
>
> * disruptive or antisocial behaviour;
> * overt parental conflict or lack of parental support/boundaries;
> * involvement in or risk of offending;
> * poor attendance or exclusion from school;
> * experiencing bullying;
> * special educational needs;
> * disengagement from education, training or employment post-16;
> * poor nutrition;
> * ill health;
> * substance misuse;
> * anxiety or depression;
> * housing issues;
> * pregnancy and parenthood. (CWDC, 2007, p. 7, original emphasis)

While the Guide pointed to a smaller group of children who had more significant or *complex needs* who were likely to be known to, or the responsibility of, statutory children's social workers, the CAF was primarily designed for 'children with additional needs' and therefore was to operate at the level of secondary prevention (or targeted services). The diagram in Figure 3, taken from the *CAF Practitioners' Guide*, provides a helpful picture of how the processes and tools designed to integrate children's services and support early intervention have been conceived, particularly in the context of Figures 1 and 2 earlier.

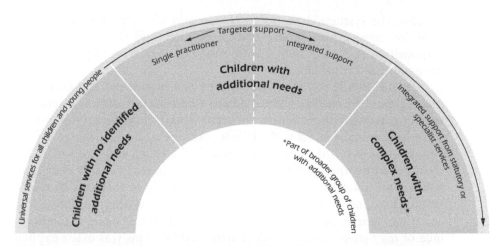

The following text labels appear within the diagram:

Targeted support

Single practitioner

Integrated support

Children with additional needs

Universal services for all children and young people

Children with no identified additional needs

*Part of broader group of children with additional needs

Children with complex needs*

Integrated support from statutory or specialist services

Note: Diagram is not to scale in representing the proportion of children and young people in each section of the windscreen. This diagram has been provided by and reproduced with the permission of the Department for Children, Schools and Families.

Figure 3 Processes and tools to support children and families

Source: The Common Assessment Framework for Children and Young People: Practitioners' Guide (CWDC, 2007, p. 8)

In parallel with the CAF, children's services are also expected to increase the sharing of information, again to identify children at risk of not fulfilling their potential and improving systems of early intervention. Section 12 of the Children Act 2004 requires local authorities to operate a national 'Information Sharing Index', now called *ContactPoint*, and covering all children. The electronic database will include information on: the child's name, address, gender and date of birth; a unique number identifying the child; the name and any contact details of any person with parental responsibility or who has care of the child at any time; the name and contact details of any educational institution, primary medical services, or any specialist or targeted services provided; the name of a nominated 'Lead Professional' if there is one; and recording whether a CAF has been carried out. Finally, where the provision of a service has ceased and a decision is made to extend the period of retention beyond the one year minimum, this would indicate that the practitioner still had information to share which they believed to be important and relevant to others.

The introduction of *ContactPoint* and the CAF clearly demonstrates how the importance of early intervention, together with the growing reliance on ICT, are seen as central for the transformation of children's services in England. However, the focus of concern has broadened considerably from those children who might suffer child abuse or 'significant harm' to include all children, particularly those who are at risk of poor outcomes and therefore may not fulfil their potential. In the process, the systems designed to screen and identify those in need of attention have grown in size and complexity and the challenges and responsibilities placed upon a wide range of agencies and practitioners have increased considerably.

However, while the focus of concern has broadened and there is a much greater emphasis on more positive notions of risk, it is important to recognise that the forensic concerns about child protection which were so dominant in the early 1990s continue to lie at the heart of the system – or, in terms of Figures 1 and 2, the sharp end or apex of the triangle. More specifically, for our purposes here, it is also clear that social work's almost exclusive responsibilities lie in this area of work. While there has been a considerable expansion in the preventive and early intervention services, these are no longer seen as being in the province of mainstream social work (Parton, 2009). This was made explicit in *Every Child Matters: Change for Children in Social Care* (DfES, 2004c) published at the same time as *Every Child Matters: Change for Children* (DfES, 2004a):

> Social workers and social care workers need to be at the heart of the *Every Child Matters: Change for Children* programme. You play a central role in trying to improve outcomes for the most vulnerable through your work with children in need including those in need of protection, children who are looked after and disabled children (DfES, 2004c, p. 2).

It is the local authority social workers who are given the key and overriding responsibility for operating the child protection system and this has changed very little from the situation in the early 1990s. In many ways, particularly following the tragic death of 'Baby Peter', social workers are more concerned than ever with forensically investigating, assessing and managing cases of child abuse in a context which is even more high profile and procedurally driven than ever before. While we have recently witnessed something of a revaluing of social work and a renewed recognition of the complexities involved, the actual focus of the work has become even more prescribed and framed by its statutory and procedurally defined roles.

Beyond this, there are some other observations I wish to make. The growing emphasis on prevention and the introduction of a range of new technologies to aid early intervention and the sharing of information between different professionals, indicates there is likely to be much greater surveillance of children, young people, parents and the professionals who operate the system (Parton, 2006; Anderson et al., 2009). In the process the boundaries between the public and the private, the State and the family begin to collapse and it becomes increasingly difficult to ensure that confidentiality is maintained and the rights of children furthered (Roche, 2008).

In broadening the focus of what is meant by risk there has been an elision of concerns about children and young people who might be *at risk* from a whole variety of threats, including abuse, with concerns about children and young people who might *pose a threat* to others, either now or in the future, particularly by falling into crime or antisocial behaviour. The agendas around the care and control of children and young people and those who might be either victims or villains are in danger of becoming very blurred (Sharland, 2006; James and James, 2008).

In attempting to widen and deepen attempts at early intervention while also trying to strengthen the systems of child protection, the aim is to integrate communication between different services and professionals and also to increase professional accountability and responsibility. In the process there is a real danger that we will see the growth in attempts at, what Michael Power calls, 'the risk management of everything' (Power, 2004). Rather than overcoming the defensiveness, risk avoidance and the blame culture so associated with the child protection system in the 1990s, the danger is that these characteristics will permeate throughout the newly integrated and transformed children's services in quite new ways.

Conclusion

In this chapter I have argued that interest in risk in social work and social care is of relatively recent origin but that this has now become a central concern to the point where much of the work is framed in these terms. However, it is a diverse and slippery concept which varies in both understanding and use, depending on its context. I have also argued, however, that until recent years risk in social work and social care was understood almost exclusively in negative terms and was often operationalised in narrow and defensive ways.

In more recent years there is clear evidence of both a broadening of the concept of risk and its application and serious attempts to recognise the importance of a much more positive and proactive approach. I have explored the recent development of these ideas about risk in the context of the *Every Child Matters: Change for Children* programme in England. In the process I have explored the complexities and tensions involved in such developments and their possible implications for both service users and professionals. Parallel critical discussions are available in relation to other areas of social work and social care policy and practice (see, for example, in relation to mental health, Brown, 2006; Sawyer, 2008; Langan, 2009).

What I have also suggested is that in many respects we can see these new and more positive approaches to risk having the effect also of both extending systems of surveillance and posing particular challenges to issues around professional confidentiality and the human rights of service users. Such challenges are heightened in a context where there is a growing emphasis on a logic of precaution which prioritises an approach to practice based on 'strict safety'. Increasingly the language of risk is in danger of being stripped of its association with the calculation of probabilities and is being used almost exclusively in terms of not just preventing future harm but also avoiding the 'worst case' scenario, and in a context where there has been a considerable broadening of those in the population for whom professionals are seen as having responsibilities.

References

Alaszewski, A., Harrison, L. and Manthorpe, J. (eds) (1998) *Risk, Health and Welfare: Policies, Strategies and Practice*, Buckingham, Open University Press.

Anderson, R., Brown, I., Dowty, T., Inglesant, P., Heath, W. and Sasse, A. (2009) *Database State*, York, Joseph Rowntree Reform Trust.

Axford, N. and Little, M. (2006) 'Refocusing children's services towards prevention: lessons from the literature', *Children & Society*, 20(4): 299–312.

Barry, M. (2007) *Effective Approaches to Risk Assessment in Social Work: An International Literature Review*, Scottish Executive Education Department. Research Findings No. 31. Edinburgh, Scottish Executive.

Beck, U. (1992) *Risk Society: Towards a New Modernity*, London, Sage.

Brearley, C. P. (1982) *Risk and Social Work*, London, Routledge and Kegan Paul.

Brown, P. (2006) 'Risk versus need in revising the 1983 Mental Health Act: Conflicting claims, muddled policy', *Health, Risk and Society*, 8(4): 343–58.

Butler, I. and Drakeford, M. (2005) *Scandal, Social Policy and Social Welfare*, Bristol, Policy Press.

Chief Secretary to the Treasury (2003) *Every Child Matters* (Cm5860), London, Stationery Office.

CWDC (Children's Workforce Development Council) (2007) *Common Assessment Framework for Children and Young People: Practitioners' Guide. Integrated Working to Improve Outcomes for Children and Young People*, Leeds, CWDC.

DfES (Department for Education and Skills) (2004a) *Every Child Matters: Change for Children*, London, DfES.

DfES (Department for Education and Skills) (2004b) *Every Child Matters: Next Steps*, London, DfES.

DfES (Department for Education and Skills) (2004c) *Every Child Matters: Change for Children in Social Care*, London, DfES.

DH (Department of Health) (1995) *Child Protection: Messages from Research*, London, HMSO.

DH (Department of Health) (2001) *Studies Informing the Framework for the Assessment of Children in Need and their Families*, London, Stationery Office.

DH (Department of Health) (2007) *Independence, Choice and Risk: A Guide to Best Practice in Supported Decision-making*, London, Stationery Office.

DH (Department of Health), Department of Education and Employment, Home Office (2000) *Framework for the Assessment of Children in Need and their Families*, London, Stationery Office.

DH (Department of Health), Home Office, and Department of Education and Employment (1999) *Working Together to Safeguard Children: A Guide to Inter-agency Working to Safeguard and Promote the Welfare of Children*, London, Stationery Office.

Douglas, M. (1986) *Risk Acceptability According to the Social Sciences*, London, Routledge & Kegan Paul.

Douglas, M. (1992) *Risk and Blame: Essays in Cultural Theory*, London, Routledge.

Dryfoos, J. G. (1990) *Adolescents at Risk: Prevalence and Prevention*, Oxford, Oxford University Press.

Ericson, R. V. (2007) *Crime in an Insecure World*, Cambridge, Polity Press.

Farrington, D. (1996) *Understanding and Preventing Youth Crime*, York: Joseph Rowntree Foundation.

Farrington, D. (2000) 'Explaining and preventing crime: The globalisation of knowledge', *Criminology*, **38**(1): 1–24.

Farrington, D. (2007) 'Childhood risk factors and risk-focused prevention', in M. Maguire, R. Morgan and R. Reiner (eds) *The Oxford Handbook of Criminology* (4th edn), Oxford, Oxford University Press.

France, A. and Utting, D. (2005) 'The paradigm of "Risk and Protection-Focused Prevention" and its impact on services for children and families', *Children & Society*, **19**(2): 77–90.

Franklin, B. (ed.) (1999) *Social Policy, the Media and Misrepresentation*, London, Routledge.

Franklin, B. and Parton, N. (2001) 'Press-ganged! Media reporting of social work and child abuse', in M. May, R. Payne and E. Brunsden (eds) *Understanding Social Problems: Issues in Social Policy*, Oxford, Blackwell.

Frost, N. and Parton, N. (2009) *Understanding Children's Social Care: Politics, Policy and Practice*, London, Sage.

Furedi, F. (2002) *Culture of Fear* (2nd edn), London, Continuum.

Goldblatt, P. and Lewis, C. (eds) (1998) *Reducing Offending*. Home Office Research Study No.187, London, HMSO.

Hacking, I. (1975) *The Emergence of Probability: A Philosophical Study of Early Ideas about Statistical Inferences*, Cambridge, Cambridge University Press.

Hebenton, B. and Seddon, T. (2009) 'From dangerousness to precaution: managing sexual and violent offenders in an insecure and uncertain age', *British Journal of Criminology*, **49**(3): 343–62.

HM Government (2006) *Working Together to Safeguard Children: A Guide to Inter-agency Working to Safeguard and Promote the Welfare of Children*, London, Stationery Office.

Home Office, Department of Health, Department of Education and Science, and the Welsh Office (1991) *Working Together Under the Children Act 1989: A Guide to Arrangements for Inter-Agency Cooperation for the Protection of Children from Abuse*, London, HMSO.

James, A. and James, A. (2008) 'Changing childhood in the UK: reconstructing discourses of 'Risk' and 'Protection', in A. James and A. James (eds) *European Childhoods: Cultures, Politics and Childhoods in Europe*, Basingstoke, Palgrave Macmillan.

Kemshall, H. and Pritchard, J. (eds) (1996) *Good Practice in Risk Assessment and Risk Management*, London, Jessica Kingsley.

Kemshall, H. and Pritchard, J. (eds) (1997) *Good Practice in Risk Management: Protection, Rights and Responsibilities*, London, Jessica Kingsley.

Kemshall, H., Parton, N., Walsh, M. and Waterson, J. (1997) 'Concepts of risk in relation to organisational structure and functioning within the personal social services and probation', *Social Policy and Administration*, **31**(3): 213–32.

Laming, Lord (2003) *The Victoria Climbié Inquiry: Report of an Inquiry by Lord Laming* (Cm5730), London, Stationery Office.

Langan, J. (2009) 'Mental health, risk communication and data quality in the electronic age', *British Journal of Social Work*, **39**(3): 467–87.

Little, M., Axford, N. and Morpeth, C. (2004) 'Risk and protection in the context of services for children in need', *Child and Family Social Work*, **9**(1): 105–18.

Lonne, B., Parton, N., Thomson, J. and Harries, M. (2009) *Reforming Child Protection*, London, Routledge.

Lupton, D. (1999) *Risk*, London, Routledge.

Mrazek, P. J. and Haggerty, K. J. (eds) (1994) *Reducing Risks for Mental Disorders: Frontiers for Preventive Intervention Research*, Washington, DC, Institute of Medicine/National Academy Press.

Mythen, G. and Walklate, S. (eds) (2006) *Beyond the Risk Society: Critical Reflections on Risk and Human Security*, Maidenhead, Open University Press.

Parton, N. (1985) *The Politics of Child Abuse*, Basingstoke, Macmillan – now Palgrave Macmillan.

Parton, N. (1991) *Governing the Family: Child Care, Child Protection and the State*, Basingstoke, Macmillan – now Palgrave Macmillan.

Parton, N. (1996) 'Social work, risk and the blaming system', in N. Parton (ed.) *Social Theory, Social Change and Social Work*, London, Routledge.

Parton, N. (ed.) (1997) *Child Protection and Family Support: Tensions, Contradictions and Possibilities*, London, Routledge.

Parton, N. (2006) *Safeguarding Childhood: Early Intervention and Surveillance in a Late Modern Society*, Basingstoke, Palgrave Macmillan.

Parton, N. (2008) 'The change for children programme in England: Towards the "Preventive-Surveillance State"', *Journal of Law and Society*, **35**(1): 166–87.

Parton, N. (2009) 'From Seebohm to think family: reflections on 40 years of policy change in statutory children's social work in England', *Child and Family Social Work*, **14**(1): 68–78.

Parton, N., Thorpe, D. and Wattam, C. (1997) *Child Protection: Risk and the Moral Order*, Basingstoke, Macmillan – now Palgrave Macmillan.

Petersen, A. and Wilkinson, I. (eds) (2008) *Health, Risk and Vulnerability*, London, Routledge.

Power, M. (2004) *The Risk Management of Everything: Rethinking the Politics of Uncertainty*, London, Demos.

Roche, J. (2008) 'Children's rights, confidentiality and the policing of children', *International Journal of Children's Rights*, **16**(4): 431–56.

Rutter, M. (1990) 'Psychosocial resilience and protective mechanisms', in J. Rolf, A. S. Masten, D. Cichetti, K. H. Nuechterlein and S. Weintraub (eds) *Risk and Protective Factors in the Development of Psychopathology*, Cambridge, Cambridge University Press.

Sawyer, A. M. (2008) 'Risk and new exclusions in community mental health practice', *Australian Social Work*, **61**(4): 327–41.

Sharland, E. (2006) 'Young people, risk taking and risk making: some thoughts for social work', *British Journal of Social Work*, **36**(2): 247–65.

Stalker, K. (2003) 'Managing risk and uncertainty in social work', *Journal of Social Work*, **3**(2): 211–33.

Taylor-Gooby, P. and Zinn, J. (eds) (2006) *Risk in Social Science*, Oxford, Oxford University Press.

Waldfogel, J. (1998) *The Future of Child Protection: How to Break the Cycle of Abuse and Neglect*, Cambridge, MA, Harvard University Press.

Warner, J. and Sharland, E. (eds) (2010) 'Risk and social work: Critical perspectives', special issue, *British Journal of Social Work*, **40**(2), February.

Gower College Swansea
Library
Coleg Gŵyr Abertawe
Llyrfgell

Chapter 6

Accountability

PENELOPE WELBOURNE

This chapter examines what is meant by accountability, with a particular focus on social work and the law. It will consider what accountability is for, how it is defined and the way in which legal accountability fits within a wider definition of accountability. More specifically it will consider the way the courts hold local authorities to account for their decisions in childcare cases, the accountability of individual social workers to their professional bodies and the role of serious case reviews in holding social work to account. This chapter explores the impact of human rights which are an integral part of contemporary social work practice. It is arguable that a balance has to be struck between holding professionals and service providers publicly accountable; protecting the privacy of children and families; and giving individual professionals protection from unfair attacks on their reputation.

Accountability is particularly important in social work because of the power that professionals have in relation to service users and other recipients of their services. The consumers of social work services are particularly disadvantaged in the professional–service-user relationship. The factors that have brought them to be users of social work services: illness, disability, or belonging to a family that is unable to care for them adequately, for example, are more often than not the very same factors that place them at high risk of social exclusion and disempowerment.

Accountability in social welfare provision, including the provision of social work services, is also an intrinsic part of the framework for promoting rights and protecting the vulnerable. Enforcing standards in social care provision is one component in the framework for upholding social rights (Cameron, 2008). Accountability takes many forms; contractual obligations to an employer; professional obligations to a professional body; and regulatory processes of inspection and audit. The judiciary also have a role in holding local authorities to account for their actions. Before considering the ways in which different forms of accountability impact on social work practice it is important to explore these different forms.

The idea of accountability

Mulgan (2000) describes 'accountability' as a complex, chameleon-like word, which crops up everywhere, to support arguments about 'rights' and 'governance'. Accountability may be *to* some person or agency to whom an explanation or justification is due, either because they provide the authority for providing the service, or because they have been delegated the task of finding out how the service is being provided (Shardlow, 1995). There is also accountability *for* services and professional activities; the things that a service provider ought to be providing (Braye and Preston Shoot, 2001, p. 43): an area that has given risen to much litigation.[1]

One recent trend in social work and in other professions which are primarily State-funded (such as the health professions) has been towards increasing accountability through working to procedures, targets and standards. This is described by Banks (2004; 2007) as the 'new accountability'. On the one hand, there are accountability systems that rely on external audit, and have the power to demand information and call to account, and a concept of accountability that is firmly tied in with targets and inspection criteria. On the other hand, there is an idea, or ideal, of accountability which relies upon the ethical values and commitment of individual practitioners, underpinned by reflection accountability to oneself and one's professional values.

The issue that is presently in contention is whether or not the balance between the two forms of accountability, the weaker and stronger forms, is correct or whether it has swung too far in the direction of intrusive external accountability systems. The Association of Directors of Children's Services' spokesperson to the 2009 Select Committee on Looked After Children said:

> the pressure on local authorities to collect information and perform in relation to it can become over-dominant. In an ideal world ... if people do the right things to try to improve what they achieve for children and young people, the performance indicators should follow behind. What can happen under pressure is that they end up chasing the indicator, not focusing on outcomes for children and young people. (UK Parliament, 2009a, para. 218)

Accountability to law and the courts

Social work is not entirely rule-bound. It is important to acknowledge that discretion is an integral part of professional practice, but this will be subject to limitation and local authorities are only permitted to do what statutes allow them to do or mandate them to do. In addition to specific duties imposed by statute (for example carrying out assessments; providing specified services), social workers are legally bound to carry out their duties in a way which does not contravene any other duties they may have to their service users. This includes legislation such as the Human Rights Act 1998.

Rights are particularly important for those who lack economic or social power. The Human Rights Act 1998 has been significant in expanding opportunities for challenging public service providers, as well as prompting providers of public services to consider what their responsibilities are in terms of the protection and promotion of individual rights. The Human Rights Act 1998 gave effect in the UK to the fundamental rights and freedoms expressed in the European Convention on Human Rights ('the Convention'). An individual who thinks that a public body has unlawfully interfered or acted incompatibly with their rights, or believes that they will do so in future, can use it to challenge the public authority. Issues about Human Rights Act rights may be raised in any existing legal proceedings, and they may also be the subject of specific legal proceedings. The 1998 Act does three things:

> [The Human Rights Act 1998] makes it unlawful for a public authority, like a government department, local authority or the police, to breach Convention rights, unless an Act of Parliament meant it couldn't have acted differently
>
> It means that human rights cases can be dealt with in a UK court or tribunal. Until the Act anyone who felt that their rights under the Convention had been breached had to go to the European Court of Human Rights in Strasbourg
>
> It says that all UK legislation must be given a meaning that fits with the Convention rights, if that's possible. If a court says that's not possible it will be up to Parliament to decide what to do. (UK Government, 2009)

Local authorities are therefore expected to have due regard for the human rights of service users. The most relevant provisions are arguably art.2, the right to life; art.3 (protection from cruel, inhuman and degrading treatment); art.6 (right to procedural fairness in decision making,) and art.8 (right to private and family life).

An example of the importance of these principles may be found in the House of Lords case of *Re W (Children: care plan) and Re S (Children: Care Plan)* (2002) which posed the government a question. The question was, how might local authorities be held accountable for protecting the rights of looked after children to family life, or privacy, or protection from harm, for example, when they are both the provider of services and the agency that reviews them? They cannot be expected to hold themselves accountable, because this ignores the principles of an accountability relationship. The government's answer was to introduce a provision under the Adoption and Children Act 2002 that all looked after children should have their cases reviewed by an Independent Reviewing Officer, who is charged with making further representations on behalf of the child if the human rights of a child are not being upheld by that authority.

One of the most draconian powers of the State is the removal of children from their parents, and the courts of appeal are part of the means available to hold local authorities and courts to account if they overreach their right of intervention in family life. *P C and S* v. *UK* (2002) is one of a number of cases in which the European Court of Human Rights considered the implications of making a care order (Children Act 1989 s.31) in light of the right to family life protected by art.8 of the Human Rights Act 1998. The important principle of *proportionality* of action is noted, as is the right of the parents to be involved in the decision-making process unless there are compelling reasons against it:

> While the authorities enjoyed a wide margin of appreciation in assessing the necessity of taking a child into care, in particular where an emergency situation arose, the court had still to be satisfied in the circumstances of the case that there existed circumstances justifying the removal of the child ... The taking of a new-born baby into public care at the moment of birth was an extremely harsh measure. There had to be extraordinarily compelling reasons before a baby could be physically removed from its mother, against her will, immediately after birth as a consequence of a procedure in which neither she nor her partner had been involved. A fair balance had to be struck between the interests of the child remaining in care and those of the parent being reunited with the child. In carrying out that exercise the court would attach particular importance to the best interests of the child. In the instant case, there was no doubt that there was an interference with P and C's rights under art.8, the only matter in dispute was whether the measures taken for S's protection were proportionate. (*P, C and S* v. *UK* [2002] All ER (D) 239)

This sets out the responsibility of the State to use its power and discretion as sparingly as possible, consistent with the welfare of the child. The rights of the parents have to be considered too, although they may be overridden by the child's need for protection. The right to family life under art.8 can legitimately be interfered with, but only if the circumstances warrant it.

A second example, this time from the UK courts rather than the European Court of Human Rights, also relates to the emergency removal of children. The case of *Re D (unborn baby) (emergency protection order: future harm)* (2009) considered the circumstances under which parents might be excluded from planning for the protection of a baby immediately after birth:

> It was established that under Art.8 of the Convention parents had a right to be fully involved in the planning, by public authorities, of public authority intervention in the lives of their family and their children, whether before, during or after care proceedings. In order to depart from that general principle, it was necessary to determine whether the step that the authority was proposing to take, namely, the step of not involving the parents in its planning and not communicating to the parents its plan for immediate removal at birth, was something that was justified by 'the overriding necessity of the interests of the child' or something that was 'essential to secure [*the child's*] safety'. *Re* D [2009]

Here it may be seen that the principle of proportionality of action is further refined to include the idea that compulsory State action without parental involvement in the planning process is only justified when exclusion of the parents from the planning process is essential to secure the child's safety. The child's and parents' rights to family life, and the parents' right to involvement in planning for their child even when child protection procedures are in train, and their right to fair and due process of law when steps are taken to interfere with the right to family life, limit what local authorities and courts may do, even with the intention of protecting the child.

Discretion is an important aspect of social work: this is partly because of the diversity of human problems and the inability for rules to cover every situation, so discretion is essential if social work is to be possible at all.[2] Social work is under-resourced, with potentially limitless demand on its resources, so discretion on the part of managers and practitioners is essential. Governments make broad policy statements about 'meeting need' or 'consumer choice', for example: individual social workers and their managers have to find ways to control budgets and share resources so slavish compliance with policy-derived rules is impossible. Social workers may be more compliant with rules in some areas of practice (Langan, 2000), and there may be more rules intended to curb discretion (Howe, 1991, 1992; Lymbery, 2001) but this does not necessarily imply an overall loss of discretion. Practitioners may find ways of working around the rules, either in the interests of service users, or in ways that run counter to their interests (Evans and Harris, 2004). The absence of clear guidance on how to manage dilemmas and the responsibility this leaves on the shoulders of social workers may be as much a problem as the proliferation of rules, leading to defensive practice.

On the other hand, the freedom that social workers necessarily have when carrying out their work means that administrative attempts to control their activities are inevitably limited by the discretion required if they are to be able to respond to complex and unpredictable situations. While practice is increasingly defined by policy directives, targets and processes, social work continues to be an activity that largely takes place in private with social workers continuing to use discretion in responding to unpredictable situations. They are arguably primarily held accountable for the aspects of their work that can be 'counted' through administrative means, unless something goes wrong, when the more private and interpersonal aspects of their work become subject to scrutiny.

That said, social work practice can be seen as taking place in the shadow of the law that is within the ever-present possibility, if not an actual requirement, that decisions taken will be reviewed and adjudicated on by a court. Some proposed actions require a decision from the court; for example removing a child from his or her parents' care without the parents' permission. To achieve this, the social worker's local authority must apply to the court for an order for an emergency protection order, care order or interim care order under the Children Act 1989. For a care order or interim care order under s.31 of the 1989 Act, they must satisfy the court that the threshold for removal of the child on a care order is met. That is, the child will suffer, or is likely to suffer, significant harm if the order is not made. Additionally, the order must be in the best interests of the child, and there must be a plan for the child that satisfies the court that a care order would bring about an improvement in the child's prospects, compared to the situation if the order were not made.

Removal of a child from its parents is widely viewed as 'draconian', not only by the public but also by academics and even by judges (see the judgement in *P, C and S* v. *UK* (2002) at 631), especially when the child is very young. There is also a high level of public and media interest in such cases, making the need for clear and effective accountability systems very pressing. Media interest has led to extensive media coverage of failures in the child protection system. High levels of political interest follow, with high-profile enquiries and reviews of child deaths making the headlines in newspapers and triggering changes in practice based on inquiry recommendations. The most well known of these in recent years have been the deaths of Victoria Climbié (Laming, 2003) and 'Baby P', which triggered a review of 'progress' in protecting children in England (Laming, 2009). There is a resulting intense interest outside as well as inside child protection social work in making it 'failsafe' and 'foolproof' by introducing systems that will minimise error and make it accountable for every action and judgement.[3]

Professional conduct and good practice

As professionals, social workers are accountable to the body that maintains the register of professional social workers, in England the General Social Care Council (GSCC) and in Wales the Care Council for Wales (CCW). No one is allowed to call themselves a social worker in a professional capacity or practice as a social worker unless they are registered. The *GSCC Code of Practice for Social Care Workers* addresses personal accountability for professional conduct in social work.

The *Codes of Practice* are aimed at practitioners and their employers. They address social workers' accountability to their professional body for their conduct, social workers' accountability to their employers, and employers' accountability for ensuring that the required professional standards are upheld. The Codes are concerned to raise standards in social care services as well as effectively regulate professional activity. They were launched in 2002: the first time there had been an attempt to set standards nationally for employers and social workers. When they were introduced they were described as 'a key step in the introduction of a system of regulation for social care.' (GSCC, 2004, p. 1). The Codes are a tool for enhancing accountability at a number of levels: *nationally,* by defining standards of practice at a national level; *organisationally,* by defining for employers what they should expect from social workers and what they should support and enforce through clear policies and practice management; and at an *individual practitioner* level, through reflection on practice, continuing professional development, and autonomous self-regulation.

The GSCC is under a duty under s.62 of the Care Standards Act 2000 to keep the Codes under review. They may be used to determine whether or not someone should be barred from practising as a social worker by suspending or removing them from the Social Care Register, the register of social workers held by the GSCC. The status of the Code is set out in the introduction:

> The General Social Care Council expects social care workers to meet this code and may take action if registered workers fail to do so.

Employers of social care workers are required to take account of this code in making any decisions about the conduct of their staff.

Since March 2008 any allegation of misconduct against a social worker is investigated through the GSCC (Conduct) Rules 2008. The GSCC Conduct Group has a duty to look into information concerning social workers who may have breached the *Codes of Practice*. Suitability to remain on the Social Care Register is examined by means of a Conduct Committee Hearing:

> usually held in public and uses the civil standard of proof. It will hear evidence and decide if the social worker has committed misconduct. If so, it will decide if action should be taken against them. (GSCC, 2008)

If misconduct is found that is judged serious enough to question the social worker's suitability to remain on the register, they can have their name removed from the register, or be suspended, or an admonishment (a mark next to their name) may be added to their entry on the register.

At the other end of the spectrum, the social care worker's *Code of Practice* is envisaged as a tool for guidance and reflection by practitioners:

> As a social care worker you will have criteria to guide your practice and be clear about what standards of conduct you are expected to meet. You are encouraged to use the codes to examine your own practice and to look for areas in which you can improve. (GSCC, 2008)

Social care workers are responsible themselves for ensuring their practice remains consistent with the standards of practice defined by the Code:

> Social care workers are responsible for making sure that their conduct does not fall below the standards set out in this code and that no action or omission on their part harms the wellbeing of service users. (GSCC, 2008)

Employers should use them to increase public confidence in the profession and in public services generally:

> Employers are responsible for making sure that they meet the standards set out in this code, provide high quality services and promote public trust and confidence in social care services. (GSCC, 2008)

Employers are responsible for monitoring the performance of their social care employees against the standards set out in the GSCC Code. The Code for Employers is not currently enforceable, meaning that employers who fail to observe it do not suffer sanctions in the way that social workers who breach the Code do. The GSCC has recommended that this should change (GSCC, 2009; Laming, 2009).

There are six practice standards applicable to social care workers:

- the protection of the rights and promotion of the interests of service users and carers;
- striving to establish and maintain the trust and confidence of service users and carers;
- promoting the independence of service users while protecting them as far as possible from danger or harm;
- respecting the rights of service users while seeking to ensure that their behaviour does not harm themselves or other people;
- upholding public trust and confidence in social care services; and
- being accountable for the quality of their work and taking responsibility for maintaining and improving their knowledge and skills.

You can see from the above how working with service users is central to good social work practice (Leung, 2008). However, if social workers are to be truly accountable to service users, service users need to have the right to question and to complain and to be able to do so in expectation of a fair hearing, impartial adjudication and a reasoned outcome. This is perhaps complemented by the view that consultation and dialogue with service users about service provision, and internal reflection and self-appraisal based on that dialogue on the part of the social work professional, are aspects of the complex web of accountability relationships to which social workers are subject (Carr, 2004).

There is debate centred on whether accountability systems in social work have reached a point at which they have become counterproductive. In 2008 Booth and Stratton commented on the current emphasis on systematic record and review systems:

> Reports by two universities have revealed that the Integrated Children's System (ICS), launched in 2005 following the death of Victoria Climbié, is so laborious it typically takes more than 10 hours to fill in initial assessment forms for a child considered to be at risk. A 'core assessment' takes a further 48 hours on average, according to government-commissioned research by York University ... the pressure on social workers, effectively tied to their desks by bureaucracy, reveals systemic problems in child protection. (Booth and Stratton, 2008)

Systems introduced with the express intention of increasing account-ability and consistency of service quality, as well as reducing the risk of another catastrophic failure, are thought by some to be having perverse effects:

'Workers report being more worried about missed deadlines than missed visits', said Professor Sue White ... 'The [computer] system regularly takes up 80% of their day.' ... Eileen Monroe, an expert on child protection ... said some local authorities are petitioning the government to allow them to drop the system. 'The programme is set up to continually nag you, and the child's misery just doesn't nag as loudly.' (Booth and Stratton, 2008)

Accountability systems need to be able to recognise human qualities as well as administrative ones. It is not always easy to define what exactly is desired in terms of an outcome from a public service. Even when it is clear what is needed, without contextual knowledge, information about service operation taken out of context can be misleading (Barton and Welbourne, 2005).

Accountability within organisations: Serious Case Reviews

Serious Case Reviews (SCRs) provide information about how the authority responded to a child and its family's need for services, and about systemic failures to protect children. Under *Working Together to Safeguard Children* (DfES, 2006) SCRs must be undertaken when a child dies (including through suicide), and when abuse or neglect is known or suspected to be a factor in the death. They can also be under-taken when:

- a child sustains a potentially life-threatening injury or serious and permanent impairment of health and development through abuse or neglect,
- a child has been subjected to particularly serious sexual abuse,
- a parent has been murdered and a homicide review is being initiated,
- a child has been killed by a parent with a mental illness,
- the case gives rise to concerns about inter-agency working to protect children from harm.

(DCSF *Every Child Matters* website: *Serious Case Reviews*)

The purpose of a SCR is to find out if any lessons need to be learned from the case, including lessons about how agencies work together to protect children, to improve inter-agency working. Ofsted should be informed of the outcome of the SCR. Ofsted also organise regular reviews of SCRs and compile data from them about (i) the adequacy of the SCR process, and (ii) lessons to be learned more generally from SCRs. These are published for wider learning. The two most recent reviews of SCRs are Rose and Barnes' (2008) study of SCRs between 2001 and 2003, and Brandon et al.'s (2008) analysis of SCRs from 2003 to 2005.[4]

SCRs are a form of 'internal' accounting in that the local authority and its partners locally examine their own practice in an effort to understand what has happened, to appraise their own role in it, and learn from this process. This raises questions about the possibility that agencies will fail to be vigorous in identifying areas of weakness in practice. Lord Laming's (2009) review of child protection called for chairs of SCRs to be independent, to counteract this possibility. SCR findings are not available to the public on grounds of confidentiality except in anonymised summary form; this has attracted criticism:

> Refusing to publish serious case reviews after a child's death is like keeping the information from an aircraft's black box secret after an aviation disaster; it prevents us all learning the lessons we need to, and debating openly how we keep children safe. We cannot have a situation where we keep terrible errors secret. (Michael Gove, Shadow Home Secretary, quoted in Horton, 2009)

A final component of a system of accountability is that it needs to complete a feedback loop (Schön, 1983) in order that lessons that may be learned and action taken to implement any change needed for future development. Accountable organisations need to be 'learning organisations', and respond to feedback, whether the feedback comes from SCRs, service users, inspectorates, or other professionals. In this way, the feedback loop can be completed. This parallels the reflection that is an important part of professional practice at an individual level:

> The Government has undertaken to ensure that all SCRs have independent chairs, and make anonymised summary information from each SCR available to the public and other agencies, while maintaining confidentiality for the subjects of the Reviews in order that this process may occur. (Balls, 2009)

One might question how useful analysis of failure is for progressing practice generally, given the specific circumstances in which each tragedy occurs. Nevertheless, repeating the errors of the past is to be avoided. Overviews of SCRs have provided particularly valuable information about vulnerability factors and the role of inter-agency working in protecting children, as well as where things can go wrong, as demonstrated by the two reviews of SCRs referenced above.

Accountability and social work – some conclusions

There has been a shift towards accountability based on outcomes, and towards inter-agency working, but making all partners share more equally the responsibility for achieving good outcomes for children seems to be a more challenging task. Children need services across a wide range of areas including health, social welfare and education, and these dimensions of welfare and development are highly interdependent. Partnership working has been mirrored by attempts to achieve accountability systems that mirror that interdependency and partnership. While some progress has been made, it seems there is still scope for further development.

The value of social work interventions is in large part determined by the skill of the analysis of the presenting problem carried out by a practitioner. Banks (2007) reflects on the role of social work:

a profession that occupies the dynamic space between social policy and civil society. As such, it is more intimately bound with politics and culture than many other professions, and has potential to tackle some of the pressing issues of social exclusion and discrimination.

This requires:

critical reflexivity on the part of social professionals: an ability to locate themselves and their work in the political and cultural climates of their countries, to recognise and resist aspects of their own roles as adjuncts of the state, while at the same time viewing their work in the context of global trends. (Banks, 2007, p. 1238)

This is a highly complex task. Social workers need excellent reflective and critical skills in order to manage their own work, much of which happens outside the gaze of managers and supervisors. At the same time, their managers, employers and professional body need to know enough about their work to be satisfied that public money is being well spent, and the public are receiving a good service. The legal requirements of the Children Acts 1989 and 2004 and the Human Rights Act 1998 add to the demand that social work be 'accountable', especially when the powers of the courts are invoked to support compulsory intervention in family life. This chapter has explored some of the ways in which that accountability is constructed.

Social and political trends, including increasing managerialism, the devolution of political powers, increased partnership working, and a new emphasis on the right to service-user choice and diversity of services and providers, all affect accountability relationships. Every organisation is affected, but the ways in which they are affected vary. It might be argued that there is a 'crisis of accountability' throughout social work, and the most acute area of crisis is child and family social work. The vulnerability of children is one reason behind this. Errors in childcare social work are so shocking that there is a strong urge to make them error-free, however difficult this is as a goal. The strongly emotive rights to family life and to family privacy are also important in making social workers and courts exercise caution when choosing when to intervene in family life against the wishes of (adult) members of families. Social workers need to be held accountable because they exercise power in a position of responsibility and authority. Both social work professionals and service users have an interest in effective processes and systems of accountability – service users because this holds out the promise of a check, a review of a decision which has perhaps transformed their lives, and social workers because, with effective managerial support and oversight, this can lead to better decision making.

References

Balls, E. (2009) Secretary of State letter to Lord Laming, available through the DCSF website, *The Protection of Children in England: A Progress Report* at: http://www.everychildmatters.gov.uk/resources-and-practice/IG00361.

Banks, S. (2004) *Ethics, Accountability and the Social Professions*, Basingstoke, Palgrave Macmillan.

Banks, S. (2007) 'Between equity and empathy: Social professions and the new accountability', *Social Work and Society* online journal, Vol. 5, 2007 www.socwork.net/2007/festschrift/esw/banks.

Barton, A. and Welbourne, P. (2005) 'Context and its significance in child protection research', *Child Abuse Review 2005*, **14**(3): 177–94.

Booth, R. and Stratton, A. (2008) 'Child protection stifled by £30m computer system – report', *Guardian* newspaper, Wednesday 19 November 2008, www.guardian.co.uk/society/2008/nov/19/baby-p-child-protection-system.

Brandon, M., Belderson, P., Warren, C., Howe, D., Gardner, R., Dodsworth, J. and Black, J. (2008) *Analysing Child Deaths and Serious Injury Through Neglect: What Can We Learn? A Biennial Analysis of Serious Case Reviews 2003–2005*, Nottingham, DCSF.

Braye, S. and Preston-Shoot, M. (2001) 'Social work practice and accountability' in Cull, L-A. and Roche, J. (eds) *The Law and Social Work*, Basingstoke, Palgrave Macmillan.

Cameron, B. (2008) *Accountability Regimes for the Federal Social Transfer*, paper presented 6 June 2008 to the Canadian Political Science Association, Vancouver, available at: www.cpsa-acsp.ca/papers-2008/Cameron,%20 Barbara.pdf.

Carr, S. (2004) *Has Service User Participation Made a Difference to Social Care Services?* London: SCIE, also available at http://www.scie.org.uk/publications/ positionpapers/pp03.pdf.

DCSF (Department for Children, Schools and Families) (n.d.) *Every Child Matters – Serious Case Reviews* website; information available at: www. everychildmatters.gov.uk/socialcare/safeguarding/seriouscasereviews/.

DfES (Department for Education and Skills) (2006) *Working Together to Safeguard Children: A Guide to Inter-agency Working to Safeguard and Promote the Welfare of Children*, London, HM Government.

Evans, T. and Harris, J. (2004) 'Street-level bureaucracy, social work and the (exaggerated) death of discretion', *British Journal of Social Work*, **34**: 871–95.

GSCC (General Social Care Council) (2004) *Code of Practice for Social Care Workers and Code of Practice for Employers of Social Care Workers*, London, GSCC. Available at: www.gscc.org.uk/NR/rdonlyres/8E693C62-9B17-48E1-A806-.

GSCC (General Social Care Council) (2008) *Conduct Rules 2008*, London, GSCC. Available at: www.gscc.org.uk/NR/rdonlyres/67F9C9D2-DE3E-4287-927C-C987911EB29D/0/2008GSCCConductRules.pdf.

GSCC (General Social Care Council) (2009) 'Poll reveals social workers feel undervalued', GSCC website, 17 March 2009. Available at: www.social-workconnections.org.uk/content.php?id=90.

Horton, C. (2009) 'Laming Report: reaction in quotes', *Guardian* 12 March 2009. Available at: www.guardian.co.uk/society/2009/mar/13/child-protection-laming-babyp-report.

Howe, D. (1991) 'Knowledge, power and the shape of social work practice', in Martin Davies (ed.) *The Sociology of Social Work*, London, Routledge.

Howe, D. (1992) 'Child abuse and the bureaucratisation of social work', *Sociological Review*, **40**(3): 491–508.

Laming, Lord (2003) *The Victoria Climbié Inquiry*, London, HM Government.

Laming, Lord (2009) *The Protection of Children in England: A Progress Report*, London, House of Commons and www.publications.everychildmatters.gov. uk/eOrderingDownload/HC-330.pdf.

Langan, M. (2000) 'Social services; managing the third way', in Clarke, J., Gewirtz, S., McLauglin, E. (eds) *New Managerialism, New Welfare,* London, Sage.

Leung, T. (2008) 'Accountability to welfare service users: challenges and responses of service providers', *British Journal of Social Work,* 38: 531–45.

Local Government Organisation (n.d.) *Complaints About Child Protection Issues.* Available at: www.lgo.org.uk/complaints-about-child-protection.

Lymbery, M. (2001 'Social work at the crossroads,' *British Journal of Social Work* 31: 369–84.

Mulgan, R. (2000) '"Accountability": An ever-expanding concept?' *Public Administration,* 78: 555–73.

Rose, W. and Barnes, J. (2008) *Improving Safeguarding Practice: Study of Serious Case Reviews 2001–2003,* Research Report DCSF – RR022, Nottingham, DCSF.

Schön, D. (1983) *The Reflective Practitioner: How Professionals Think in Action,* London, Temple Smith.

Shardlow, S. (1995) 'Confidentiality, accountability and the boundaries of client–worker relationships', in Hugman, R. and Smith, D. (eds) *Ethical Issues in Social Work,* London, Routledge.

UK Government (2009) *Your Rights and Responsibilities.* Available at: www. direct.gov.uk/en/Governmentcitizensandrights/Yourrightsandresponsibilities/ DG_4002951?cids=Google_PPC&cre=Government_Citizens_Rights.

UK Parliament (2009a) *House of Commons Children, Schools and Families Committee: Looked After Children – Third Report of Session 2008–9,* HC 111-I, London, The Stationery Office. Also available at: www.publications. parliament.uk/pa/cm200809/cmselect/cmchilsch/111/111i.pdf.

UK Parliament (2009b) 'The performance framework for the care system', in the Conclusions and recommendations of the House of Commons Select Committee on looked-after children, www.publications.parliament.uk/pa/ cm200809/cmselect/cmchilsch.

Cases

AK v. *Central & North West London Mental Health NHS Trust & Another* [2008] EWHC 1217.

G, R (on the application of) v. *London Borough of Southwark* [2008] EWCA Civ 877.

Hansraj Chavda v. *Harrow LBC* [1997] 2 WLR 459.

P C and S v. *UK* [2002] All ER (D) 239 (Jul).

R v. *Gloucestershire County Council ex parte Barry* [1997] 2 All ER 1, [1997] 2 WLR 459.

Re D (unborn baby) (emergency protection order: future harm) [2009] EWHC 446, p.6, (Fam).

Re W (Children: care plan) and Re S (Children: Care Plan) [2002] UKHL 10.

Notes

1. See for example, *R* v. *Gloucestershire CC ex parte Barry* and *Hansraj Chavda* v. *Harrow LBC* (right to adult services); *G* v. *London Borough of Southwark* (right of care leaver to housing); *AK* v. *Central & North West London Mental Health NHS Trust and Another* (right of former psychiatric patient to after-care provision).
2. Evans and Harris (2004) point out that professional discretion is inherently neither good nor bad.
3. In addition to the possibility of judicial scrutiny, service users and carers may also be able to make a complaint. If the service user is still dissatisfied with a decision they can then complain to the Public Ombudsman's Office. The Public Ombudsman is an independent 'watchdog' for users of public services. Complaints may be made directly to the Ombudsman, although the Ombudsman will not usually become involved unless all other avenues of complaint have been exhausted (Local Government Organisation, (n.d.)). This includes internal complaints under the Children Act 1989 complaints procedures. This means that the Ombudsman is unlikely to become involved until a problem has been unresolved for some period of time, which is not helpful when timeliness of action is important, as it often is for children. 'Neither the Children Act 1989 complaints process nor the office of the local government ombudsman appears to be particularly child-friendly.' (Howard League for Penal Reform in evidence at UK Parliament, 2009b, para. 139).
4. When failures of practice are very serious, as in the cases of Victoria Climbié (Laming, 2003) and 'Baby P' (Laming, 2009); an 'external' inquiry may be set up with an independent chair and wider dissemination of findings rather than an SCR set up by the area Local Safeguarding Children Board.

Chapter 7

Remedies

JANE WILLIAMS

Introduction

This chapter considers some of the key judicial and administrative remedies available to service users and carers when they believe that their rights have been breached or their needs not met. There may be many instances where service users are dissatisfied with the availability of a service or the quality of that service but none the less are able to resolve the matter by informal means. In some cases however this will not be possible and it is important for professionals and service users alike to know the range of remedies available – even though in the circumstances some will be more relevant than others.

Judicial and administrative remedies

The mechanisms within which remedies may be sought can be categorised as either judicial or administrative: judicial mechanisms can result in a legally binding decision while administrative mechanisms empower bodies, other than the courts, to investigate, report and make recommendations – usually the outcomes are not directly legally enforceable.

The judicial mechanisms are the same throughout England and Wales but the administrative mechanisms have been separated as a result of devolution. Since 1998, separate institutions have been established in Wales – not only a government (the Welsh Ministers) and Parliament (the National Assembly for Wales) but also inspectorates, commissions, tribunals and other administrative bodies. This has been achieved by incremental changes in several Acts of Parliament. Whether the processes are devolved or non-devolved, they all have their own particular purpose and outcomes. Many do not result in tangible compensation or indeed any individual remedy. When something goes wrong, those affected do not always seek a personal remedy but just as often, or also, seek to have errors acknowledged and to know that something will be done to prevent recurrence of the problem – to make sure it does not happen again.[1]

This chapter first examines the function of complaints and the importance of inspection, audit and review, the system of statutory complaints and the role of the ombudsman before examining judicial remedies including judicial review and breach of statutory duty.

Function of complaints

Complaints could be seen as a positive feature of social work practice. Having the right to complain is in itself empowering and service users and carers have a right to be listened to, to have their concerns taken seriously and to see that action is taken where necessary to rectify the problem and prevent its recurrence. Complaints highlight problems and can lead to an improvement in services. In this sense complaints are an essential aspect of a constructive relationship between service providers and service users and their carers. A commitment to improving services is important to the relationship between social services and the general public as well as between social workers and the individual service user.[2]

Government guidance on dealing with complaints emphasises key principles including care, fairness and respect for complainants and timely, transparent responses (DfES, 2006; WAG, 2006; DH, 2009a and b). Complaints are portrayed as a valuable component of a modern, user-focused administration. In practice, however the experience can be less than positive. At the same time, many social work professionals have to deal with the ever-present possibility of media criticism. Literature catalogues the adverse impact of the fear of blame and public criticism on individual social workers and local authorities (for example, Harris, 1987; Macdonald, 1990). There is an issue over where blame and criticism should be directed – whether at individual caseworkers, operational managers, strategic decision makers or those who set the broad framework of policy (for example Masson, 2006). When there is a public outcry over social work practice (for example over the death of a child registered as at risk) it often appears that there is an irresistible demand that an individual professional be held to account. The result of laying the blame at the door of individual social workers can cause a retreat into defensive practice with the consequence that there may seem little space for the practitioner between the 'vice' of defensive practice and the 'virtue' of service-user empowerment and reflection on one's own practice. The trend is towards ever greater scrutiny and for this, if no other, reason it is advisable to have a strategy for keeping on the side of virtue; this entails knowing the legal basis for social work action as well as the criteria for review, the standards required and the remedies available.

Inspection, audit and review

Inspection, audit and review are not designed to be triggered or even much participated in by individuals who have a complaint to make. Local complaints procedures are designed for individual complaints but are not well-equipped to address systemic failings. An individual complaint to an ombudsman is more likely to generate investigation of systemic failings or even failures in policy, but still will not result in a legally enforceable remedy although compensation is often paid following the recommendation of the ombudsman. The same applies to the work of the Commissions discussed below for children, older people and for equalities and human rights. These are hybrid mechanisms with powers of investigation and review as well as (varied) powers to take up individual grievances.

Since devolution there has been an incremental but quite rapid separation out of this administrative process for Wales and England. Some inspectorates that have collateral importance for social work, notably on criminal justice, still cover England and Wales, reflecting the fact that governmental powers in that field are not as yet devolved. Bodies concerned with social care, education, local government and health are mainly separated out, the Welsh bodies being accountable to the Welsh Assembly Government and the National Assembly for Wales and the English bodies being accountable to the relevant UK government department and to the UK Parliament. This is demonstrated in the table below.

For England, the Care Quality Commission (CQC) subsumed from March 2009 the previous remit of the Commission for Social Care Inspection, the Healthcare Commission and the Mental Health Service Commission in relation to health and adult social care services in England (whether provided by the NHS, local authorities, private companies or the voluntary sector) and the protection of the interests of persons detained under mental health legislation. The CQC has powers under the Care Standards Act 2000 and the Health and Social Care Act 2008 to register, inspect, review and take one or more of a range of enforcement measures against a service provider. The enforcement measures range in severity from a mere warning to criminal prosecution and a fine for specific offences including obstruction of the Commission when seeking to carry out an investigation.

Table 7.1 Administrative processes: England and Wales

	England	Wales	England and Wales	England, Wales and Scotland
Inspection and review	Care Quality Commission (adult social care and health) Ofsted (HMI Education, Children's Services and Skills: also covers CAFCASS)	Care and Social Services Inspectorate for Wales Health Inspectorate Wales Estyn (HMI Education and Training in Wales)	HMI Prisons HMI National Probation Service HMI Constabulary HMI Courts Administration HMI Crown Prosecution Service	
Audit	Audit Commission	Wales Audit Office		
Complaints	Statutory complaints (local authorities, NHS bodies) Local government ombudsman Parliamentary and health service ombudsman	Statutory complaints (local authorities, NHS bodies) Public services ombudsman: unified service covering the Welsh Assembly Government as well as health, local government and social housing		
Commissions	Children's Commissioner	Children's Commissioner for Wales Commissioner for Older People		Commission for Equalities and Human Rights

The CQC undertakes a programme of inspections or reviews, liaising with other relevant inspectorates and the Audit Commission to try to avoid an excessive burden falling on the organisation concerned. However the CQC can also undertake an investigation as a result of direct contact from service users, staff, the public or the media. This can therefore be seen as a possible avenue for an aggrieved service user to pursue and one which has the potential to attract significant consequences for the organisation concerned. It will not result in a remedy or compensation for the service user but may result in recommendations or enforcement action designed to ensure that the failing will not reoccur and to improve the service user experience for others.

Children's services in England are, since 2007, subject to review and inspection by Ofsted – or, to use the title conferred by the Education and Inspections Act 2006, 'Her Majesty's Inspectors of Education, Children's Services and Skills'. This inspectorate, like the CQC, has investigative and enforcement powers in relation to children's services provisions, for example under the Care Standards Act 2000 and the Childcare Act 2006 but, also like the CQC, is designed for service improvement generally and not to provide remedies for individual grievances.

For Wales, since devolution there has been a gradual move towards unified inspection and review of all public services. Three main bodies have emerged: the Care and Social Services Inspectorate for Wales (CSSIW), the Wales Audit Office and Health Inspectorate Wales. The CSSIW, an operationally independent department of the Welsh Assembly Government, carries out reviews and inspections of social care providers in relation to both adult and children's services. Taking into account the investigative role of CSSIW and the various enforcement powers conferred on the Welsh Ministers, a similar range of options is available in Wales as in England when a service is found to be wanting.

The role of audit is often overlooked. Like the inspectorates, the national audit commissions for Wales and for England (the Wales Audit Office and the Audit Commission respectively) are not designed primarily to respond to individual grievances or to promote service-user involvement (see Cope and Goodship, 2002). However the interest of these bodies – which conduct inspections and reviews and have wide powers of investigation – might be engaged as a result of a direct communication from a service user or member of the public. They also influence the coordination and timing of inspections and reviews by the inspectorates, applying the 'Hampton principles' (Hampton, 2005). These principles state that no inspection should take place without a reason: concerns raised by a service user or member of the public could provide a reason.

Specialist commissions

In the early years of the twenty-first century specialist commissions have become a growth industry. The concept of a commissioner is one of specialist supervision of governmental activity on behalf of a category of people who for one reason or another are deemed to have less power. There are specialist commissioners at all levels of governance – local, devolved, national, European, global – dealing with a wide range of matters from refugees to racial equality. In the UK, since 2001, four separate children's commissioners have been established, followed by commissioners for older people in Wales and Northern Ireland. At the same time the former race, sex and disability equality commissions have been consolidated in a single Commission on Equalities and Human Rights with a broadened remit on equalities and human rights generally.

The precise role and functions of these commissions varies but they all have investigative and reporting powers and some capacity to respond to individual complaints. The most active in individual case work has been the Children's Commissioner for Wales, this commissioner having a relatively wide remit in that regard (for a comparison with the role of other commissioners see Williams, 2005).

Statutory complaints

For children's services, complaints procedures and advocacy services must be provided by the local authority under Pt. III Children Act 1989. Section 26 Children Act 1989 requires each local authority to have a complaints procedure to deal with complaints about any aspect of local authority functions under the 1989 Act. For children looked after by a local authority there is also a system of regular review of the implementation of the care plan regardless of whether any complaint has been made. This procedure was introduced by the Adoption and Children Act 2002 as a response to judicial recognition, in *Re S, Re W* [2002], that the previous lack of formalised regular review could lead to breaches of article 8 ECHR.

For adult services, local complaints procedures are mandatory under ss.113 and 114 of the Health and Social Care (Community Health and Standards) Act 2003. As in the case of complaints relating to children's services, the details are set out in regulations made separately for Wales and England. There are also provisions ensuring that complaints may be made about the handling of complaints under these provisions.

In practice the effectiveness of these measures depends very much on the spirit in which they are implemented and, crucially, on the accessibility and quality of advocacy services. Support for advocacy is important to avoid marginalisation of service users, especially those lacking independent capacity. As argued by Pithouse and Crowley (2007) in relation to children, for example, it should not be necessarily assumed that a family member who may take the lead in making a complaint either represents the authentic voice of the service user or has synonymous interests.

Where a person remains dissatisfied after the end of a statutory complaints process, there may be recourse to the relevant Ombudsman. For England this would be the Local Government Ombudsman[3] or, in the case of a complaint concerning a health body, the Parliamentary and Health Service Ombudsman. For Wales it would be the Public Services Ombudsman (appointed under the Public Services Ombudsman (Wales) Act, 2005). The complaints regulations for both Wales and England require that at the end of the local complaints process the complainant be informed of the right to take the case to the relevant ombudsman.

The courts expect these statutory complaints procedures to be used before any application for judicial review (see below) is made. It is, however, possible to seek a judicial review of the decision at the end of the complaints process or of an authority's decision whether or how to implement any recommendation. The latter situation was the subject of *Re T (Accommodation by Local Authority)* [1995] where it was held that the local authority could not be compelled to follow a recommendation that a looked-after child should reside with particular foster carers.[4]

Judicial remedies

This chapter deals with these under five headings:

- human rights;
- negligence;
- breach of statutory duty;
- judicial review;
- deliberate acts or omissions.

Human rights

This is considered first because it affects all other remedies and processes – whether judicial or administrative – as well as constituting a separate judicial remedy in its own right. The Human Rights Act 1998 (HRA) affects the legality of everything done by any public authority in the UK with the exception of the UK Parliament. This includes the courts, tribunals, commissions and inspectorates as well as the local authorities and NHS bodies that deliver front-line services. This dramatic result was achieved by the simple provision in s.6 HRA:

> It is unlawful for a public authority to act in a way which is incompatible with a Convention right.

'Convention rights' refer to the rights contained in European Convention on Human Rights (ECHR) articles set out in Schedule 1 to the HRA and made part of UK law as a result of the enactment of the Human Rights Act 1998. Section 7 HRA entitles a person who claims to be a victim of a breach of s.6 to rely on 'Convention rights' in any legal proceedings or to make a free-standing legal claim.[5] The courts, as public authorities themselves under s.6 of the Act, must act compatibly with the Convention rights and they are also subject to the requirement in s.3 to interpret legislation in a way that gives effect to Convention rights.

Some Convention rights are of widespread application in social work. Article 8 (right to respect for home, private life, family life and correspondence) is likely to be relevant to any intervention. Judicial interpretation of art. 8, importing both positive and negative obligations on the State, means that it is relevant not only to decisions to take coercive action (for example seeking a care order or seeking compulsory hospital admission) but also to decisions whether and what services ought to be provided. In general, procedure is critical: the great majority of successful human rights claims affecting social work have concerned some procedural defect: a failure to disclose all relevant evidence, to involve service users and their families adequately or to consider properly the balance to be struck between competing human rights.

Negligence

Negligence claims are the best-known means of seeking compensation for harm caused by defective professional practice. For a negligence claim to succeed the claimant has to prove that:

- the defendant owed a duty of care to the claimant;
- the defendant breached the duty;
- the claimant suffered loss or damage as a result of the breach;
- the loss or damage was foreseeable.

Each of these elements has been developed and refined by the courts: negligence is a common law, rather than statutory remedy and sometimes this form of potential liability is referred to as the 'common law duty of care'. The general test for a duty of care is:

- it must be reasonably foreseeable that a person (the claimant) will suffer harm if another person (the defendant) acts or fails to act;
- there must be a relationship of sufficient proximity between claimant and defendant for it to be fair, just and reasonable to impose a duty on the defendant.

Social workers often develop a relationship which puts them in the position where they owe a duty of care to the service user. If the social worker then breaches the duty by failing to act in accordance with the standard of a reasonably skilled and competent social worker, and foreseeable harm results, the social worker is potentially liable to pay damages to the aggrieved service user or client. In practice it is usually the local authority that will be held accountable since it is the local authority, not the individual social worker, that bears the relevant statutory power or duty and, in practice, will have the funds to pay damages.

Historically, succeeding in a claim for negligence against a local authority when the fault arose from the exercise of a statutory power or duty, is fraught with difficulties. The courts developed what was effectively a 'public interest immunity' which meant that social work decisions pursuant to statutory functions could not give rise to negligence claims. The reasons were first, that the duties owed by a social worker were owed to the public generally, not to the individual client and second, that it would be contrary to the public interest to place the burden of risk of litigation on professionals carrying out very difficult and sensitive work in areas such as child protection and mental health. It was thought that imposing liability in damages might encourage defensive practices to the detriment of service users generally. In contrast Guthrie (1998) has argued that potential liability can operate to ensure that high standards are secured and maintained. It is important to note that the standard of care is not absolute: the 'Bolam' test, derived from the leading case on medical negligence, states that if a responsible body of professional opinion supports the practice that caused the injury then the professional (in this case the doctor) would not be guilty of negligence.[6]

Whatever the merits of 'public interest immunity', it did not survive challenges from the mid-1990s deploying arguments derived from the ECHR. A line of cases starting with *X (Minors) v. Bedfordshire* [1995], which went to the European Court of Human Rights as *Z v. UK* [2001], established that there could be no blanket immunity for statutory social services functions. Furthermore, it became clear that a failure to intervene, as well as over-zealous interference, could give rise to liability not only for negligence but also as a breach of s.6 of the HRA which, as noted above, states that 'it is unlawful for a public authority to act in a way which is incompatible with a Convention right'.

So far the courts have not been prepared to extend the common law duty of care beyond the immediate social work client. Thus in a child protection investigation the duty is owed to the child concerned, not to family members. For example in *JD (FC)* v. *East Berkshire Community Health Trust and others* [2005], three separate cases were heard, in each of which a child was separated from the family because of suspicion of abuse at home. In each case it transpired that the symptoms giving rise to the suspicions were attributable to wholly innocent medical causes which arguably should have been identifiable before the children were removed. The question arose whether the parents, as well as the children, could claim damages for negligence. Four of the five law lords dealing with the case held that they could not: the fifth, Lord Bingham, thought the law in this area was 'on the move' under the influence of the ECHR and ought to be allowed to develop incrementally. He was not prepared to say that a duty could never be owed to parents. The case law that has followed, however, suggests a distinct lack of enthusiasm for any such further incremental development. In *D* v. *Bury Metropolitan Borough Council* [2006] the Court of Appeal followed the majority in *JD (FC)* (*supra*), holding that the authority's duty of care could only be owed to the child concerned throughout the entire investigative stage, that is, right up until the making of a final care order: in childcare cases the interests of the child and parents are in potential conflict (for example because the parents might be abusing the child) and in such circumstances priority has to be given to the welfare of the child and the duty to investigate.

Beyond child protection investigations, local authority social work involves a range of assessment activity which is a gateway to the provision of services and facilities for people of all ages. In *Phelps* v. *Hillingdon London Borough Council* [1999], the local education authority was held liable for the failure of an educational psychologist to identify that a child was suffering from dyslexia. It was argued that the psychologist owed a contractual duty as an employee of the local authority but no duty beyond that to persons assessed. The House of Lords disagreed, finding no principled reason why a common law duty of care should not arise; the House of Lords therefore found that the LEA could be liable in negligence if there is a breach of that duty, in this case for the failure of the educational psychologist to carry out the assessment properly.

Despite these movements in the courts' attitude to claims arising out of statutory casework, it will still be an exceptional case that meets all the criteria for a claim in negligence. Even if all the requirements for a duty of care are made out, cases may still founder on issues of whether the duty was in fact breached, whether the damage was caused by the breach or was unforeseeable.[7]

Breach of statutory duty

To establish a claim for damages for breach of statutory duty[8] it must be shown that a person (the defendant) was under a duty imposed by statute and that the statute should be so interpreted as to confer a right of individual action on a person (the claimant) who was intended to benefit. Then, if it can be shown that the defendant breached the statutory duty and if the claimant can show that s/he suffered damage as a result, the claimant may be entitled to compensation.

On the whole, however, statutory social work functions do not give rise to actions of this kind: this aspect of the decision in *X (Minors)* v. *Bedfordshire* (*supra*) remains intact notwithstanding the subsequent developments in relation to the common law duty of care. This is either because duties are general duties (like s.17 Children Act 1989 – to provide services to children in need generally, not to provide a specific service to a specific child) or because the courts take the view that in passing the legislation Parliament did not intend to confer an individual right of action.

Judicial review

Judicial review enables the court to scrutinise the way in which administrative decisions are made. Judicial review is not designed for compensation, nor can the court substitute its own decision for that of the administrative authority, usually a local authority or government department, under review. The purpose of judicial review is to ensure that decisions are properly and fairly made. Judicial review is an important remedy in which the executive (government at national and local level) is subject to legal review, protecting the citizen from arbitrary government action. Social work decisions made in the exercise of statutory functions are a part of the executive function of the State and the task of the court in judicial review is to safeguard the rule of law by ensuring the decisions are properly made. The scope of judicial review has been developed by the courts over centuries but as with other areas of domestic law, the courts have had to absorb the law of the ECHR, especially since the HRA.

An application for judicial review may be brought with the leave of the court by a person having a sufficient interest in the decision. This could include a service user but may also encompass other family members and interest groups. While taking a relatively generous view of the sufficiency of interest test, the courts interpret strictly the requirement that an application must be brought without delay – and within a maximum of three months from the date of the decision. The court's scrutiny is directed at certain established criteria: whether the decision was within the scope of the powers conferred on the decision maker, was reached rationally and followed a fair process. Furthermore, if a Convention right is engaged, any interference must be proportionate to a legitimate aim. Remedies in judicial review proceedings are discretionary, unlike in most civil claims in which the general rule is that if you can prove your case, you get the remedy. They include quashing of the decision, mandating the authority to take specified steps or prohibiting it from taking specified action, or simply declaring the legal position.

While all social work decisions pursuant to statutory functions are in principle amenable to judicial review, it is possible to categorise them into those which are more and less likely to be the subject of a challenge. Local authorities carrying out inspection, audit, review and statutory complaints functions are potentially open to legal challenge by way of judicial review. The purpose of judicial review is to ensure that services are carried out lawfully and effectively; it can and is often used to force a local authority to provide services to an individual. Generally, judicial review is not appropriate where there are other means by which a court can determine whether a particular social work decision is legally sound. For example, it would not normally be appropriate to seek judicial review of a care plan drawn up in contemplation of care proceedings. The court will decide whether the plan satisfies the welfare test but it can also deal with issues about the legality, fairness or rationality of the plan. Similarly once a care order is made, questions about the implementation of the care plan would normally be dealt with in the statutory review system under the Children Act 1989 (as amended by the Adoption and Children Act 2002) which allows for a return to the court if implementation is unsatisfactory.

Another category of decisions less amenable to judicial review are those which strike a balance between competing claims for public resources in accordance with a power given to the decision maker by an Act of Parliament. Many examples in the field of health care provision show the courts refusing to second-guess a commissioning body as to the availability of specific treatments and the reasoning is readily transferable to decisions about the provision of social services. A lot depends, however, on whether the particular statutory provision is interpreted so as to generate a duty to supply a particular service to an individual as opposed to merely a general duty to provide services. Where a duty is owed to an individual, judicial review has been successfully used to show that a refusal to carry out the duty is unlawful, even where the reason for the refusal is lack of resources. This happened in *R* v. *East Sussex County Council ex parte Tandy* [1998], a case concerning the duty of a local education authority to provide suitable education where a child is too ill to attend school. By contrast, the courts have held that s.17 of the Children Act 1989 does not normally generate a duty to provide a particular service in an individual case: *R* v. *Bexley LBC, ex p. B (Care Hours Provision)* [2000]. This means that it will be more difficult for an individual service user to succeed in an application for judicial review of a decision not to provide services under that section.

However, where a person's ECHR rights are engaged, the position may be different; here, to borrow Lord Bingham's phrase in the *JD* case the law may well be 'on the move'. In *R (G)* v. *Barnet London Borough Council and others* [2003] and *R(J)* v. *Enfield London Borough Council* [2002] the courts accepted that the positive obligation on the State to ensure respect for ECHR rights could effectively mean the authority could be legally compelled to make particular provision in order to avoid a violation of the Convention right. This is a controversial development both at European and UK level because it brings greater judicial control over areas of administrative or even political discretion touching on public resource allocation (see for example, Palmer, 2003).

Decisions more likely to be successfully challenged by way of judicial review are those which could not otherwise be scrutinised by a court and which do not concern resource allocation policy, for example a decision to place information about a suspected abuser on the Integrated Children's System (formerly the child protection register): *R* v. *Norfolk County Council ex parte M* [1989], although usually there should first be recourse to the complaints procedure under s.26 Children Act 1989: *R* v. *Hampshire CC ex parte H* [1999]. Another type of decision not otherwise subject to the court's scrutiny would be one relating to a care plan where services are being provided by a local authority whether under the National Assistance Act 1948 or Chronically Sick and Disabled Persons Act, and so on. An example is *CD* v. *Isle of Anglesey* [2004] where a judicial review succeeded on rationality grounds in the case of a 15-year-old girl with multiple disabilities whose care package the local authority proposed to change: the judge making the graphic comment that 'like a computer virus, some demon has ... come to infect the local authority's decision-making referable to C in the course of the last two years'. In general, decisions to alter an established package of support need to be approached with great care and with meticulous attention to service users' Convention rights.

Actions for damages for deliberate acts or omissions

It is important to remember that a legal action can arise from even the most well-intentioned interference in a person's private life if the interference is not authorised by law. This finds modern expression in the remedies that flow from the ECHR, but there are much older legal remedies for trespass (assault, battery, false imprisonment). Indeed, these remedies were developed by the courts as an important constitutional protection from arbitrary government interference and it is for that reason that there is no requirement for a claimant to show that damage resulted from the interference. Thus, where a service user lacks mental capacity to make a decision, the lawful authority of another person to make that decision on behalf of the service user is of critical importance. Normally, the situation is covered by statute – for example the Mental Capacity Act 2005 or, in the case of children, by the notion of parental responsibility or the authority of an order under the Children Act 1989. Obviously, where social work action involves overriding a person's objections, as will often be the case where a care order is implemented, lawful authority is provided by the court's order.

Conclusion

The processes summarised above provide for a variety of responses to follow allegations of defective, or merely 'not good enough', social work practice. This account has not embraced the public inquiries that are commissioned and responded to by government, but has been confined to the judicial and administrative machinery that can be accessed or stimulated into action by the citizen. Many are not service-user-friendly (see, for example, Murphy, 2006) although increased recognition of the need for advocacy support coupled with the work of the specialist commissioners might be expected to yield some improvement in time. All of the machinery discussed here contributes to the accountability of social work and can generate investigation, identification of problems – and, potentially, improvement for the future. Some, but not all, also carries the possibility of a just settlement for an aggrieved individual. These are genuine virtues and consistent with social work principles.

References

Cope, S. and Goodship, J. (2002) 'The Audit Commission and public services: delivering for whom?' *Public Money and Management*, **22**: 33–40.

DfES (2006) *Getting the Best from Complaints: Social Care Complaints for Children, Young People and Others*, London, Department for Education and Skills.

DH (Department of Health) (2009a) *Making Experiences Count*, London, HMSO.

DH (Department of Health) (2009b) *Listening, Responding, Improving: A Guide to Better Customer Care*, London, HMSO.

Fairgrieve, D. and Green, S. (eds) (2004) *Child Abuse Tort Claims Against Public Bodies: A Comparative Law View*, Aldershot, Ashgate Publishing.

GLS/TSols (2006) *The Judge Over Your Shoulder*, London, Government Legal Service and Treasury Solicitors Department.

Guthrie, T. (1998) 'Legal liability and accountability for child-care decisions', *British Journal of Social Work*, 28: 403–22.

Hampton, P. (2005) *Reducing Administrative Burdens: Effective Inspection and Enforcement*, London, HM Treasury.

Harris, N. (1987) 'Defensive social work', *British Journal of Social Work*, 17: 61–9.

Macdonald, G. (1990) 'Allocating blame in social work', *British Journal of Social Work*, 20: 525–46.

Masson, J. (2006) 'The Climbié inquiry – context and critique' *Journal of Law and Society*, 33(2): 221–43.

Murphy, J. (2006) 'Children in need: the limits of local authority accountability', *Legal Studies*, 23: 103–34.

Palmer, E. (2003) 'Courts, resources and the HRA: reading section 17 of the Children Act 1989 compatibly with article 8 ECHR', *European Human Right Law Review*, 3: 308–24.

Pithouse, A. and Crowley, A. (2007) 'Adults rule? Children, advocacy and complaints to social services', *Children and Society*, 21: 201–13.

WAG (Welsh Assembley Government) (2006) *Listening and Learning: A Guide to Handling Complaints and Representations in Local Authority Social Services in Wales*, Cardiff, Welsh Assembly Government.

Williams, J. (2005) 'Effective government structures for children? The UK's four children's "commissioners"', *Child and Family Law Quarterly*, 17: 37–53.

Notes

1. The mechanisms for complaints are set out in government guidance and have to be publicised. Part of a commitment to empowering service users and their carers may entail directing the service user to a clear account of the remedy and its associated process.
2. Government guidance proclaims similar virtues for judicial review, with the law seen as essentially supportive of good administration (GLS/TSols, 2006).
3. Technically, a 'Local Commissioner' appointed under the Local Government Act 1972.

4. Judicial review would be limited to the legality of the decision in question rather than the substantive outcome.

5. In general the courts prefer Convention arguments to be raised in the course of existing legal proceedings rather than starting separate proceedings, but a free-standing claim can be brought if there are no other suitable proceedings in train.

6. A doctor is not guilty of negligence *if he has acted in accordance with a practice accepted as proper* by a responsible body of medical men skilled in that particular art. *Bolam* v. *Friern Hospital Management Committee* [1957] (emphasis added).

7. In addition it has to be the 'right type' of damage. It remains very difficult to establish negligence liability if the only damage sustained is either emotional distress or pure economic loss, which is often the case.

8. A claim for damages for breach of statutory duty may be made alongside a claim in negligence or independently.

Chapter 8

The Role of Assessment in Social Work

JANE ALDGATE

Introduction

From very early days, social workers have drawn on knowledge and observations to make professional judgements about how best to help people who are using their services. In her groundbreaking book, *Social Diagnosis*, published in the USA 1917, Mary Richmond wrote about social workers building up a body of knowledge from their cases, and being able to draw on this to inform their practice (Richmond, 1917). She successfully created a model for social casework and the approach now known in the social work field as the person-in-environment or ecological approach to assessment.

This chapter considers briefly what constitutes assessment in social work, looking at a definition of what it is, the processes that it involves and some of the key theories that are used in assessments in social work. It will then use the assessment framework for *Children in Need and their Families* (DH, 2000) implemented in England and Wales to discuss the strengths and weaknesses of having a national, 'one size fits all' framework.

What is assessment?

From the early beginnings of social work arose the idea that, in order to provide the best possible social work services, workers needed to be able to gather information about a person and his or her environment, make sense of this information using knowledge and research and then use their professional judgement to decide upon a course of action. From early on, assessment has been seen as a process not an event. Meyer (1993, p. 2) suggests assessment is a complex skill. It is:

> The thinking process that seeks out the meaning of case situations, puts the particular case in some order and leads to appropriate interventions

... Assessment is the intellectual tool for understanding the client's psycho-social situation, and for determining 'what's the matter?'.

Meyer goes on to outline the process of assessment in five steps:

1. Exploration
2. Inferential thinking
3. Evaluation
4. Problem definition
5. Intervention planning. (Meyer, 1993, quoted in Austrian, 2002, p. 204)

(1) *Exploration* involves listening to what the service user defines as the problem that has brought them to social work. This is an initial stage in which engaging the service user is critical. Techniques at this stage involve using open-ended questions to gain a picture of the person in the environment perspective. Exploration will continue throughout intervention.

(2) *Inferential thinking* is the stage that reflects the social worker's knowledge about the issues the service user is concerned about. In this stage the worker will draw on a wide range of theoretical frameworks to make sense of the data being gathered. They will also use their professional knowledge base, for example, of what is possible within the legal framework in which they are working.

(3) *Evaluation* involves weighing the severity of the problems and the strengths and challenges for the service user and should take into account strengths and barriers in their environment. Austrian suggests that:

assessment of the person's adaptive capabilities obtained from exploration and inferential thinking should result in an understanding of the client's motivation for change, inner resources, resources in the person's environment, and a realistic assessment of the person's adaptive capabilities. (Meyer, 1993, quoted in Austrian, 2002, p. 206)

(4) *Problem definition* demands careful negotiation between worker and service user about what are the agreed issues to be worked on. In cases where worker and service user disagree, such as may happen sometimes where compulsory action is deemed necessary by the worker but not by the service user, the worker may have to invoke the mandatory authority invested in them by law. But this should be a rare occurrence. Research on child protection has shown it is

possible for worker and service user to agree on a course of action (DH, 2001). As Austrian (2002) suggests:

> The mutually agreed on problem definition should always represent the thinking of, and be acceptable to the worker and the client. It may vary from the presenting request and the worker may see a more complex situation, but only with understanding and agreement can the focus of attention be arrived at and a productive intervention planned. (Austrian, 2002, p. 206)

(5) *Intervention planning* is the final stage of assessment and represents the outcome of the previous four stages. This stage should represent practical details about time frames, who is to do what and what the outcomes might be. Any plans made will have been guided by the shared information and exploration stages and by the mutually agreed areas that require intervention. The intervention planning should also build in review of progress.

Austrian summarises the different components of assessment and how each assessment needs to be tailored to the individual person and their situation:

> Assessment, while grounded in professional knowledge and skill, is an individualized process that demands recognition of the uniqueness of person and situation. It is an ongoing process, with intervention possibly subject to some modification as new data emerges. Knowledge of cultural, class, and gender differences and perceptions of problems, emotional or situational is essential to providing a thorough assessment and good intervention planning. Knowledge of developmental stages, personality theories, and a range of family structures can also be important. (Austrian, 2002, p. 206)

Two key points emerge from this summary:

- The actual process of conducting the assessment, including the relationship between service user and worker will be as important as the outcome
- Assessment will always be underpinned by knowledge and research and informed by professional judgement.

The process of how assessments are conducted

Rose has suggested that assessment is a relational activity and that to develop trust and confidence between family members and the social worker will influence the process. It is necessary that everyone has a clear understanding of the purpose of the assessment, how it is to be done, the information being sought, who will see this and what will happen next (Rose, 2009).

In their research on parental participation in child protection, Cleaver and Freeman (1995) found that families appreciated being kept informed at all stages of the investigation and being treated with courtesy. Writing about empowerment and participation of families, Shemmings and Shemmings (2001) point out that professionals and families may have different preoccupations:

> Professionals tend to stress procedural aspects of empowerment – for example, sharing records, attending meetings, knowing about complaints procedures – whereas family members usually stress both the procedural and the relational aspects – typically developing trust, being transparent, genuine and even-handed, and being direct, yet sensitive. (Shemmings and Shemmings, 2001, p. 116)

The contemporary knowledge base for assessment

There are many contemporary theories that underpin assessment in social work. These have been evolved over time and are subject to some degree of social construction. There has been a revolution in thinking about mental health and learning disability with a move from a medical model of 'what's wrong with this person?' to a social model that recognises the issues may lie in the circumstances surrounding the person and the reaction of others to them (French and Swain, 2002). Psychological theory has also embraced a more positive approach, moving from a negative diagnostic model to one which emphasises strengths rather than weaknesses (Aldgate, 2006). Related to a strengths approach is the emergence of the theory of resilience (Daniel and Wassell, 2002; Seden, 2002). Resilience has been described as:

> the power of recovery and in the ability to return again to those patterns of adaptation and competence that characterized the individual, prior to the pre stress period. (Garmezy, 1993, p. 129, quoted in Seden, 2002, p. 202)

One enduring theory, which has basically not changed as a foundation for assessment, is ecological theory, described earlier as the 'person-in-environment' approach (Bronfenbrenner, 1979). The interplay between person and environment permeates much developmental theory relating both to children and adults (see, for example, Walker, 2002; Aldgate et al., 2006) and has become integral in assessing the well-being of individuals.

The law and assessment

Legislation that relates to protecting the rights and promoting the well-being of individuals has increasingly played a part in influencing the way social work is practised. Children's legislation since the Children Act 1989 in the UK has embraced the UN Convention on the Rights of the Child and has incorporated a social justice perspective into the law, emphasising the rights of children to be consulted about decisions affecting their lives. The law makes connections between eligibility for services and the well-being of individuals; children are defined as 'in need' if their health and development is impaired or likely to be impaired without the provision of services. The legislation also allows for immediate intervention if risk of harm is high. Similarly, laws relating to the care of adults, notably the Community Care Act 1990 and the Mental Health Act 1983 (as amended by the Mental Health Act 2007), set thresholds for intervening to protect individuals from harm.

Legislation also helps to shape the standards for attitudes and behaviour towards certain groups of individuals.[1] Sometimes what policymakers intended through the law has not been interpreted correctly. A good example is the assessment of children in need. Aldgate and Tunstill, for example, found that after the implementation of the Children Act 1989, there was considerable variation on the interpretation of a child 'in need' (s.17 Children Act 1989) in many cases, using assessment to restrict services to children who were at risk of significant harm, even though this was against both the spirit and letter of the law (Aldgate and Tunstill, 1995).

Assessment of risk

Assessing risk is an important part of the social work role across different areas of practice. The principle of identifying risk, responding immediately and looking towards protection of individuals in the long term is embedded in much of the legislation implemented by social workers.

What needs to be assessed therefore is the risk of *current* and *future* harm to an individual and what services need to be put in place to address that risk. Furthermore, there needs to be consideration of the risk to the individual if services are not available, as the risk from not providing services may be extremely serious.

The context of risk assessment

Since assessing risk is so important, it is helpful to look at the most commonly used models of risk assessment, highlighting their strengths and weaknesses.

Stalker (2003) suggests that risk has taken priority over welfare in social care services. The increasing emphasis on risk in social work is a reflection of 'the impact of globalisation' which has 'dislocated many areas of social and economic life, giving rise to uncertainties, fears and insecurities: more importance is now attached to calculating choices of individuals' (Stalker, 2003, p. 216). Additionally, professionals in health and social work working in this 'risk society' have become 'increasingly reliant on complex systems of audit, monitoring and quality control' (Stalker, 2003, p. 217). Models of risk assessment have tended to focus on this bureaucratic approach (see, for example, literature reviews on the subject by Cleaver et al., 1998; Hagell, 1998).

As Seden (2000) points out, the development of models of risk assessment has also been influenced by a quest for more certainty in predicting harm. Highly publicised 'failure' to protect children from danger, for example, has led professionals to develop checklists of indicators and predictors which claim to measure the safety of a child within a family or the recurrence of offending behaviour (Seden, 2000, p. 10). This approach also lends itself to a concentration on immediacy, neglecting areas of risk where effects may be more evident in the longer term.

The desire to seek a fail-safe method of risk assessment has led to a move towards defensible decision making. Parton (1998) and Stalker (2003) have suggested that 'defensible' has been interpreted as workers wanting to defend their backs. In a more measured context of risk assessment, defensible decision making has an important part to play in managing risk.

Recently, some writers have suggested a move away from a negative approach to one that includes an emphasis on recognising 'signs of safety' as well as risk (Turnell and Edwards, 1999). Calder (2002, p. 8) suggests that, in realms other than social work, a risk equation also calculates possible benefits. He urges therefore that any risk assessment should include weighing up the pros and cons of an individual's circumstances 'in order to inform decision-making as to what should happen with regard to intervention and protection'. While Calder is talking about children, his views apply equally well to adults who are at risk.

Different approaches to risk assessment

As Calder (2002, p. 13), has suggested, 'there is no ideal risk assessment method or framework'. Practitioners wanting a fail-safe checklist will fail to find one and practitioner judgement will always need to play a part in identifying and responding to risk. In spite of this, there are several identifiable approaches to risk assessment. These include the following three approaches.

Unstructured clinical assessment

This approach relies on assessments being made without any structured aides-memoires, relying on the clinical judgement of professionals. Decisions are justified on the basis of the qualifications and experience of the professional making them, but this has led to criticisms of subjectivity and lack of reliability and validity. However, its strength is that it allows assessments to take into account the particular circumstances and context of the situation, and interventions to be tailored accordingly. This approach gives considerable professional discretion but, as Douglas and Kropp (2002, p. 624) suggest, it 'is vulnerable to missing important factors that require intervention'.

Actuarial methods of risk assessment

Actuarial methods are designed to predict specific behaviours within specific time scales. Interest in this approach has grown to counteract what was seen as an idiosyncratic and intuitive approach of individual clinical assessments. It has also been influenced by the wish to find a way to predict and prevent the likelihood of serious harm to children and adults. (Seden, 2000). In youth justice, actuarial scales have been used to predict rates of reoffending. Barry (2007) suggests such scales may foster a culture of blame towards individuals, for example those with mental health difficulties or parents of children at risk and fail to bring into the equation external factors in the individual's ecology, such as poverty or neighbourhood.

Munro (2002, p. 881) suggests that actuarial calculations 'have an air of authority and objectivity that can mislead people into crediting them with more accuracy than they deserve'. There are a number of disadvantages to the actuarial approach. First, although there is merit in using factors that have been shown to be predictors in research studies, use also needs to be made of the theory of human growth and development, for example, understanding about the relationship between patterns of attachment in childhood and their application in adults who are parents.

Second, actuarial models tend to develop an inflexible list of factors that cannot take into account the unique set of circumstances for a particular individual 'To properly apply the actuarial approach, the evaluator is forced to consider a fixed set of factors and cannot consider unique, unusual, or context specific variables that might require intervention' (Douglas and Kropp, 2002, p. 625). The 'dynamic' risk factors Douglas and Kropp are talking about need to be taken into account and cannot always be accurately predicted.

Third, one of the most significant omissions of the actuarial model is that the checklist can only be applied to the specific current or past situations and does not allow for patterns of interactions and transactions over time. Current thinking suggests that risk is more contextual, dynamic and continuous (Seden, 2000).

Fourthly, writing about children who have been abused, Jones et al. (2006) suggest that there is no reliable way of weighting the scores for particular factors to develop an aggregated picture of risk. The evidence base can do no more than guide decision making and is not 'a short cut to be reduced to mere numbers' (Jones et al., 2006, p. 278). Furthermore, the scores do not provide a fail-safe way of predicting that an individual is unsafe (Seden, 2000). Calder (2002) concludes that risk assessment is not an exact science. There will be consequential dangers of false positives and false negatives which could have serious consequences for child and family because actions taken by professionals could be based on false premises.

A structured professional judgement approach

Because of the limitations of actuarial approaches to risk assessment, Kempshall (2002) suggests that a combination of approaches to risk assessment may in the end be most helpful. Douglas and Kropp (2002, p. 651) have taken forward this idea in what they call a prevention-based approach to risk assessment 'characterised by the use of structured professional judgement'. Their work has been developed in relation to risk assessment of violent behaviour but has application to other service users in social work. The model uses scales or tools judiciously, but does not rely on them entirely. An important part of the assessment will be to look at an individual's ecology. The professionals will need to work in partnership with the service user to identify all the strengths and risks. They will then need to weigh the information gathered and bring their professional judgement into the decision making. This model has been adopted by the Scottish Government in the *Getting it right for every child* practice model of assessment and planning (Aldgate and Rose, 2008).

Moving towards national frameworks for assessment

Prior to the 1980s, there were very few frameworks of tools for assessment which were related specifically to the intentions of legislation and, consequently, assessment was very much a matter for individual workers and their organisations, mirroring the fragmentation of individual services with their differences in ideological approaches and training (Ward, 2002).

Changes in assessment for children since the 1980s provide a good case study of how increasingly governments have moved towards the introduction of standardised frameworks for assessment of need. Gray (2002) suggests that, prior to the late 1980s, assessment of children tended to relate to children in the care system, with assessment taking place in specially designed residential assessment and observation centres. A report from the Department of Health and Social Security in 1981 loosely defined assessment as 'a continuous process whereby problems are identified and appropriate responses decided upon' (DHSS, 1981, p. 2).

As Gray points out, the first government practice guidance that attempted to provide a framework for assessment for social workers nationally was introduced in the 1980s 'to assist social workers undertaking comprehensive systems of assessments for long-term planning where child protection issues had been identified' (Gray, 2002, p. 170). This had been prompted by concerns from a number of child abuse enquiries and several inspections of services which found too much emphasis on procedures and not enough on evidence-based assessments and practice. The 'Orange Book', as the comprehensive assessment guidance published by the Department of Health in 1988 came to be known, was widely used but subsequent inspections and research found that 'it was being used mechanistically and as a checklist, that practice in assessments was widely variable and that too often child protection plans were not informed by comprehensive assessments' (Gray, 2002, p. 170). There was also a growing concern that many children 'in need' within the terms of the Children Act 1989 were only getting help if they met narrow child protection criteria (DH, 1995). The government's response was to develop a strategy for refocusing services for children in need through its *Quality Protects* programme, introduced in 1997, which had improved assessment as a central objective. Government thinking was influenced by research studies showing that various groups of children in need were not getting appropriate help. These included those living in poverty (Utting, 1995; Holman, 1998), children who were disabled (Lawton, 1998) and those needing family support services (Aldgate and Tunstill, 1995). See also Rose (2009).

The Framework for the Assessment of Children in Need and their Families

It was a logical step forward to produce a framework for all children in need, which incorporated child protection cases. The aim was:

> to ensure that referral and assessment processes discriminate effectively between different types and levels of need and produce a timely service. (DH, 1999, p. 20)

The framework was underpinned by several key principles:

Assessments:

- are child centred
- are rooted in child development
- are ecological in their approach
- are a continuing process not a separate event
- ensure equality of opportunity
- involve working with children and families
- build on strengths as well as difficulties
- are inter-agency in their approach to assessment and the provision of services
- are grounded in evidence based knowledge. (Department of Health et al., 2000, p. 10)

The theory underpinning the assessment framework built on several decades of evidence and research about child development. It also took into account research on service-user participation and methods that would be empowering to both children and families (see Rose and Aldgate, 2000; DH, 2001). Being child centred was an important social justice innovation to combat the criticisms about social workers never seeing a child with whom they were working. Subsequent child abuse enquiries revealed that the assessment framework had done little to combat this problem and that children continued to be invisible, which sometimes contributed to their untimely demise (see, for example, the Victoria Climbié Inquiry (Cm. 5730). The framework emphasised the value of the ecological approach to assessing children and families and that children will flourish best if all agencies recognise the part they can play in contributing to good outcomes.

The issue of how far the assessment framework could promote equality of opportunity for children is worth further scrutiny. Certainly, the Children Act 1989 is founded in the view that children and young people and their parents should all be considered as individuals with particular needs and potentialities (DH, 1990) and recognises there are many different ways of bringing up children. The framework allows for this diversity in the domains of children's developmental needs and parenting capacity, and its emphasis on environmental factors, which gives an opportunity to identify the inputs of schools and the impact of long-term poverty, and invites workers to use their skills and networks to improve the situation (Jack and Gill, 2003).

The framework is sound in its principles and the developmental and ecological theory that supports it but is only as good as the practice that underpins it. There is ample opportunity to promote the rights of children, but much will depend on the skills of social workers to communicate with children. Children are very clear about what makes a good social worker, including reliability and listening to them (DH, 2001).

Research on working in partnership with parents since the implementation of the Children Act 1989 has shown that, given the appropriate attitudes and behaviour from social workers, parents can respond positively and can separate their own needs from those of their children, even in circumstances where compulsion is necessary (DH, 2001).

Framework or practice tool?

The assessment framework was just that, a framework for assessment, planning action and review, very much in line with classic assessment models, like that developed by Meyer described earlier. It was never intended to be used mechanistically, as a checklist and it was expected that practitioners would use the framework judiciously, according to the individual problems with which they were presented. The documentation underpinning the framework was therefore explanatory rather than instructive. With hindsight, policymakers may have assumed too much sophistication on the part of practitioners to read, digest and adapt the theory to their own circumstances.

One special aim was to promote early intervention through early identification of problems. Rose (2009) points out that it had been recognised for several decades that early intervention in health was essential to remedy impairment such as hearing problems, while research into preventive schemes to combat antisocial behaviour had also highlighted the value of an early preventive approach (Cleaver, 1991). It was very much the intention that use of the framework could apply to any child in need, from those where environmental factors such as housing or living in a dangerous neighbourhood were posing risks to a family, to include factors such as health or educational issues that were impeding a child's development and, where appropriate, to enable practitioners to assess risk of significant harm where children were in need of protection. To reinforce this latter point, when relaunching guidance in England on safeguarding in 2006, *Working Together to Safeguard Children* (HM Government, 2006a) the use of the assessment framework was included in a key chapter on managing risk. In short, it was a framework for all circumstances, which relied on the professional judgement of social workers and their managers to use it appropriately. This separation of the framework from practice, in some senses, may have been the factor that has most impeded implementation.

Perhaps unwittingly recognising that they were expecting too much of practitioners, policymakers took the view that workers might need some help with deciding how much or how little assessment they undertook. Accordingly:

In order to ensure that, in practice, work with children and families is proportionate and timely, the assessment process has been divided into two stages – an *initial assessment* to be completed within seven working days of referral which may be followed by a *core assessment*, if a more in depth, detailed assessment is required, for completion within thirty-five working days. (Rose, 2009)

Although the underlying intention of timescales was to prevent children waiting for help for a long time, this complexity introduced challenges in terms of meeting targets which have tended to override the purpose and quality of the assessment in some cases.

The situation was further complicated by the introduction of a second assessment framework in 2006, *The Common Assessment Framework* (HM Government, 2006b). This was designed to strengthen early identification of problems by a range of agencies beyond social work and provide a means by which all agencies could identify and share concerns.

Working together and sharing information

The *Common Assessment Framework* came out of the government's major policy initiative, *Every Child Matters* (Cm. 5860, 2003). Section 27 of the Children Act 1989 had placed a duty on other services to cooperate with social services to provide appropriate help for children in need. In 2003, the government published its Green Paper, *Every Child Matters* which set out its approach to the well-being of children and young people from birth to age 19. The aim of the *Every Child Matters* programme was to give all children the support they needed to be healthy, stay safe, enjoy and achieve, make a positive contribution and achieve economic well-being.

After a consultation process, legal underpinning for *Every Child Matters* was introduced through the Children Act 2004. The duty of cooperation was strengthened and became law, finally giving clout to the 'whole child' approach within the assessment framework.

Such a whole child approach has proved difficult to achieve, mainly because the whole framework is seen as being social services led. Although it makes sense for information about a child to be shared in order to gain the whole picture, issues about 'confidentiality' have made it difficult in some local areas for social workers to gain important information relating to children's health or educational progress unless the child is formally 'looked after' by the local authority. Such barriers to cooperation undermine the principles of early identification and early intervention. Arguments against sharing information are made on the grounds that child and family need protecting. This approach is not based on research evidence. One of the complaints of families who seek help is that they are passed from agency to agency and that they have to repeat their stories many times over (DH, 2001). Families have indicated to researchers that they would be happy for information to be shared providing it is done with their consent and they know why the information is to be shared.

Implementing the framework

The main assessment framework was launched with an accompanying guidance and practice guidance, which included an exposition of the knowledge base of the framework, detailed guidance on assessment with black children and with disabled children (DH, 2000). Subsequently, there have been several key publications to help implementation. Notable among them is a book and accompanying training materials entitled *The Child's World* (Horwath, 2001).

Recognition that the framework might require more detailed practice tools to support assessments led to publication of accompanying scales and questionnaires, designed to help assess special aspects of children's well-being (DH et al., 2000a). Many of these have been widely used, not only in practice but also in research and practice evaluation (see for example, Aldgate et al., 2007). This has been a useful development which has helped workers to see the value of bringing different sources of information to their whole child assessment, as suggested in the structured professional judgement model described earlier.

To embed the framework in practice, curriculum for a post-qualifying course in childcare was commissioned by the Department of Health (Aldgate and Colman, 1999) and launched by CCETSW, the then training council for social work. Students had to complete an assignment on assessment as part of this course, as well as academic assignments on the knowledge base underpinning the framework. In theory, all these activities should have helped embed the framework across the country.

What are the strengths and weaknesses of having a national framework?

Undoubtedly, one of the strengths of using a common approach to assessment nationally is that social workers and others in health and social care services are using a shared language, describing factors in the same way. For this to work well there needs to be a common understanding between professionals as to the meaning of descriptors and definitions.

One major problem has been the use of, in effect, three parts of an assessment framework, the *Common Assessment Framework*, the Initial and Core Assessments. Such complexities, and accompanying demands in terms of the forms and procedures which have been issued nationally, have led some to question whether the aims of providing a framework to promote therapeutic work as originally suggested in the guidance accompanying the original assessment framework have been sabotaged to 'embody an ethos of bureaucratic regulation with stultifying effects on social work' (Millar and Corby, 2006, p. 887).

A further complication has been introduced through the *Integrated Children's System* (Cleaver et al., 2008), designed to bring together all the different frameworks and provide a coherent process of recording from first contact to planning and review, supported by an electronic case record system. However, implementing a national ICT system has created considerable demands on both agencies and individual workers and is yet another challenge and diversion for workers away from the actual purpose of assessment.

To some extent, critics of the complexity of the assessment framework have acknowledged that introducing a new system and embedding it in practice will take time. Cleaver and Walker (2004), who looked at implementation in 24 local authorities, found variation in implementation. In a summary of the study, Cleaver acknowledged the challenges but was also able to identify 16 essential features that made for successful implementation (DH and Cleaver, 2003). A case study by Rose et al. (2007) in one local authority showed how management investment was a key factor in changing practice. Inspection reports early after implementation in 2002 highlighted the demands the assessment framework had made on agencies and workers. Later reports in 2005 (Commission for Social Care Inspection, 2005) showed that the use of the assessment framework was making a positive difference to children and families in the quality of information used to inform decision making, but more recent reports showed that there was considerable variation in quality of assessments (Ofsted, 2008).

One major area of criticism of the assessment framework has been the omission of risk as a separate category (Calder and Hackett, 2003; Garrett, 2003; Davies, 2008). Calder and Hackett (2003) believe a needs-led approach can lead to underestimating risks, while Davies (2008, p. 33) believes that the assessment framework 'is not an appropriate tool for investigative work'. It is interesting that the recently developed Scottish national practice model for assessing children does pay equal attention to risk and need, saying they are two sides of the same coin (Scottish Government, 2008).

Another major omission is the absence of practice help for social workers to make sense of the often extensive information they have gathered. Not only does the information gathered need to be analysed, but workers need to make judgements based on that analysis of what needs to be done to ensure assessment leads to clear plans for action. The main documentation for the assessment framework contains three pages describing analysis and judgement (DH et al., 2000b, pp. 54–7). While this is useful, it provides no tools which workers can use to help them make sense of the information they have gathered. Scotland has learned from the experience of England and has introduced a Resilience Matrix through which information can be filtered and clustered to identify both strengths and vulnerabilities and the degree to which the environment around the child is adverse or supportive (Daniel and Wassell, 2002; Scottish Government, 2008).

Can a national framework for assessment in social work be helpful?

This chapter on assessment in social work has looked at the definitions and use of assessment in social work practice, using the assessment framework for children in need and their families as a case study to illustrate the strengths and challenges of introducing a national system of assessment. It has shown that it is helpful to have a common under-pinning theoretical model and a shared language that all practitioners can use for assessment.

What has been difficult in practice is not so much the ethos and prin-ciples behind the framework, but the complexity in its implementation. Criticisms have included the complexity of having what amounts to three systems of assessment, which do not entirely relate to each other and duplicate some recording. Some key areas, such as risk of harm, are in the framework implicitly but do not invite the worker to address risk factors explicitly. The introduction of the *Integrated Children's System* has attempted to bring coherence to the frameworks but the introduc-tion of an accompanying ICT recording system has introduced yet another challenge. The verdict must be that while the theory and aide-memoire domains of the assessment framework triangle are helpful, the complexity of the practice systems introduced to help implementation has provided a layer of challenge for the practitioner that was never intended. The solution might be to keep the heart of the framework but think again about a simpler implementation, using a structured profes-sional judgement approach which allows social workers to draw on the research and knowledge which underpins the framework but, above all, recognises that the relationship between worker and service user is at the heart of any social work practice and that time needs to be built into any system to make sure the trust and relational activity are not taken over by bureaucracy and technology.

References

Aldgate, J. (2006) 'Children, development and ecology', in Aldgate, J., Jones, D. P. H., Rose, W. and Jeffery, C. (eds) *The Developing World of the Child*, London, Jessica Kingsley Publishing, pp. 17–34.

Aldgate, J. and Colman, R. (1999) *The Post Qualifying Award in Childcare: A Conceptual Framework*, Leicester, University of Leicester School of Social Work.

Aldgate, J. and Rose, W. (2008) *A Systematic Practice Model for Assessing and Managing Risk*, Edinburgh, Getting it right for every child team, Scottish Government.

Aldgate, J. and Tunstill, J. (1995) *Making Sense of Section 17: Implementing Services for Children in Need within the Children Act 1989*, London, Her Majesty's Stationery Office.

Aldgate, J., Rose, W. and McIntosh, M. (2007) *Changing Directions for Children with Challenging Behaviour and their Families: Evaluation of Children 1st Directions Projects*. Edinburgh: Children 1st. www.children1st.org.uk.

Aldgate, J., Jones, D. P. H., Rose, W. and Jeffery, C. (eds) (2006) *The Developing World of the Child*, London, Jessica Kingsley.

Austrian, S. G. (2002) 'Guidelines for conducting a biopsychosocial assessment', in Roberts, A. R. and Greene, G. J. (eds) *Social Workers' Desk Reference*, Oxford, Oxford University Press, pp. 204–8.

Barry, M. (2007) *Effective Approaches to Risk Assessment in Social Work: A Literature Review*, Edinburgh, Scottish Executive.

Bronfenbrenner, U. (1979) *The Ecology of Human Development: Experiments by Nature and Design*, Cambridge, MA, Harvard University Press.

Calder, M. C. (2002) 'A framework for conducting risk assessment', *Child Care in Practice*, 8(1): 7–18.

Calder, M. C. and Hackett, S. (2003) 'The Assessment Framework: a critique and reformulation', in Calder, M. C. and Hackett, S. (eds) *Assessment in Child Care. Using and Developing Frameworks for Practice*, Lyme Regis, Russell House Publishing, pp. 3–60.

Cleaver, H. (1991) *Vulnerable Children in Schools*, Aldershot, Dartmouth.

Cleaver, H. and Freeman, P. (1995) *Parental Perspectives in Cases of Suspected Child Abuse*, London, HMSO.

Cleaver, H. and Walker, S., with Meadows, P. (2004) *Assessing Children's Needs and Circumstances, The Impact of the Assessment Framework*, London, Jessica Kingsley.

Cleaver, H., Wattam, C. and Cawson, P. (1998) *Assessing Risk in Child Protection*, London, NSPCC.

Cleaver, H., Walker, S., Scott, J., Cleaver, D., Rose, W., Ward, H. and Pithouse, A. (2008) *The Integrated Children's System: Enhancing Social Work and Inter-Agency Practice*, London, Jessica Kingsley.

Cm. 5730 (2003) *The Victoria Climbié Inquiry*, London, The Stationery Office.

Cm. 5860 (2003) *Every Child Matters*, London, The Stationery Office.

Commission for Social Care Inspection (2005) *Safeguarding Children – The Second Joint Chief Inspectors' Report on Arrangements to Safeguard Children*, Newcastle, Commission for Social Care Inspection.

Daniel, B. and Wassell, S. (2002) *Assessing and Promoting Resilience in Vulnerable Children: 1. The Early Years; 2. The School Years; 3. Adolescence*, London, Jessica Kingsley.

Davies, L. (2008) 'Reclaiming the language of child protection: mind the gap. Family support versus child protection: exposing the myth', in Calder, M. (ed.) *Contemporary Risk Assessment in Safeguarding Children*, Lyme Regis, Russell House Publishing, pp. 25–39.

DH (Department of Health) (1988) *Protecting Children: A Guide for Social Workers Undertaking a Comprehensive Assessment*, London, Her Majesty's Stationery Office.

DH (Department of Health) (1990) *The Care of Children: Principles and Practice in Regulations and Guidance*, London, Her Majesty's Stationery Office.

DH (Department of Health) (1991) *Child Abuse: A Study of Inquiry Reports 1980–1989*, London, Her Majesty's Stationery Office.

DH (Department of Health) (1995) *Child Protection: Messages from Research*. London: Her Majesty's Stationery Office.

DH (Department of Health) (1999) *The Government's Objectives for Children's Social Services*, London, Department of Health.

DH (Department of Health) (2000) *Assessing Children in Need and their Families: Practice Guidance*, London, The Stationery Office.

DH (Department of Health) (2001) *The Children Act Now: Messages from Research*, London, The Stationery Office.

DH (Department of Health) with Cleaver, H. (2000) *Assessment Recording Forms*, London, The Stationery Office.

DH (Department of Health) and Cleaver, H. (2003) *Assessing Children's Needs and Circumstances: The Impact of the Assessment Framework. Summary and Recommendations*, London, Department of Health.

DH (Department of Health), Cox, A. and Bentovim, A. (2000a) *The Family Pack of Questionnaires and Scales*, London, The Stationery Office.

DH (Department of Health), Department for Education and Employment and Home Office (2000b) *Framework for the Assessment of Children in Need and their Families*, London, The Stationery Office.

DHSS (Department of Health and Social Security) (1981) *Observation and Assessment. Report of a Working Party*, London, Department of Health and Social Security.

Douglas, K. S. and Kropp, P. R. (2002) 'A prevention-based paradigm for violence risk assessment: Clinical and research applications', *Criminal Justice and Behaviour*, 29: 617–58.

French, S. and Swain, J. (2002) 'The perspective of the disabled person's movement', in Davies, M., (ed.) *The Blackwell Companion to Social Work* (2nd edn), Oxford, Basil Blackwell, pp. 394–400.

Garrett, P. M. (2003) 'Swimming with dolphins: the New Assessment Framework, New Labour and New Tools for Social Work with Children and Families', *British Journal of Social Work*, 33: 441–63.

Gray, J. (2002) 'National policy on the assessment of children in need and their families', in Ward, H. and Rose, W. (eds) *Approaches to Needs Assessment in Children's Services*, London, Jessica Kingsley Publishing, pp. 169–94.

Hagell, A. (1998) *Dangerous Care: Reviewing the Risks to Children from their Carers*, London, Policy Studies Institute.

HM Government (2004) *Every Child Matters: Change for Children*, London, Department for Education and Skills.

HM Government (2006a) *Working Together to Safeguard Children. A Guide to Inter-agency Working to Safeguard and Promote the Welfare of Children*, London, The Stationery Office.

HM Government (2006b) *Common Assessment Framework for Children and Young People: Practitioners' Guide*, London, Department for Education and Skills.

Holman, B. (1998) *Faith in the Poor*, Oxford, Lion Publishing.

Horwath, J. (ed.) (2001) *The Child's World*, London, Jessica Kingsley.

Jack, G. and Gill, O. (2003) *The Missing Side of the Triangle*, Barkingside, Barnardo's.

Joint Chief Inspectors (2002) *Safeguarding Children. A Joint Chief Inspectors' Report on Arrangements to Safeguard Children*, London, Department of Health.

Jones, D. P. H., Hindley, N. and Ramchandani, P. (2006) 'Making plans: assessment, intervention and evaluating outcomes', in Aldgate, J., Jones, D. P. H., Rose, W. and Jeffery, C. (eds) *The Developing World of the Child*, London, Jessica Kingsley, pp. 267–86.

Kemshall, H. (2002) 'Risk assessment and management', in Davies, M. (ed.) *The Blackwell Companion to Social Work* (2nd edn), Oxford, Basil Blackwell, pp. 123–31.

Lawton, D. (1998) *The Numbers and Characteristics of Families with More than One Disabled Child*, York, University of York, Social Policy Research Unit.

Meyer, C. H. (1993) *Assessment in Social Work Practice*, New York, Columbia University Press.

Millar, M. and Corby, B. (2006) 'The Framework for the Assessment of Children in Need and Their Families – A basis for "therapeutic" encounter?', *British Journal of Social Work*, 36(6): 887–99.

Munro, E. (2002) *Effective Child Protection*, London, Sage Publications.

Ofsted (2008) *Safeguarding Children. The Third Joint Chief Inspectors' Report on Arrangements to Safeguard Children*, London, Ofsted.

Parton, N. (1998) 'Risk, advanced liberalism and child welfare: the need to rediscover uncertainty and ambiguity', *British Journal of Social Work*, 28: 5–27.

Richmond, M. (1917) *Social Diagnosis*, New York, Russell Sage Foundation.

Rose, W. (2009) 'The assessment framework', in Horwath, J. (ed.) *The Child's World* (2nd edn), London, Jessica Kingsley.

Rose, W. and Aldgate, J. (2000) 'Knowledge underpinning the assessment framework', in Department of Health, *Assessing Children in Need and their Families: Practice Guidance*, London, The Stationery Office, pp. 7–15.

Rose, W., Aldgate, J. and Barnes, J. (2007) 'From policy visions to practice realities: the pivotal role of service managers in implementation', in Aldgate, J., Healy, L., Malcolm, B., Pine, B. A., Rose, W. and Seden, J. (eds) *Enhancing Social Work Management. Theory and Best Practice from the UK and USA*, London, Jessica Kingsley, pp. 263–90.

Scottish Government (2008) *A Guide to Getting it Right for Every Child*, Edinburgh, Scottish Government.

Seden, J. (2000) 'Assessment of children in need and their families: a literature review', in Department of Health (2000) *Studies Informing the Framework for the Assessment of Children in Need and their Families*, London, The Stationery Office.

Seden, J. (2002) 'Underpinning theories for assessment of children's needs', in Ward, H. and Rose, W. (eds) (2002) *Approaches to Needs Assessment in Children's Services*, London, Jessica Kingsley, pp. 195–216.

Shemmings, Y. and Shemmings, D. (2001) 'Empowering children and family members to participate in the assessment process', in Horwath, J., (ed.) *The Child's World*, pp. 114–28.

Stalker, K. (2003) 'Managing risk and uncertainty in social work – a literature review', *Journal of Social Work*, 3(2): 211–33.

Turnell, A. and Edwards, S. (1999) *Signs of Safety: A Solution and Safety Oriented Approach to Child Protection*, New York, W.W. Norton.

Utting, D. (1995) *Family and Parenthood: Supporting Families and Preventing Breakdown*, York, Joseph Rowntree Foundation.

Walker, J. (2002) 'The human life cycle: partnership and parenting', in Davies, M. (ed.) *The Blackwell Companion to Social Work* (2nd edn), Oxford, Basil Blackwell, pp. 370–7.

Ward, H. (2002) 'Introduction' in Ward, H. and Rose, W. (eds), *Approaches to Needs Assessment in Children's Services*, London, Jessica Kingsley Publishing, pp. 15–30.

Note

1. See, for example, the Disability Discrimination Act 1995, the Sex Discrimination Act 1975 (amended 2008) and the Race Relations legislation (see Race Relations Act 1975 and Race Relations Act 2000).

Chapter 9

Youth Justice

HEATHER KEATING[1]

Introduction

The aim of this chapter is to introduce the competing and conflicting agendas, values and interests inherent in the youth justice arena by providing an overview of the youth justice system. While primary emphasis is upon the child[2] as offender it will also consider the child as victim of offending and as witness, to reflect upon the usefulness of such labels. The chapter will examine government approaches to individual and parental responsibility, and consider whether the criminal court is the appropriate forum to resolve issues surrounding children's criminal and antisocial behaviour.

From the outset, it should be recognised that such troublesome behaviour by children is highly politicised, that it is far from certain that English law[3] satisfies international standards and that it has one of the highest rates of juvenile detention in Western Europe. Much media coverage portrays the poor behaviour of youth as a social crisis. As a result, it is not surprising that surveys reveal that antisocial behaviour, such as that of 'teenagers hanging around the streets', is a matter of public concern. While it is undeniably true that some people and communities are profoundly affected by the behaviour of children, it is also necessary to look behind the headlines, and thus the chapter opens with a discussion of the nature of children's offending.

Levels of offending and victimisation

Successive generations have condemned the deterioration in children's behaviour (Pearson, 1983). But reliable information, both about how much crime and antisocial behaviour children commit, and their level of victimisation, has been lacking historically and is still patchy. The two main sources of information about crime rates and victimisation are the offences reported to and recorded by the police and the annual British

Crime Survey (BCS) (see, for example, Home Office, 2009), with the BCS suggesting that much crime goes unreported and unrecorded. In the past, the BCS has not included those aged under 16 in its sample, so less is known about the victimisation of this age group. In addition, the creation of new offences (of which there have been many in recent years, for example antisocial behaviour orders (ASBOs)) for which children are then prosecuted can misleadingly suggest that behaviour is worsening. Finally, the concept of antisocial behaviour is in itself problematic: its definition as 'behaviour which is likely to cause harassment, alarm or distress to others'[4] is both broad and vague. It is also clear that people have different expectations of acceptable behaviour and different levels of tolerance.

Bearing in mind such limitations, recent research does provide an insight into the criminal and antisocial behaviour of children. The latest survey of young people and crime found that almost 80% of its respondents stated that they had not committed a criminal offence within the previous year (Roe and Ashe, 2008). Those who had committed offences had generally done so occasionally or had committed relatively trivial offences, the most common offences being theft and assault. Offences such as criminal damage, drug selling or vehicle related thefts were less common. Three per cent of children reported carrying a knife (overwhelmingly for 'protection'). General levels of offending had remained stable over the previous five years of the survey. As far as antisocial behaviour is concerned, just over a fifth of respondents had behaved in such a way; the most common forms were being rude or noisy in a public place. The peak age for offending was 14–17, and 14–15 for antisocial behaviour. Males were more likely than females to have engaged in criminal or antisocial behaviour. Research suggests that most children will at some point commit a criminal offence and that the majority will 'grow out of crime' (although males do so rather later than females). Identifying and responding to those whose offending is not transient is one of the most intractable problems of the youth justice system, as is avoiding the harmful effects of 'labelling' youthful indiscretions as criminal. Much research has been conducted into the risk factors associated with offending and certain factors consistently emerge as significant. Prominent among these is the nature of family life. More important than whether the family is intact or not is parenting style: the level of attachment, supervision, disruption and parental attitudes towards crime all figure as key factors. Of late, much governmental policy has been targeted towards persistent offenders, but the use of different definitions of persistence makes research difficult to interpret. In terms of risk factors, research does demonstrate that children who offend repeatedly are likely to have multiple problems, are likely to be known to social services for reasons unrelated to crime, have a record of poor school attendance and in many cases will have experienced local authority care (Whyte, 2009).

Often crime or antisocial behaviour is committed against other children. Sometimes it is almost a matter of chance who becomes the victim and who the offender. Where, rarely, serious violent crime is committed, again the victims may be other children. One such crime – the killing by Jon Venables and Robert Thompson (both aged ten at the time) of two-year-old James Bulger in 1993 – has had, as will be seen, a profound impact upon public attitudes and governmental policy towards offending by children.

Youth justice in context

In considering how society should respond to the criminal and antisocial behaviour of children a preliminary issue arises: how does society perceive childhood itself? If it is accepted that being a child is in some way different from being an adult then consequences should flow for both the family and the State. Although the concept of childhood remains deeply contested, the State has accepted this difference in a number of significant ways, including, as we shall see, the creation of a legal age of criminal responsibility below which children cannot be prosecuted for what would be offences if committed by an adult. But this does not mean that youth justice policy is coherent in its approach to children's troublesome behaviour, nor that it has remained constant. Instead, different models of youth justice can be seen to underpin different aspects of policy at any one time and adherence to each of the models swings, sometimes dramatically, over time. Much has been written about the two main models of youth justice, commonly referred to as the 'welfare model' and the 'justice model'. The welfare model reached its zenith in the 1960s and culminated in the Children and Young Persons Act 1969. The philosophy underpinning this legislation was that offending by children was to be regarded as a sign that they were 'in trouble': crime was a symptom of wider problems and disadvantages affecting their development. Children became objects of concern. Intervention was meant to be supportive and therapeutic. Many of the protective, welfare-based measures of the 1969 Act were not uncontroversial and raised the problem (very familiar today) that what may be designed to be 'supportive' (or is presented as such) may be experienced as coercive, and may further disempower members of society. Further, some provisions (including one to increase the age of criminal responsibility) were never implemented. Since then the justice model has gained ascendancy, although some elements of the welfare model still remain. For instance, the provision that in criminal proceedings courts should have regard to the welfare of the child before them has never been repealed,[5] although its influence has reduced and it is, in any event, a diluted form of the welfare principle that applies in family law.

Unlike the paternalistic philosophy of the welfare model, the justice model takes responsibility as its cornerstone. The thesis is that once children are old enough to be regarded as responsible for their behaviour, they should be held to account for their criminality and punished. After a period during the 1980s when, despite governmental rhetoric about being tough on young criminals, significant (and often successful) measures were introduced to divert offending children from formal court processes, the 1990s mark the real beginning of the current approach to youth crime – and the present preoccupation with antisocial behaviour began to emerge. Supported by unsubstantiated perceptions that were fuelled by media accounts of large numbers of communities living in terror of young 'yobs' and of children becoming increasingly feral (in the wake of the killing of James Bulger), the incoming Labour government of 1997 made youth crime a key issue in its agenda. Driven by beliefs that welfare-based measures were too lenient and that the criminal justice system was expensive, wasteful and unsuccessful, the government declared:

> Young people who commit offences must face up to the consequences of their actions for themselves and for others and must take responsibility for their actions. ... No young person should be allowed to feel that he or she can offend with impunity. ... Punishment is important as a means of expressing society's condemnation of unlawful behaviour and as a deterrent. (Home Office, 1997, pp. 1–2)

The government's view was that much of the problem with the youth justice system was caused by confusion and conflict between welfare and punishment. Its policies were designed to remove this and to stop the pendulum swinging between the two models of youth justice policy. Although it did not believe notions of welfare to be incompatible with punishment, it stressed that ultimately the individual needs of a young offender could not outweigh society's interest in being protected from harm. The government established the Youth Justice Board to oversee youth justice services and has placed the prevention of offending at the heart of official policy: s.37 of the Crime and Disorder Act (CDA) 1998 states that 'it shall be the principal aim of the youth justice system to prevent offending by children and young persons.'

While the prevention of offending is unquestionably a desirable objective, many of the measures introduced since 1997, targeting the responsibility of children, have been very heavy-handed. Further, parents are also increasingly held to account for the behaviour of their children by way of, for example, parenting orders and parenting contracts.[6] This strategy of 'responsibilisation' is open to challenge on a number of levels. It assumes that parents should be blamed for matters, when they may well have been doing their utmost, in the midst of what research reveals may be very troubled and chaotic lives, to care for their children (Koffman, 2008). Compulsion is often disguised behind the language of support. Finally, if children are responsible for their behaviour, then why should parents also be held to account? (See Stephenson et al., 2007 for discussion on controversy around the introduction of the Parenting Order.) This question will be considered shortly.

In the meantime, while it is true that many of the measures introduced since 1997 do reflect a justice model, it is not the case that all the contradictions have been removed. The system today is undoubtedly much more punitive, but also contains measures which are preventative, diversionary and restorative. Further, although the government's views seem to be entrenched in relation to the appropriate policies to be pursued in relation to children's criminal and antisocial behaviour, increasingly its actions have to be judged against international standards.

International standards

England and Wales (as part of the United Kingdom) is a signatory to the European Convention on Human Rights and although this was incorporated into English law by the Human Rights Act 1998, it offers little direct guidance in relation to children accused of crime. We are also a signatory to the United Nations Convention on the Rights of the Child (UNCRC). This latter convention has not been incorporated into English law, although it has been adopted in Wales, but in the appeal following the conviction of Jon Venables and Robert Thompson for murder, the European Court used the UNCRC for guidance as to the appropriate standards to be employed.[7] The UNCRC states that the welfare of the child is a primary consideration in all actions concerning children, including those of the courts. Of course, the fact that the wording adopted is 'a' primary consideration rather than 'the' primary consideration (or paramount as in family law) permits States to argue that other considerations, such as the interests of society, can, if necessary, outweigh the interests of an individual child. The UNCRC also requires governments to establish special laws and procedures for dealing with children accused of crimes, and it further requires the setting of a minimum age of criminal responsibility.

The UNCRC is not the only international instrument against which individual States' laws and practice should be judged. The Beijing Rules (the Standard Minimum Rules for the Administration of Juvenile Justice 1985) stipulate that in those States 'recognising the concept of the age of criminal responsibility for juveniles, the beginning of the age shall not be fixed at too low an age level, bearing in mind the facts of emotional, mental and intellectual maturity' (Rule 4.1). The explanatory note to the rule states that 'in general, there is a close relationship between the notion of responsibility for delinquent or criminal behaviour and other social rights and responsibilities (such as marital status, civil majority and so on) but no specific age limit is identified. The Beijing Rules place emphasis upon children's rights and welfare, the need to consider diversion from formal court processes and, if prosecution is necessary, for the use of custody to be a last resort. Among the other international standards it is worth highlighting the Vienna Guidelines (Economic and Social Council Guidelines for Action on Children in the Criminal Justice System 1997): these encourage States to develop child-oriented youth justice systems and also stress the importance of diversion from the criminal justice system and of dealing with the underlying social issues affecting children's behaviour to prevent crime.

The United Nations Committee on the Rights of the Child regularly monitors the performance of States against these international instruments. In each of its reports it has noted the improvements made in the United Kingdom but has also expressed grave concerns about the increase in punitive policies, the low age of criminal responsibility and the high rate of detention. Similar findings emerge in the reports from the European Commission of Human Rights, but one comment stands out in particular: the 2005 report concluded that some of the more positive steps taken by the UK government could have been 'undermined by the introduction of a series of civil orders aimed at reducing urban nuisance, but whose primary effect has been to bring a whole range of persons, predominantly the young, within the scope of the criminal justice system (European Commission, 2005). It is to these developments that discussion now turns.

Antisocial behaviour

Since 1998 the government has introduced a range of measures designed to address the fear that children were engaging in much persistent low-level criminal or antisocial behaviour that was making life a misery for communities. The most important such measure is the antisocial behaviour order (ASBO)[8] although other measures include acceptable behaviour contracts, curfews and group dispersal powers (under the Antisocial Behaviour Act 2003). In a very short period of time the term 'antisocial behaviour' has entered everyday language.

ASBOs are civil orders which may be made in respect of anyone aged ten or above. Although not designed only with children's behaviour in mind, it is clear that they are used disproportionately against them. The orders are made in civil courts upon application by a body such as the local authority, police or registered social landlord (housing associations).

No 'guilty mind' has to be proved in proceedings. No allowance need be made for children with, for example, mental health problems or learning difficulties despite the fact that they might not understand the order. ASBOs last for a minimum of two years and may contain severe restrictions upon the freedom of movement. Official guidance states that publication of names should be the norm. Challenges against ASBOs based upon arts.6 and 8 of the European Convention (the right to a fair trial and the right to respect for private and family life respectively) have been unsuccessful, but even more worrying is the fact that breach of an antisocial behaviour order is automatically a criminal offence (ASBOs are described as 'hybrid' orders). Not surprisingly, given the duration of ASBOs and the restrictions often imposed, approximately 60% of them are breached. This can then lead to the child being sentenced to custody for behaviour which was not even criminal, let alone seriously harmful (although sentencing guidelines do now state that custody is to be regarded as a last resort). In sum, the current use to which ASBOs are put is a blight on the youth justice system: while society is clearly entitled to protect itself, these measures are draconian, ineffective in changing behaviour and possibly counterproductive (Ashworth, 2004).

The age of criminal responsibility

As noted above, the law sets a fixed age below which children are exempt from criminal liability. At common law the age of criminal responsibility was seven. This was raised to eight in 1933 and to ten in 1963.[9] As indicated above, the Children and Young Persons Act (CYPA) 1969 would have raised the age to 14 but this was never implemented.

Below the age of criminal responsibility the child is irrebuttably regarded as *doli incapax* (incapable of wrong). However, this has not precluded the introduction of controlling measures for children under the age of ten. Measures such as child safety orders (which can be imposed, for example, where a child under the age of ten has acted in an antisocial manner) under the CDA 1998 have been justified on the basis that '[c]hildren under 10 need help to change their bad behaviour just as much as older children'. (Home Office, 1997, para. 99). Critics warn, however, that this constitutes a dangerous blurring of the ambit of the criminal justice system and renders almost meaningless the concept of the age of criminal responsibility.

Above the age of ten, children are legally liable for their actions. It is true that the criminal law and criminal justice system do make certain allowances for youthful immaturity in some contexts (most notably, as will be seen later, in relation to mode of trial and sentencing) but a child aged ten or above who commits an offence is liable to prosecution. The idea of a fixed cut-off point is not exclusive to this area of law, of course. Law is riddled with different age levels, relating to the age at which one may marry or drink or drive and so on. Although one can certainly criticise the arbitrariness and artificiality of such age limits this is not the most important criticism of the law. The overwhelming objection is that ten is too low an age to hold an individual answerable to a criminal court for his or her behaviour. There are several strands to this argument that need now to be examined.

The age of criminal responsibility in this country is lower – sometimes significantly lower – than in many other countries. In Belgium it is 18; in Spain it is 16; throughout Scandinavia it is 15; in Germany it is 14; in France it is 13 while in the Netherlands and Ireland it is 12. There are countries with lower age limits than England and Wales, such as Scotland, but the welfare-oriented system of children's hearings there places it apart from our system. Disturbing though these comparisons are for those interested in child welfare in this country, they raise questions rather than answers in terms of the relationship between child development, responsibility and criminal justice policy.

It is important to consider what we know from child development studies because until individual children have gained the capacity to understand right and wrong, and to weigh up the consequences of actions, liberal theories of responsibility argue that it is morally indefensible to hold them responsible for their behaviour. Child development studies stress the difference between the thought processes of a 10- to 12-year-old and those of an older adolescent. Younger children have less well-developed cognitive abilities, have less well-developed control over emotions and are highly impressionable. Law has been deeply influenced by this developmental construction of the child. In family law, in determining whether a child's wishes in relation to, say, medical treatment, should be consulted or decisive, the *Gillick* test of competency is employed.[10] This requires the court to consider whether the child has sufficient understanding and intelligence to enable her fully to understand what is proposed, and sufficient discretion to enable her to make a wise choice. So protective are the courts of a child's vulnerability that this test sets a very high benchmark of competency. While it is in family law that the *Gillick* test has taken strongest hold, versions of it have been adopted elsewhere, as will be seen later in relation to child witnesses giving sworn evidence in criminal trials. And this is not the only way in which the criminal law took note of childhood as a process of development. For hundreds of years, running in tandem with the fixed age of criminal responsibility was the presumption of *doli incapax*. This presumption applied to children between the age of criminal responsibility (currently, as we have seen, ten) and their 14th birthday. If such a child was prosecuted it was presumed that she did not understand that her behaviour was gravely, morally wrong (rather than simply naughty) and it was for the prosecution to rebut this presumption before she could be tried.[11] Evidence suggests that it was very easy to do so. It is also accepted that the test was flawed (Keating, 2007). Nevertheless, the presumption could operate as a welfarist safeguard and was symbolically very significant: it acknowledged that children develop at different rates; that capacity is important for the criminal law; and that children are a special case for the criminal justice system. This all came to an end when s.34 of the CDA 1998 abolished the presumption of *doli incapax*, the government having taken its lead from a failed attempt in the courts to do so.

The reasons given by the government for this change bear scrutiny because they suggest that an important shift in thinking is taking place. At times the government supports the imposition of criminal responsibility on children aged ten and above on the basis that such children are old enough to understand the difference between right and wrong (without supplying much in the way of evidence for this assertion) and thus *are* 'responsible' agents. One might well disagree with this in the light of all the research evidence from child development studies, but at least the government seems to accept the principle that the criminal law addresses itself to people who are 'responsible' – in the sense of having the capacity to make sense of, and answer for their behaviour. But there are times when the government justifies the use of the criminal law on the basis that it will help children to *become* responsible members of society. This is deeply worrying for a number of reasons, not least being the sleight of hand employed with nurturing words, such as 'help' when many of the interventions are punitive in nature or will be experienced as such. More fundamentally, to use the criminal law as a tool to instil responsibility is to subvert the liberal origins of modern criminal law: put simply, we do not punish people who lack the capacity, say through mental illness, to understand and conform to the law, and young children have traditionally been exempt from punishment on a similar basis. Responsibility is thus firmly linked with capacity and to sever this link is to remove justice from 'youth justice'.

In fact, the shift here is part of a much wider transformation. Whereas traditional liberal thinking stresses the importance of the individual and of autonomy, current Labour policy has been deeply influenced by communitarian approaches to responsibility. Central to this way of thinking is the idea that individual rights need to be balanced with social responsibilities. Individuals are expected to behave in accordance with community values, and departure from these values can be censured by other members of the community so as to reinforce the shared values (Etzioni, 1995). However, while communitarian theorists stress the role of the community in regulating itself, the government has transformed this into a punitive, 'top down' form of control that runs the risk of further alienating those who already feel excluded by society. It has also led to the measures taken against parents of children who commit crimes or antisocial behaviour. Parents who fail to train or supervise their children are failing in their role as parents: it is in this sense that the government is able to assert that children are responsible or must become responsible and that parents are also responsible. As the Commission on Families and the Well-being of Children has commented, this blurs the distinction between parents' duty of care and their responsibility for conduct (Commission on Families and the Well-being of Children, 2005, p.6). The abolition of the presumption of *doli incapax*, as part of the government's strategy against youth crime, is profoundly to be regretted. It has left us with an age of criminal responsibility that by international standards is low and has been the subject of criticism domestically (by bodies such as the Royal College of Psychiatrists) and by international human rights organisations, such as the United Nations Committee on the Rights of the Child. There is much support for reform, with most commentators proposing that the age of criminal responsibility be raised, say to 12 or 14. This would indeed be a significant improvement. Consideration ought, however, to be given to an alternative reform, even though some commentators have dismissed it as impractical: the reintroduction of a test similar to that in *Gillick* which reflects the view that children develop at different rates.

Court processes and disposals

The majority of lesser offences by children are not dealt with through the formal processes of prosecution and trial, but by various diversionary methods. Principally, this involves the police administering reprimands and warnings (ss.65 and 66 of the CDA 1998). Neither the consent of the child nor her parents is required. Prosecution results in cases where a reprimand or warning has been used previously and failed to prevent the young person reoffending.

Most children who are prosecuted for offences appear before the youth court (part of the magistrates' court). In such cases certain allowances are made for the youth of the offender: the magistrates have particular relevant experience and receive additional training; the proceedings are not open to the public[12] and any media reporting must not identify the defendant.[13] Proceedings are meant to be less formal than those in other courts: magistrates sit at a table rather than raised on a dais; the child does not sit in a dock and her parent(s) (who must be present if the child is under 16 under s.34 of the CYPA 1933) and social worker (if there is one) sit nearby. Magistrates refer to the child by her first name and must explain matters in ordinary language.[14]

Children charged with serious offences (defined by s.90 of the Powers of the Criminal Courts (Sentencing) Act 2000) are tried in the Crown Court. Further, if the youth court believes that the likely outcome of a case before them is custody, then the case will be heard in the Crown Court. Proceedings in the Crown Court make fewer allowances for the youth of the defendant. Those that are made were introduced in the light of criticism from the European Court of Human Rights arising from the trial of Venables and Thompson. Guidelines now provide, for example, for children to have access to social workers, to have regular breaks, and for judges to remove wigs and so on.[15] Child defendants cannot give evidence under the special measures that exist, as we shall see in the next section, for witnesses. Despite the concessions that have been made, it is far from clear that the youngest defendants are able to participate effectively in the trial process as is their right under art.6 of the European Convention on Human Rights.

A large number of special sentencing provisions exist for young offenders that are dependent upon the age of the child and the severity of the offence; ranging from community to custodial disposals. They are complex and change very rapidly. It is not within the ambit of this chapter to provide an explanation of such disposals; however, it is important to reiterate that the increased range of custodial sanctions and the increased use of custody for longer periods has attracted criticism both domestically and internationally. It is here that the punitive dimension to the youth justice system is at its most obvious.

In contrast to the manifest problems with the current use of custody, one recent, potentially more positive, development will be considered briefly. The referral order was introduced in 1999 and is now governed by ss.16–20 of the Powers of the Criminal Courts (Sentencing) Act

2000. This is a compulsory order for children (aged 10–17) who plead guilty to what is their first offence before a court. Courts make a referral order of between three months and one year, dependent upon the seriousness of the offence. The child is referred to a Young Offender Panel (YOP). The meeting of the panel is less formal than that of the court and parents are expected to attend with their child. The panel draws up a 'contract' with which the child has to agree. The contract consists of actions that the child is required to take. This is likely to include an element of reparation (such as writing a letter of apology) and should include measures to help prevent further offending (which may include educational activities, curfews and so on). Referral orders should be seen as part of the government's acceptance of principles of restorative justice (although subsequent research reveals little evidence of victim engagement in the process). As parents and children are both involved, the disposal is also part of the responsibilisation strategy. It is clear from research that the process may, in fact, deliver much needed help to children. Indeed, referral orders have been described as 'the jewel in the crown' of the youth justice system (Morgan, 2007). But one has to question why a child should have to appear before a criminal court before help can be unlocked. Further, although the child has to 'agree' to the contract, the fact that refusal leads to a return to the court for re-sentencing means that the process is potentially coercive. Finally, as was seen in the context of court proceedings, evidence is beginning to emerge that the very youngest children coming before YOPs find much of the process beyond their powers of understanding (Newbury, 2008).

Children as victims and witnesses

While most of this chapter has focused upon the child as offender, children are, of course, frequently the victims of crimes. A recent survey conducted by the Howard League revealed that 95% of 3,000 children who had been surveyed over a period of seven years had been a victim of crime on at least one occasion. Most of the offences were low level and took place in schools and playgrounds, involving theft, property damage or assault. Only one-third reported incidents to the police or teachers. The survey also revealed a fear of crime among children and that they felt that adults 'demonised' them as criminals when they should be viewed as victims of crime (Howard League, 2008).

While much crime against children is thus hidden, more serious offending against children by adults or other children can lead to prosecutions being brought, and the victim may then be called as a witness to give evidence. The law draws a distinction between the competence of a witness to give evidence and the issue of whether she can be compelled to do so. In relation to the competence of children, attitudes have changed in recent times: it used to be thought that if a child was too young to swear an oath in relation to the truth of her evidence that it should not be heard at all. Now even uncorroborated evidence will be heard if the court is satisfied that the child understands the questions and can give meaningful answers.[16] But child witnesses may not give sworn evidence in criminal trials until they are 14 years old and then only if they are found to possess 'a sufficient appreciation of the solemnity of the occasion and the particular responsibility to tell the truth which is involved in taking an oath'.[17] As far as compellability is concerned, children can be summonsed to give evidence. As noted above, s.44 of the CYPA 1933 is still in force and it is possible (although unlikely as the interests of justice might well prevail) that it could be found not to be in the child's interests for her to be compelled to give evidence.

   The experience of giving evidence in court can be an ordeal that is deeply distressing to both adult and child witnesses and in recent times, often in the wake of cases where victims have been exposed to unacceptable and humiliating treatment by both prosecution counsel and the defendant (when defending himself), special protective measures for child and other vulnerable witnesses have been introduced. The law here has to strike a difficult balance: on the one hand, art.6 of the European Convention on Human Rights states that the defendant has the right to challenge the evidence as a fundamental aspect of the right to a fair trial, but on the other hand, witnesses must be protected from being further harmed by their experiences in court. The key provisions are contained within the Youth Justice and Evidence Act 1999. Under s.35 it is no longer possible for the defendant himself to conduct the cross-examination of a child. Sections 23–25 provide for evidence to be given behind screens, by live link or in private. The proceedings can be made less intimidating by the removal of wigs and gowns under s.26, and ss.27–28 enable the giving of evidence and cross-examination to be video recorded in advance. These are very considerable safeguards but there are matters of concern. Section 28 is not yet in force. After the trial of the killers of Baby Peter, the boyfriend was also convicted of the rape of another child. By the time of the trial the child was four years old and she was cross-examined fairly robustly for some 40 minutes, by live video-link, causing an outcry. Levels of protection are thus imperfect (and many have not yet been extended to magistrates' courts). On the other hand, the fact that a child witness in the Crown Court is automatically extended special measures removes that choice from the child – denying any autonomy to the older child (Hall, 2009). Once again, the contrast between the child as victim and offender is clear.

Summary

As the House of Lords has commented, 'ignoring the special position of children in the criminal justice system is not acceptable in a modern civil society'[18] but the extent to which the law actually does offer protection, as we have seen, varies, depending on a number of factors, including the government policy being pursued and whether the child is categorised as offender or victim. The reality is that children are neither devils nor angels and categorisations of them as 'thug' or 'troubled' or 'innocent victim' do not assist in the development of a sufficiently nuanced youth justice system. This is not to deny that the behaviour of some children is dangerous, nor that society is entitled to protect itself against it; further, although there are instances when victimisation occurs as part of a tit-for-tat dispute between children, this is far from being universally true, as child protection cases tragically remind us.

But in addressing the complex issues surrounding children's criminal and antisocial behaviour, measures based upon populist punitiveness are unlikely to do more than temporarily appease certain elements of the media. It has been rightly said that 'the political climate in the UK stresses individual responsibility as if somehow reduction in reoffending and personal and social reintegration is the sole personal and moral responsibility of young people, with scant regard to structural barriers and broader social justice requirements of shared responsibility' (Whyte, 2009). Until more consideration is given to our obligations under international conventions and the findings from research on children and crime; until it is accepted that the criminal law should be a weapon of last and not first resort, and that children who offend are still children, there is grave cause to be concerned for the future of youth justice policy in this country.

References

Ashworth, A. (2004) '"Social control" and "Antisocial behaviour": the subversion of human rights', *Law Quarterly Review*, **120**: 263.

Commission on Families and the Well-being of Children (2005) *Families and the State: An Inquiry into the Relationship Between the State and the Family*, Bristol, Policy Press.

Etzioni, A. (1995) *New Communitarian Thinking: Persons, Virtues, Institutions and Communities*, Charlottesville, VA, University Press of Virginia.

European Commission (2005) *Report by Mr Alvaro Gil-Robles, Commissioner for Human Rights on his visit to the United Kingdom*, European Commission, para. 83.

Hall, M. (2009) 'Children giving evidence through special measures in the criminal courts: progress and problems' *Child and Family Law Quarterly* **21**(65).

Home Office White Paper (1997) *No More Excuses – A New Approach to Tackling Youth Crime in England and Wales*, Cm 3809, London, TSO, pp. 1–2.

Home Office (2009) *Findings from the British Crime Survey and Police Recorded Crime 2008–2009*, London, TSO.

Howard League for Penal Reform, (2008) *Children as Victims: Child-sized Crimes in a Child-sized World*, Howard League.

Keating, H. (2007) 'The "responsibility" of children in the criminal law', *Child and Family Law Quarterly*, **19**(183): 190–5.

Koffman, L. (2008) 'Holding parents to account: tough on children, tough on the causes of children', *Journal of Law and Society*, **35**: 113.

Morgan, R. (2007) 'A new direction' *Safer Society*, **32**: 5–8.

Newbury, A. (2008) 'Youth crime: whose responsibility?', *Journal of Law and Society*, **35**: 131.

Pearson, G. (1983) *Hooligan: A History of Respectable Fears*, London, Macmillan – now Palgrave Macmillan.

Roe, S. and Ashe, J. (2008) *Young People and Crime – Findings from the 2006 Offending, Crime and Justice Survey* (H.O.S.B. 09/08), Home Office. The survey covered 20 core offences.

Stephenson, M., Giller, H. and Brown, S. (2007) *Effective Practice in Youth Justice*, Cullompton, Willan.

Whyte, B. (2009) *Youth Justice in Practice: Making a Difference*, Bristol, Policy Press, pp. 37–9.

Youth Justice Board (www.youth-justice-board.gov.uk).

Notes

1. With thanks to Laurence Koffman for reading a draft of this chapter.
2. The law distinguishes between children (those aged 10–13) and young people (those aged 14–17). But for simplicity and because the age of majority is 18 the term child will be used throughout.
3. This chapter focuses upon the criminal justice system of England and Wales.
4. Crime and Disorder Act 1998 (CDA 1998), s.1.
5. Children and Young Persons Act 1933 (CYPA 1933), s.44.
6. CDA 1998, s.8; Antisocial Behaviour Act 2003.
7. *T and V* v. *The United Kingdom* (1990) 30 EHRR 121.
8. CDA 1998, s.1.
9. CYPA 1933, s.50 as amended by the Children and Young Persons Act 1963, s.16.
10. *Gillick* v. *West Norfolk and Wisbech Area Health Authority and Department of Health and Social Security* [1986] AC 112.
11. *R* v. *Gorrie* (1919) 83 JP 136.
12. CYPA 1933, s.47(2).

13. Youth Justice and Criminal Evidence Act 1999 (YJCEA), s.44.
14. See Magistrates' Courts (Children and Young Persons) Rules 1992.
15. Practice Note (trial of children and young persons: procedure) [2000] 2 ALL ER 285.
16. YJCEA 1999, s.53.
17. YJCEA 1999, s.55(2).
18. *R* v. *G and Another* [2004] 1 AC 1034, para. 53 per Lord Steyn.

Chapter 10

Can You Keep a Secret? Children, Human Rights, and the Law of Medical Confidentiality

JOAN LOUGHREY*

The existence of competent children's right to medical confidentiality was confirmed in *R (Axon)* v. *Secretary of State for Health (Family Planning Association Intervening).*[1] However, a number of important questions remained unanswered including: whether non-competent children have a right to medical confidentiality against their parents as well as third parties; when it would be legitimate to override competent and non-competent children's medical confidentiality; whether parents can rely on article 8 of the European Convention for the Protection of Human Rights and Fundamental Freedoms 1950 to claim a right to disclosure of their children's medical information; and, if so, what approach should be adopted where that right comes into conflict with children's article 8 rights to privacy and confidentiality. These questions will be explored, taking into account the development of the law of confidentiality as a means of protecting article 8 rights to privacy. It will be argued that children's right to, and decisions regarding, medical confidentiality require greater respect and protection.

Introduction

In *R (Axon)* v. *Secretary of State for Health (Family Planning Association intervening)* (hereafter *Axon*), Silber, J confirmed that competent children have a right to medical confidentiality exercisable even against their parents. This was unsurprising, given that this right was recognised, albeit implicitly, as long ago as 1986 by the House of Lords in *Gillick* v. *West Norfolk and Wisbech Area Health Authority and Department of Health and Social Security (Gillick),*[2] a case which *Axon*

---

* First published in *Child and Family Law Quarterly* 20(3), 2008. Reproduced with the kind permission of Jordan Publishing.

strongly resembled.[3] Nevertheless, many aspects of the legal duty of confidence owed to children remain uncertain. For example, the link made in both *Axon* and *Gillick* between adolescent autonomy, the capacity to consent to treatment and the right to confidentiality leaves open the question of whether, and the extent to which, minors who are not competent to consent to treatment possess a right of medical confidentiality. Meanwhile, in relation to competent children, there are outstanding questions concerning when the courts may consider it permissible to override the right.

This article will address these questions by first considering the difference between confidentiality and privacy, the extent to which the law has developed to protect both and the values underpinning the law of confidence. It will then consider in more detail the law of medical confidentiality and in particular whether the law should, and the extent to which it does, recognise that non-competent children possess a right to confidentiality, including the right to have medical information withheld from their parents. The final sections consider when both *Gillick* competent and non-competent children's right to medical confidentiality can be overridden to protect their welfare, or may be outweighed by a parental right to disclosure.

The article identifies three broad categories of child. First there are *Gillick* competent children, that is those children who possess sufficient maturity to be able to consent to treatment. The second category comprises children who are not competent to consent to treatment, but who desire confidentiality. These will be referred to as non-competent children, although this is not entirely accurate, since some will be sufficiently competent to make decisions about confidentiality. The third category comprises children who are neither competent to consent to treatment nor have the capacity to understand nor want confidentiality. These will be termed 'the very young'. In practice the boundaries between the categories will be fluid. Which a child belongs to will depend not only on his age and cognitive development, but also his life experiences and the nature of the information at issue. A young child with a medical condition may be capable of wishing information relating to that condition to be kept secret, whereas others of his age may lack the capacity to seek secrecy. Again the same child may lack this capacity in relation to other types of information.[4] Furthermore, it is possible that children may develop the ability to desire secrecy from outsiders earlier than they acquire the capacity to desire secrecy from parents: if so, the category a child falls into could also depend on to whom disclosure was to be made.

It will be argued that children in all three categories are entitled to medical confidentiality both vis-à-vis third parties and parents. However, the extent to which children's decisions about medical confidentiality should be respected, the circumstances in which their right to medical confidentiality can be overridden and how the right plays out a vis-à-vis parents will vary depending upon the category a child falls into at the time in question.

Confidentiality and privacy

Prior to the Human Rights Act 1998, the traditional formulation of the action for breach of confidence was that:

> The information ... must have the necessary quality of confidence about it. Secondly, that information must have been imparted in circumstances importing an obligation of confidence. Thirdly, there must be an unauthorized use of that information to the detriment of the party communicating it.[5]

This formulation focused on the existence of a relationship of confidence, and the action for breach of confidence was directed at protecting such relationships.[6] The courts articulated public interest rationales to explain the law's concern, recognising a public interest in protecting medical confidentiality in order to encourage people to come forward for treatment, with the consequent protection of public health.[7] Another explanation was that the action was designed to protect the trust inherent in relationships of confidence.[8] Although the courts had taken some steps towards protecting informational privacy as a separate value,[9] this was not the focus of the action.

The introduction of the Human Rights Act 1998, and the incorporation of article 8 rights to respect for a private life under the European Convention for the Protection of Human Rights and Fundamental Freedoms 1950 into UK law, altered this. The courts developed the law of confidence as the main vehicle for protecting these rights, and, in doing so, redirected the focus of the action towards protecting informational privacy.[10] The transformation of the action for breach of confidence into a remedy for breach of privacy was endorsed by the House of Lords in the leading case of *Campbell* v. *MGN Ltd* (*Campbell*), when the House of Lords recognised that the action could be maintained when private information was disclosed without authorisation, regardless of whether it was originally imparted in trust.[11]

As a result of these developments, courts and commentators have articulated a new set of values underpinning the law of confidence. Notably there is a growing emphasis on protecting informational autonomy,[12] meaning the ability 'to control what is known (and by whom) regarding oneself and one's activities'.[13] It has also been recognised that article 8 privacy rights, and so the law of confidence, function to protect psychological and physical integrity,[14] and dignity.[15] Again, it has been argued that privacy per se is a key value underlying article 8, since the preservation of a private sphere is essential for personal development.[16]

The courts increasingly appeal to these rationales but, at least in relation to medical confidentiality, consequentialist public interest justifications for protecting such information remain important.[17] The courts also continue to attach great significance to the protection of relationships of confidence where these exist. At times, in fact, the courts appear to regard invasions of privacy accompanied by betrayals of trust more seriously than those unaccompanied by such betrayals.[18]

Thus, in *McKennitt* v. *Ash,* the court indicated that in determining whether a breach of confidence had occurred, to focus on the question of whether the information disclosed was private, while disregarding the fact that it was imparted in the course of a relationship of confidence, was likely to lead to 'a distorted outcome'[19] Buxton LJ went on to say that, while medical information was obviously private, the fact that it was imparted in the course of a relationship of confidence made it *'doubly private'* (emphasis added).[20]

These developments have led the writers of a leading text to argue that the action for breach of confidence encompasses two very different types of action, one being an action for the protection of privacy, the other being the action for breach of confidence. In relation to the latter they argue that:

> Where there is an underlying relationship of confidence, the law has not changed as a result of the Human Rights Act ... The basic value which underlies the law in such circumstances is that a person ought to be able to entrust information to another without having that trust abused.[21]

In the light of these developments, there is now a basis for explaining the existence of children's legal right to medical confidentiality. Prior to the Human Rights Act 1998, although it was established that doctors owed a legal duty of confidence to all child patients, even the very young,[22] the foundation of this duty was unclear, since young children could not form relationships of confidence.[23] One possibility was that this duty was simply an aspect of the doctor's duty of care.[24] If so, a doctor could not disclose confidential information about a child patient to the media, because such disclosure would be against the child's interests and a breach of the duty of care to him.[25] This was not, however, the approach adopted by the courts, who articulated the doctor's duty as one of confidence rather than care.[26] Now that the law has developed to protect privacy, it is easier to explain the law's concern with even the very young, because there is no doubt that they possess article 8 rights to privacy, including the right to informational privacy.[27] These children are obviously not autonomous, and so article 8 and the action for breach of confidence cannot be functioning to protect their informational autonomy. However, other values underpinning article 8 will be in play, such as the protection of dignity, physical and psychological integrity and the protection of the private sphere to enable personal development. Helen Fenwick has argued that this last value is particularly significant for children, whose development may be adversely affected by invasions of privacy.[28]

To summarise, in response to the Human Rights Act 1998, the courts have developed the action for breach of confidence to protect article 8 rights to privacy, but continue to emphasise their role in protecting confidential relationships. The privacy of children in all three categories is protected by the law. In addition, by respecting the wishes of *Gillick* competent children concerning the disclosure of their confidential information, the law respects their informational autonomy.[29] Furthermore, unlike the very young, it operates to protect their confidential relationship with the doctor, and the trust that they place in him. The precise values which the law of confidence protects by respecting the confidence of non-competent children is more controversial and will be considered in the next section, which examines the right to confidentiality of the non-competent child and the very young. In contrast to *Gillick* competent children, whose right to confidentiality, including the right to have information withheld from parents, is now established,[30] the extent to which non-competent children and the very young do, or should, possess a right to confidentiality is much more uncertain. It has even been argued that such children have no right to confidentiality at all.[31] As a description of positive law this is untenable, since the courts have recognised that even babies have a right to medical confidentiality. However, since such arguments raise the normative question of whether the law is correct to recognise this right, they will be addressed, together with the controversial question of whether these children have a right to have medical information withheld from their parents. This question – whether such a legal right exists – needs to be distinguished from the question of whether it is justifiable in a particular case to override it. The latter question will be examined separately in the last part of the article.

The next section is divided into three parts – the first will examine the position of the non-competent child, the second the very young, while the third considers developments in the law of confidence pertaining to detriment and remedies which affect both groups.

The legal right to confidence of non-*Gillick* competent children

The non-competent child

Some have argued that only *Gillick* competent children have a right to confidentiality, whether as against their parents or at all.[32] The link between *Gillick* competence and the right to confidentiality may have been made because, in the context of children, and increasingly in the context of adults, the right has been conceived of as an autonomy right. If children do not possess autonomy, there is no need to accord them such a right.[33] Indeed to do so may be harmful, both to the project of children's rights, and to children themselves. Jane Fortin has argued strongly against claiming autonomy rights for children who, for developmental reasons, are unable to assert them. To do so both devalues the importance of children's rights; can deflect attention from other, more important rights that children have, such as the right to care and protection; and can foist responsibilities on them before they are mature enough to assume them.[34] Such an argument makes the existence of the right to confidentiality conditional upon the capacity for autonomy and could exclude a child from claiming a right to confidentiality not only as against parents but also as against third parties.

A second reason for linking the right to *Gillick* competence is that, not unusually, where the child is not competent to consent to treatment, information has to be disclosed to parents in order to obtain their consent to treatment. This practical argument would exclude children possessing a right to confidentiality against their parents, although it would not exclude the existence of the right in other cases.

This latter reason can be rejected rapidly. It is correct that if a non-competent child requires treatment, it will usually be necessary to disclose the child's medical information to parents in order to obtain consent to treatment. However, it does not follow that it is necessary for a doctor to disclose all the information the child has confided, although he needs to disclose whatever is relevant to an assessment of the benefits and risks of treatment. Again, where treatment is not indicated, and so parental consent is not required, it is not at all clear why the child's right to confidentiality should depend on whether he can consent to treatment. There is, therefore, not always a practical link between the absence of *Gillick* competence and the need to make disclosure to parents.

The argument that non-competent children cannot have a right to confidentiality because they lack autonomy is vulnerable on two further grounds. First, children who are not competent to consent to treatment may still be sufficiently autonomous to make decisions about confidentiality. As Munby J commented, 'The question of capacity ... is always issue specific'.[35] The standard for *Gillick* competence to consent to treatment can be set very high. In *Axon,* for example, Silber J, citing Lord Scarman in *Gillick,*[36] stated that, in order for a medical professional to be able to give advice and treatment on abortion without notifying a girl's parents, the girl would need to understand all aspects of the advice and treatment, including moral and family questions, the long-term implications of the options available, and the emotional impact of termination.[37] It seems very likely that many children who could not meet this test would be perfectly capable of understanding the concept of confidentiality, which provides a good reason for recognising their right to, and respecting their decisions regarding, confidentiality.

Second, the assumption that the right to confidentiality can only arise where the child is autonomous is incorrect. Until the advent of the Human Rights Act 1998, the courts were able to accord adults a right to medical confidentiality without appealing to the principle of respect for autonomy. There consequently seems to be no reason for the law to require children to be autonomous in order to possess the right.[38] As discussed above, the courts explained – and continue to explain – the rationale for protecting medical confidences by reference to public interest considerations, or the need to protect the trust inherent in the doctor–patient relationship. These provide very strong grounds for recognising children's confidentiality, even where the child lacks autonomy.

Thus, in *Axon,* Silber J placed particular emphasis on evidence that failing to accord young people a right to confidentiality would have a public health impact by deterring them from coming forward for treatment. These concerns are as applicable to non-competent as to *Gillick* competent children.[39] It can be argued that this public interest does not require information to be withheld from parents. Rather, insofar as younger children rely on parents to bring them for treatment, and insofar as parental consent is needed before giving treatment, it requires disclosure. However, not every non-competent child is dependent on their parents to access medical services, and even where parents are aware of, and have consented to treatment, treatment may not be possible, or may be undermined, if children cannot be sure that their confidentiality will be respected.[40] An obvious example would be psychotherapy, where trust and openness is essential for the therapeutic process to work.[41]

Again, since the right to confidentiality protects the trust inherent in the therapeutic relationship, the mental integrity of the confider and dignitary interests, it seems difficult to justify making the child's competence to carry out a risk–benefit analysis of the consequences of non-disclosure a condition of holding the right. There is evidence that non-competent children can form relationships of trust with health care professionals and can feel betrayed if disclosure occurs, even to parents. Thus in *Re R (A Child) (Disclosure)*,[42] a primary care trust was sued on a child's behalf for negligently failing to diagnose Attention Deficit Hyperactivity Disorder and Asperger's Syndrome. An application was made by the claimant for pre-action disclosure of documentation, including the child's confidential psychotherapy notes. The child was aged between five and eight at the time of treatment. The psychotherapist gave evidence that the child had understood that the therapy was confidential and had been annoyed when he had thought that she had discussed his case with others.[43] In *Re B (Disclosure to Other Parties)* children aged 10 and 12 indicated strongly that they did not want their mother's violent ex-partner to have access to confidential information about them.[44] Munby J attached considerable weight to these views.[45] He accepted that the children would be harmed if they discovered that the ex-partner could access this information.[46] As a result the ex-partner was prevented from seeing a range of papers, including material relating to a psychologist's work with the children.[47] It is conceivable that disclosure to parents could, in certain circumstances, have a similar impact.

Finally, disclosure may result in physical harm to children. It has been reported that girls as young as 13 are thrown out of home when their parents discover that they are pregnant.[48] Although parents ultimately will discover a pregnancy in a 13-year-old who, on the *Axon* test, might be assessed as non-competent to consent to an abortion, to deny that the child possesses a right to confidence against her parents does not appear to be an appropriate response to her dilemma.[49] For a start, fear of disclosure could deter such children from seeking advice and support which, again, could have a public health impact.[50] While there are strong grounds for overriding the child's right to confidentiality in such extreme cases, so as to safeguard her welfare for example, that is a separate issue. It is important to recognise the right in the first place.

This is because, if a right to confidentiality is not recognised, there may be little incentive, and some disincentive, for practitioners to take children's views properly into account, since this could bring practitioners into conflict with parents. Again, if no right is recognised, the onus is shifted from justifying disclosure of confidential information, to justifying non-disclosure. It is possible that health care professionals will themselves feel obliged to disclose to parents even though they may have misgivings about doing so. Finally, recognising that children have this right may be the best way of promoting not only their right to privacy under article 16 of the United Nations Convention on the Rights of the Child 1989, but also their right under article 12 to be consulted about decisions affecting them.[51] Article 12 does not require a child's views on a matter be treated as conclusive. Nor does recognising that a child has a right to confidentiality conclude the question of whether disclosure should occur.

There is, therefore, a strong normative case for recognising that non-competent children have a right to confidence against both third parties and their parents. However, while the law recognises the right of confidence against third parties, the courts have not directly considered whether confidentiality can be claimed against parents, nor is it clear how the current law of confidentiality would be applied were this question to arise.

In *Campbell* the House of Lords set out three different tests for determining whether an obligation of confidence attached to information: where the recipient of the information knows, or ought reasonably to know, that information is fairly and reasonably to be regarded as confidential;[52] where information is obviously private or, where it is not obviously private, its publication would be offensive to a person of ordinary sensibilities;[53] and where the information is such that the person to whom it related had a reasonable expectation of privacy. Applying these tests to medical information about non-competent children, it seems clear that the first two would give rise to an obligation of confidence, since medical information is fairly and reasonably to be regarded as confidential and is obviously private. Furthermore, there seems to be no reason why this obligation would not arise simply because it was proposed to disclose it to parents. However, the third test, which is objective, presents more difficulties. It is possible to anticipate an argument that, from an objective perspective, any expectation children have that their medical information will be kept confidential from their parents is unreasonable. If so, no right to confidentiality would arise vis-à-vis parents, even though, contemporaneously, there could be a reasonable expectation that disclosure would not be made to third parties, and so a right to confidence could be claimed against them.

On the other hand, as Lord Hope of Craighead stated in *Campbell,* 'If the information is obviously private, the situation will be one where the person to whom it relates can reasonably expect his privacy to be respected'.[54] Since medical information is the paradigm example of 'obviously private' information, it must follow that children possess a reasonable expectation of privacy in relation to such information, and therefore a right to confidentiality in respect of it.[55] If, despite this, it is intended to disclose the information, it will be necessary to justify this – but the reasonable expectations of privacy test does not provide an answer to whether a sufficiently strong justification exists.[56]

In summary, where children are capable of forming their own opinions regarding disclosure, and the information is obviously private, it is submitted that a legal obligation of confidence attaches to their medical information, which can be asserted even against parents. It should be recognised that in many cases, if not most, children will expect their parents to be fully involved in their medical treatment,[57] and their consent to disclosure can be implied. However, where children do not wish information to be disclosed, the reasonable expectations test should not be used to override their wishes. This would misuse the test and would result in a failure to recognise that disclosure is an invasion of privacy, requiring justification. Any disclosure against the wishes of the child in these circumstances must be justified.

The very young

Historically there was a great deal of uncertainty regarding how and why the law of confidence protected the very young. This was because these children seemed unable to meet the requirements of the traditional test for establishing breaches of confidence set out in *Coco* v. *AN Clark (Engineers) Ltd.*[58] While that test has been replaced by the reasonable expectations of privacy test, this has not eliminated all the uncertainties regarding how the law applies to this group. In particular, although the reasonable expectations test is objective, it requires an assessment of whether someone in the position of the person to whom the information relates would have a reasonable expectation of privacy in relation to the information.[59] It was difficult to see how this could be satisfied by the very young, since arguably no one in their position could possess an expectation of privacy.[60]

The issue was confronted in *Murray* v. *Express Newspapers,* both at first instance and on appeal (*Murray* v. *Big Pictures (UK) Ltd*).[61] This was an application to strike out a claim, brought on behalf of the infant child of J. K. Rowling, that his right to privacy and confidentiality had been breached by the publication of a photograph showing him being pushed by his parents in a buggy along a street. At first instance the defendants' strike out application was successful, but the action was reinstated on appeal.

The Court of Appeal held that the first instance judge, Patten J, had failed to clearly distinguish between the parents' privacy rights and the child's. At times he did not seem to fully acknowledge the child as a rights holder with interests separate from his parents. Rather he viewed the action as artificial, a device directed at protecting the famous parent's privacy, rather than the child's.[62] The Court of Appeal rejected this and emphasised that, even at 19 months, a child's right to privacy was distinct from his parents' and that the child could have a claim to privacy when his famous parents might not.[63] The Court of Appeal confirmed that, because the reasonable expectations test was objective, a baby could be treated as possessing a reasonable expectation of privacy in respect of private information.[64]

This judicial recognition of the child as a rights holder distinct from his parents is welcome. Unfortunately, however, the Court of Appeal expressly agreed with another troubling aspect of Patten J's judgment, where he stated that: 'The court can attribute to the child reasonable expectations about his private life based on matters such as how it has in fact been conducted by those responsible for his welfare and upbringing'.[65] The reasonable expectations test therefore, as applied to infant children, is shaped by the behaviour of their parents and the degree to which the parents have exposed themselves and their children to publicity, or have consented to disclosure of their children's private information.[66]

However, it seems wrong to hold that parental actions, which are themselves an invasion of a child's privacy, can modify the child's expectation of privacy and so limit the degree of protection he can expect from the law. This compounds the wrong done to the child and fails to adequately distinguish his rights from his parents. It also fails to take into account that parents owe their children duties of confidentiality, can act in ways that wrongfully invade children's privacy and that children have rights against their parents that they should not behave in this way.[67] It is questionable, therefore, whether the law should accept that a young child's right to privacy can be eroded by the status or actions of his parents.

The facts of the case obviously did not require consideration of whether a very young child's right to privacy can ever require that his medical information should be withheld from his parents. It was argued earlier with reference to non-competent children that disclosures of medical information are, in the absence of express or implied consent, breaches of confidentiality which must be justified. It seems to follow that disclosures of medical information to the parents of the very young in order to obtain consent to treatment would also be breaches of confidence. Perhaps this is unproblematic, since these disclosures would be easily justifiable as necessary for the child's protection. On the other hand, it seems wrong to treat these as prima facie breaches of a professional's duty of confidence which require justification.[68] Non-disclosure would seem to require rather more justification. It may be defensible, therefore, in the context of the very young only, to modify the reasonable expectations test to avoid this conclusion. Thus, no breach of the legal obligation of confidence would occur where information relating to a child was disclosed to his parents for the purposes of obtaining treatment for the child, because a person in that child's position would reasonably expect disclosure to occur. It could also be argued that such disclosures are not sufficiently serious interferences with privacy to engage a child's article 8 rights at all.[69]

This application of the reasonable expectations test bears superficial similarities to the way it is used to determine whether information disclosed in a public place is nevertheless protected from publication by the law of privacy.[70] When making this assessment the courts have considered whether the person to whom the information related had a reasonable expectation that information would not be published. Such claims have significant freedom of speech implications, since they limit discussion of events which occurred in the public sphere, and so, in that context, the test is aimed at keeping claims for breach of privacy within acceptable limits.[71] Such policy reasons do not apply in the present context: the information is obviously private, and is disclosed in the private sphere. Given this, the proposed modification must not be used to undermine the privacy of the very young. Its limits must be noted: only disclosures necessary for the care of the child should satisfy the reasonable expectations test. Disclosures for the parents' purposes, rather than for care of the child, would breach the child's article 8 rights and right to confidentiality, and would thus require justification. Some may consider that this modification fails to properly acknowledge and protect the privacy interests of the very young, while others may resist the idea that the very young have privacy rights at all. Nevertheless it is suggested that this represents a compromise which both recognises the very young as separate rights holders while promoting their welfare, alongside avoiding an approach which many might regard as out of touch with reality.

Detriment and remedies

We will now turn to other aspects of the law of confidentiality that have developed in recent years. Under the old law, the question of whether it was necessary to establish that a breach of confidence had caused detriment was unsettled. This requirement would have been problematic since it was unclear that non-competent children and the very young suffered any detriment through disclosure of their medical information. It is now generally accepted that detriment is not, if it ever was, a separate requirement. It is sufficiently detrimental that information is disclosed where the person to whom it relates had a substantial interest in it remaining confidential.[72] This would usually be the case in relation to the disclosure of medical information.[73]

It was also unclear whether a remedy for mental distress was available and, even if it was, what remedy might be available to the very young, who were unaware of disclosure and so might not suffer actionable harm. In relation to the first point, this uncertainty has been resolved: damages for mental distress are available,[74] although debate continues over the precise basis and quantification of damages awards in breach of confidence actions.[75] In *A (A Child)* v. *Newham London Borough Council*, an action in confidence was brought on behalf of a 10-year-old child whose photograph was taken at nursery, and used without parental knowledge to illustrate brochures about HIV. Damages of £5,000 were awarded.[76]

As for the second point, it has been recognised that even where children are unaware of a disclosure, they may still suffer harm as a result of it: the impact on their carers of disclosure could impair the carers' ability to look after the children, and the carers' distress could be communicated to the children.[77] Children could be stigmatised and bullied, for example, if it was revealed that they were HIV positive.[78] Such harm would infringe their physical and psychological integrity, and thus constitute a breach of article 8. Finally, other equitable remedies may be available to these children, such as injunctions to prevent publication or, where their medical information is published, an account of profits.[79]

Thus the action for breach of confidence, even in the case of the very young, has the potential to be an effective remedy for invasions of privacy. This potential will not, however, be fulfilled if the child's legal right to confidentiality is too easily overridden, either on the basis of the child's own welfare or in the face of assertions that parents have a 'right to know'. It is to these matters that the next section turns.

Overriding the child's right to confidentiality

The background

Children, like adults, have no absolute right to confidentiality. Confidentiality can be compulsorily overridden by court order or by statute. In addition, it is a defence to an action for breach of confidence that disclosure to appropriate persons was necessary in the public interest.[80]

Just as with the right to confidence, so the right to privacy under article 8 is not absolute. Article 8(2) permits disclosures that are in accordance with the law and are 'necessary in a democratic society in the interests of national security, public safety or the economic well-being of the country, for the prevention of disorder or crime, for the protection of health or morals or for the protection of the rights and freedoms of others'.

Consequently, recognising children's legal right to confidentiality does not settle the question of whether it may be legitimate to breach confidentiality and disclose information to parents or third parties. This raises difficult questions in relation to all three categories of children which the following discussion will address. It will focus on two particularly important issues: first, when it may be permissible to disclose information to parents or third parties in order to safeguard children's welfare; and, second, whether parents possess a right to have their children's medical information disclosed to them and, if they do, how the law should resolve conflicts between that right and children's rights to privacy and confidentiality.

Disclosures to protect children's welfare

The *Gillick* competent child and disclosures in the public interest

The General Medical Council *0–18 Guidance for All Doctors* (the Guidance) provides that the right to confidentiality of *Gillick* competent children can be overridden where disclosure is justified in the public interest. The Guidance's statement that disclosure can occur where the benefits of disclosure outweigh children's and society's interests in medical confidentiality provides little direction to doctors.[81] Nevertheless, at law also, the boundaries of the public interest defence are vague and uncertain.[82] Cases in which the defence has been successful include where disclosure served the public interests of protecting others from a real risk of serious harm, or the prevention and detection of crime or other serious wrongdoing, or the public interest in free speech.[83] At first blush the Guidance appears to mirror the law. Thus it advises that disclosure of information should occur where it is necessary to protect the child from the risk of death or serious harm such as in cases of abuse and neglect, or where the child is placing himself at serious risk of harm.[84] However, at law, the defence has not been relied on to justify paternalistic disclosures aimed at protecting the interests of the adult confider. Rather the public interest has been established where disclosures were intended to protect third parties. Using it paternalistically would be controversial. It has, for example, been argued that a competent woman's confidentiality should be respected if she reveals that her partner is abusing her, since disclosure against her wishes would be an impermissible violation of her autonomy.[85] Again, the public interest may not justify disclosing a competent adult's medical information against his wishes where he poses no risk to others, just to save him from himself, such as where the adult has an addiction. Yet the Guidance stipulates that children's confidentiality should be overridden in this situation.[86] It seems therefore that competent children's right to confidentiality is more vulnerable than that of competent adults. While the public interest in the prevention and detection of child abuse may justify disclosures against children's wishes, given the serious child welfare implications and the seriousness of the crime, it is highly debateable whether the public interest in child welfare should legitimate disclosures aimed at protecting competent teenagers from the consequences of their own actions. This is arguably too great a violation of their autonomy. Furthermore it has been cautiously argued that *Axon* marks a renewed emphasis on respecting adolescent autonomy.[87] Certainly Silber J reaffirmed that *Gillick* competent children are entitled to obtain medical advice and treatment without parental knowledge or consent even for matters as serious as an abortion.[88] Further he cited and emphasised Thorpe LJ's comments in *Mabon* v. *Mabon* that 'we must, in the case of articulate teenagers, accept that the right to freedom of expression and participation outweighs the paternalistic judgment of welfare'.[89] These dicta could be interpreted as suggesting that the courts will now recognise that *Gillick* competent children's decisions about confidentiality will be respected, even though their welfare may be harmed as a result.[90]

On the other hand, *Axon* was a case in which children's rights and welfare coincided, and so the court's commitment to adolescent autonomy was not tested. It is also worth noting that Silber J, citing Toulson and Phipps' assertion that 'the doctor stands in a confidential relationship to every patient of whatever age including a baby but the purpose of the relationship is the welfare of the patient',[91] warned: 'In my view, that purpose must not be forgotten or under-estimated'.[92] It is at least implicit in this that where a competent child's right to confidentiality comes into conflict with his welfare, there may be times when a child's welfare could prevail over confidentiality.

However, paternalistic disclosures are serious interferences with children's article 8 right to respect for private life. Such interferences may be justifiable under article 8(2) and possibly under article 2 where they are directed at protecting children's health or life, or the prevention of crime as in cases of child abuse. Even then though, interferences must be limited to what is necessary and proportionate to achieve these ends. Thus disclosure must only be made to those who can act to avert the risk to the child, which will not necessarily be the child's parents. Again, as Silber J commented in *Axon*, the duty of confidence that health care professionals owe to competent children is a high one, which can only be overridden for very strong reasons.[93] He appeared to recognise that overriding a *Gillick* competent child's medical confidentiality would, of itself, usually be contrary to his welfare.[94] Given this, and given the weight of the right, and the seriousness of the interference, there would need to be a grave threat to the *Gillick* competent child's welfare before disclosure could be considered proportionate.

Non-competent children and best interests

The Guidance provides that the confidentiality of children who cannot make decisions about disclosure can be overridden both on public interest grounds and where disclosure is necessary to protect their best interests.[95] It advises that disclosures can be made not only to parents to enable them to make important decisions relating to children, or to provide proper care, but also to appropriate third parties.[96]

There is no case law directly on these points and there is a risk that a broad best interests ground may make it relatively easy for doctors to justify disregarding children's wishes regarding confidentiality. Nevertheless, since such disclosures breach children's article 8 rights, they must again be justifiable under article 8(2).[97] While the aims of protecting children's welfare[98] or health fall within article 8(2), again interferences to achieve these aims must be necessary and proportionate. Doctors should therefore limit disclosures to those necessary to obtain properly informed parental consent. They should consider whether treatment is necessary. To determine whether disclosure is proportionate, doctors will need to balance the factors in favour of disclosure against the harm to children and the therapeutic relationship if disclosure occurs against children's wishes. Where a child opposes disclosure, this should weigh heavily in favour of finding that his decision should be respected, and his right to confidentiality upheld. Nevertheless, non-competent children's opposition would carry less weight than that of competent children due to their comparative immaturity and greater dependence and need for care. Finally, where it is proposed to disclose to third parties who do not have care of the child, but the reasons for disclosure are not sufficiently weighty to amount to a public interest justification, it may be rare for it to be necessary and proportionate to disclose information on the best interests basis.

In summary, if it is justifiable to override *Gillick* competent children's confidentiality to serve the public interest in child welfare, this should be exceptional and restricted to disclosures directed at averting serious harm. As for non-competent children, less serious threats to welfare would suffice, but disclosure must still be a necessary and proportionate response. The younger the child, the stronger the case will usually be for disclosure.

The parental right to disclosure

In addition to disclosures that are necessary in the public interest and on grounds of children's best interests, it can be argued that parental rights require disclosure.

Insofar as a parental right to disclosure exists, it seems to be an aspect of the parent's right to respect for family life under article 8.[99] In *Axon*, however, in the context of *Gillick* competent children, Silber J held that a parent's right to respect for family life was not violated by non-disclosure.[100] He stated that the parental right to be informed of the child's medical information, and to participate in medical decisions affecting the child, existed for the benefit of the child, not the parent.[101] Once the child possessed sufficient autonomy to make decisions about medical treatment herself, the need for these parental rights vanished, as did the rights.

It is, however, implicit in Silber J's judgment that, in relation to non-competent children who cannot consent to treatment, a failure to disclose information which parents need to give consent could violate parents' article 8 rights.[102]

If this right exists, it does not follow that parents can automatically access their children's information.[103] Rather, since disclosure would violate children's article 8 right to privacy, the dilemma is how the conflict of rights between parents and children should be resolved. The first issue is whether children's interests should be treated as paramount, or whether children's and parents' interests must be balanced against each other. If the latter, the second issue is how the balancing exercise should be conducted.

Children's rights and welfare: balance or paramountcy?

Under domestic law, where a particular decision has been categorised as relating to the upbringing of a child under section 1(1) of the Children Act 1989, the child's welfare has been treated as paramount, and no balancing exercise has been carried out between the child's rights and those of the parents.[104] It is not clear whether withholding a non-competent child's medical information from his parents should be classified as a matter relating to upbringing. However, when parents consent to a child's treatment, that decision does relate to upbringing.[105] It must follow that a decision not to disclose information that would enable parents to give informed consent to treatment must also be a decision that affects the child's upbringing.

If, however, treatment is not required, the decision to withhold information may not relate to upbringing. If it does, according to domestic case law, the child's interests would be deemed paramount, and the question of whether disclosure should occur would turn on an assessment of the child's best interests, rather than on the parental right to be consulted. Much has been written about the extent to which the paramountcy principle is consistent with the requirements of article 8 of the

Convention.[106] Suffice it to say that Strasbourg case law clearly establishes that a fair balance should be struck between the interests and rights of the child and those of the parents, albeit that particular importance (if not paramount)[107] must be attached to the best interests of the child, which may (not must), depending on their nature and seriousness, override those of the parents.[108] It has also been established that parents' article 8 rights do not entitle them to measures that would harm the child's health and development.[109]

If the decision to withhold information does not relate to the child's upbringing, then, as discussed below, the child's rights and interests would have to be balanced against those of the parents'.[110]

Balancing the rights of parents and child

An interference with a child or a parent's article 8 rights which occurs in order to respect the other's article 8 rights, or to protect the child's interests, is potentially justifiable under article 8(2) as being necessary to protect the rights and freedoms of others, or to protect health or child welfare. This does not, however, resolve how the balance is to be struck between these competing rights and interests.

Fenwick argues that, in order to carry out the balancing exercise, it is first necessary to identify what values underpin the rights claimed and then to assess whether, and to what extent, these values are at stake in any given case.[111] Insofar as they are not fully at stake, then either there may be no breach of the article 8 right, or the interference with the right will be more easily justifiable.[112]

If the values underpinning the rights are at stake then, as we have seen, it is necessary to consider whether the interference with the child's rights (for example), was prescribed by law, necessary in a democratic society and proportionate to the legitimate aim of protecting the parents' article 8 rights. In particular the interference with the child's rights (or the parents') must go no further than is necessary to protect the rights of the other.[113]

Not all the values underlying the protection of children's article 8 right to privacy will be affected where disclosure is made to parents. If the child is not autonomous, informational autonomy will obviously not be relevant; but other values may be, such as dignity, the protection of mental and psychological integrity, as well as the protection of the public interest in public health. In addition, certain types of medical information are considered particularly sensitive, and therefore particularly in need of protection. These include information about sexual health and psychiatric medical notes.[114]

Turning to the parental right to respect for family life, *Axon*, following *Gillick*, strongly suggests that, in this context, it is child-centred. That is, it exists for the child's benefit, and to advance the child's welfare.[115] If the child does not need his parents to exercise the right, either because he possesses sufficient autonomy to make his own choices, or his welfare does not require it, it falls away. There is no residual parent-centred right to be informed, that is, a right that serves the parents' own interests and needs. On the other hand, Mrs Axon, relying upon the well-known and controversial decision in *Nielsen* v. *Denmark (Nielsen)*, argued that she had a right to disclosure under article 8, even though her children were competent. In *Nielsen* it was held that a mother's right to respect for family life entitled her to arrange the compulsory detention of her 12-year-old son in a closed psychiatric ward.[116] That decision certainly appears to give parents a broad parent-centred right of control, which could encompass a right to disclosure of their children's medical information in order to facilitate the exercise of control. In *Axon*, in the context of competent children, Silber J refused to interpret *Nielsen* in this manner.[117] Arguably, though, *Nielsen* could still be applied to non-competent children, and the very young, particularly given the European Court of Human Right's comments that: 'Regarding the weight which should be given to the [child's] views as to his hospitalisation ... he was still of an age at which it would be normal for a decision to be made by the parent even against the wishes of the child'.[118] Such a parent-centred right could require disclosures to be made to parents of a non-competent child, even though the child opposed this and it was not necessary for his care.

Nevertheless, *Nielsen* can be read as recognising only child-centred parental rights: it was a key step in the reasoning that the mother's objective was to protect her child's health – in other words the right was exercised for the child's benefits.[119] Further, it has been argued convincingly that *Nielsen* no longer represents the law under the European Convention for the Protection of Human Rights and Fundamental Freedoms 1950, given the age of the decision, changing social attitudes to children, and the division of opinion between the judges in the case.[120]

In contrast, in *A* v. *United Kingdom* a mother successfully argued before the European Commission that overriding a parent's bona fide and reasonable decision regarding whether a course of action served her child's best interests was an interference with her article 8 right to respect for her family life,[121] although the interference was justified as necessary to protect the child's best interests.[122] This formulation of the right to family life does appear to be parent-centred, in that it exists for the parent's benefit by facilitating the exercise of the parent's discretion over raising a child.[123]

Although *Axon* and *Gillick* support the view that the recognition of a parental right to know is conditional on the need to obtain parental consent to medical treatment, these decisions were not concerned with non-competent children.[124] In relation to these children it is possible that the courts will follow a similar approach to that adopted in *A v. United Kingdom*, and identify a parent-centred right. Although there was no consideration of such article 8 rights in *Re R (A Child) (Disclosure)*,[125] a decision discussed above, Sumner J's assumption that a child's medical information had to be disclosed to those with parental responsibility, even though it was known that the 11-year-old child would probably object,[126] further supports a parent-centred approach.

If the right were parent-centred, disclosure would have to be considered even though it was not required to protect the child's welfare. Given the child's conflicting right to privacy, a complex balancing exercise would be needed to determine whether disclosure should occur. If the right was only child-centred, the balancing exercise would be simpler. Where disclosure was not necessary to obtain parental consent to treatment, or take other steps to protect the child's welfare, the child's article 8 right to privacy should easily outweigh any parental right to disclosure, insofar as such a right was recognised at all.

In any event, a parent-centred right would probably be more easily outweighed when it stood alone than when the child-centred aspect of the right was also in play. For example, in *Brent London Borough Council v. N (Foster Carers) and P (by her Guardian)*, the issue was whether the HIV status of a two-year-old child's foster parent should be disclosed to the child's father.[127] Sumner J held that a local authority would usually be under an obligation to disclose relevant health information relating to a child to his parents.[128] However, the risk that the child had been exposed to HIV infection was negligible. Because disclosure was therefore unnecessary and would infringe the foster parent's article 8 rights, it was not permitted.[129] The case is under-reasoned and did not explore the parties' article 8 rights, but it could arguably be concluded that the parental right to be informed is weaker where disclosure is not necessary, for example, to obtain treatment for the child, and where gaining access to such information would infringe another's article 8 rights, including, it is suggested, the child's.

The final question is whether, if the child's welfare does not require disclosure, his right to privacy could outweigh the parental right to disclosure. There is much case law in which children's rights to privacy and family life have had to be balanced against other interests, such as parents' article 8 and 10 rights, the media's article 10 rights and public interests, including the open administration of justice.[130] These cases must, however, be treated with caution. The balancing act is fact sensitive and requires, in each instance, a close scrutiny and assessment of the comparative importance of the rights at issue.[131] In the case law referred to, children's article 8 rights came into conflict with extremely weighty rights and so publication was permitted to proceed despite the risk that it would cause very serious harm to the children.[132] Insofar as parents possess an article 8 right to be informed of children's medical information, it is unlikely to be given the same weight.

Bearing this in mind, some conclusions might be drawn about factors that a court will consider significant in deciding whether to uphold the child's right to privacy. The most significant will be the degree of harm resulting from disclosure.[133] The most serious harm would be injury to the health or development of the child. As noted earlier, a parent's article 8 rights will not be permitted to override the child's rights where this harm would result.[134] Although not every disclosure of medical information against the child's wishes would cause such harm, disclosures relating to the child's mental health, for example disclosures of counselling notes, or disclosures relating to the child's sexual health, could well have this impact. In relation to the former the betrayal of trust could result in the breakdown of the therapeutic relationship and result in the child being deprived of treatment required to restore him to health.[135] In relation to the latter, the fear of betrayal could deter the child from seeking treatment and counselling, with a consequent detrimental impact on his health. Even the very young, who may be unaware of disclosure, and unable to comprehend its implications, may suffer as a result, such as where disclosure disrupts their care or treatment or distresses their primary carer (for example, where the parents are estranged).[136]

Even if the health and development of the child would not be impaired, he might suffer harm through interference with his mental integrity when he is aware that his trust has been betrayed. Again, if the child is sufficiently autonomous to understand the concepts of confidentiality and privacy, his informational autonomy will be violated if disclosure occurs against his wishes. These consequences are not only violations of the child's rights, but may also be contrary to his interests and welfare, which the European Court of Human Rights has indicated must be treated as being of crucial importance in cases involving conflicts between the article 8 rights of the child and those of his parents.[137]

Finally, the public interests in child welfare and the protection of public health will, where relevant, also weigh against the parent's right to disclosure. For example, in *Axon*, Silber J held that even if the parent's article 8 right to family life had been infringed by non-disclosure, the public interest in promoting sexual health among adolescents justified the interference.[138]

It is therefore suggested that, in the main, where a child, even one who is non-competent, wants his medical information to be withheld from his parents, and disclosure is neither necessary to obtain parental consent to treatment nor justifiable by reference to the child's best interests, there are strong grounds for allowing the child's right to privacy to outweigh a parent-centred right to disclosure. Even in relation to the very young, the parental right must be balanced against the child's and particular care should be taken to avoid harming the child. However, where a young child would suffer no harm then, given the child's inability to desire confidentiality, the parent's claim to disclosure will be stronger. Each case is fact specific, but it should not be assumed that non-competent children can never have a right to confidentiality against their parents, nor that parental rights must be respected over children's, nor, indeed, that children's rights should be treated as paramount in a conflict with parents' rights.

Conclusion

Both non-competent and *Gillick* competent children should have a right to confidentiality against their parents and third parties. Informational autonomy provides a strong reason for recognising the right if children are sufficiently autonomous. But there are other equally compelling reasons for doing so, including the protection of trust and the preservation of the utility of medical treatment, the protection of dignitary interests and psychological integrity, as well as public health reasons. As for when the right can be overridden, while the confidentiality of *Gillick* competent children can, like that of adults, be overridden on public interest grounds, it is much more controversial to rely on this to justify purely paternalistic disclosures where no child abuse or other serious crime has been committed. Non-competent children meanwhile will rarely wish to have information withheld from parents,[139] but when they do their decision should be respected, although it need not be determinative. Disclosure must occur if it is necessary to obtain parental consent to treatment and it would be negligent not to treat. Otherwise disclosure may occur where there are sufficiently pressing welfare or public interest considerations, or the protection of the child's rights requires it. However, appeals to best interests should not be used to emasculate the right to confidentiality of non-competent children and the very young. It should be recognised that violating a non-competent child's right to confidentiality, and betraying his trust, of itself harms his welfare. In any event, arguably the right to confidentiality of the very young will not be breached if disclosure is confined to what is required for the care and treatment of the child. As for the argument that non-disclosure violates a parental right, generally no such right will be recognised in the case of *Gillick*

Gower College Swansea
Library
Coleg Gŵyr Abertawe
Llyrfgell

competent children. In relation to non-competent children and the very young, this right probably exists, but if the child's welfare does not require disclosure, so that only a parent-centred version of the right is at stake, it should usually be rare for it to be sufficiently weighty to override the child's right to confidentiality if the child opposes disclosure.

The decision on whether to disclose will usually be made by practitioners, who can differ widely in their responses to children's claims to confidentiality.[140] Better practitioner training is needed to avoid this problem and to safeguard confidentiality. Professional guidelines also have a part to play. Finally, it is essential that the courts should consider more carefully than they have done hitherto whether a non-competent child's medical information should be disclosed to his parents, explaining more fully their reasoning, while giving due weight to the rights of both parents and children.

Notes

1. [2006] EWHC 37 (Admin), [2006] QB 539.
2. [1986] AC 112, at 174 (Lord Fraser of Tullybelton), 189 (Lord Scarman).
3. For a detailed discussion see A. Hall, 'Children's Rights, Parents' Wishes and the State: the Medical Treatment of Children' [2006] *Fam Law* 317; J. Bridgeman, 'Young People and Sexual Health: Whose Rights? Whose Responsibilities?' (2006) 14 *Medical Law Review* 418; R. Taylor, 'Reversing the Retreat from Gillick? R (Axon) v. Secretary of State for Health' [2007] *CFLQ* 81.
4. I thank the anonymous referee for drawing my attention to this point.
5. *Coco* v. *AN Clark Engineers Ltd* [1969] RPC, at 47.
6. Toulson, R. G. and Phipps, C. M. (2006) *Confidentiality* (2nd edn), Sweet and Maxwell, p. 23.
7. *X* v. *Y* [1982] 2 All ER 648; *W* v. *Egdell* [1990] Ch 359, at 416 and 420. See the discussion in Montgomery, J. (2002) *Health Care Law* (2nd edn) Oxford University Press, pp. 99, 257–8; Loughrey, J. (2005) 'The Confidentiality of Medical Records; Informational Autonomy, Patient Privacy, and the Law' *Northern Ireland Legal Quarterly*, 293.
8. Toulson, R. G. and Phipps, C. M. (2006) *Confidentiality* (2nd edn), Sweet and Maxwell, p. 23. See also Kennedy, I. (1991) 'The Doctor, the Pill and the 15-Year-Old Girl' in *Treat Me Right: Essays in Medical Law and Ethics*, Oxford University Press, pp. 64–5.
9. For example, *Attorney-General* v. *Guardian Newspapers Ltd (No 2)* [1990] 1 AC 109, at 281 (Lord Goff of Chieveley).
10. G. Phillipson and H. Fenwick, 'Breach of Confidence as a Privacy Remedy in the Human Rights Act Era' [2000] 63 MLR 660, at pp. 671–2.
11. *Campbell* v. *MGN Ltd* [2004] UKHL 22, [2004] 2 AC 457, at 465 (Lord Nicholls of Birkenhead), 472–3 (Lord Hoffmann). The case law is now

extensive: see Fenwick, H. and Phillipson, G. (2006) *Media Freedom Under the Human Rights Act*, Oxford University Press, pp. 722–4.

12. *Douglas v. Hello! Ltd* [2001] QB 967, at 1001; *Campbell v. MGN Ltd* [2004] UKHL 22, [2004] 2 AC 457, at 472–3; *HRH Prince of Wales v. Associated Newspapers Ltd* [2006] EWCA Civ 1776, [2008] Ch 57, at 90. See G. Phillipson and H. Fenwick, 'Breach of Confidence as a Privacy Remedy in the Human Rights Act Era' (2000) 63 MLR 660, at pp. 662–3 and H. Fenwick, 'Clashing Rights, the Welfare of the Child and the Human Rights Act' (2004) 67 MLR 889, at p. 919.

13. Pennock, J. R. (1971) 'Introduction', in Pennock, J. R. and Chapman, J. W. (eds), *Privacy*, NOMOS XIII, Atherton, p. xiii.

14. *X (a woman formerly known as Mary Bell) v. SO* [2003] EWHC 1101 (QB), [2003] EMLR 850, at para [20]; *Campbell v. MGN Ltd* [2004] UKHL 22, [2004]2 AC 457, at p. 501. See also *Re S (A Child) (Identification: Restrictions on Publication)* [2003] EWCA Civ 963, [2004] Fam 43, at p. 71; *Re X, Y (Children)* [2004] EWHC 762 (Fam), [2004] EMLR 607, at pp. 629–30.

15. *Campbell v. MGN Ltd* [2004] UKHL 22, [2004] 2 AC 457, at 472 and 473; *HRH Prince of Wales v. Associated Newspapers Ltd* [2006] EWCA Civ 1776, [2008] Ch 57, at 90; *Lord Browne of Madingley v. Associated Newspapers* [2007] EWCA Civ 295, [2007] 3 WLR 289, at 301; *T v. British Broadcasting Corporation* [2007] EWHC 1683 (QB), [2008]1 FLR 281, at para [16].

16. H. Fenwick, 'Clashing Rights, the Welfare of the Child and the Human Rights Act' (2004) 67 MLR 889, at p. 919; *Campbell v. MGN Ltd* [2004] UKHL 22, [2004] 2 AC 457, at para [12] (Lord Nicholls).

17. *Ashworth Hospital Authority v. MGN Ltd* (2001)1 WLR 515, at 535; *Ashworth Hospital Authority v. MGN Ltd* (2002) UKHL 29, [2002]1 WLR 2033, at 2051–2, citing *Z v. Finland* (1998) 25 EHRR 371. See also *X v. A Health Authority* [2001] EWCA Civ 2014, [2002]2 All ER 780, at 784; *H (A Healthcare Worker) v. Associated Newspapers Ltd* [2002] EWCA Civ 195, [2002] EMLR 425, at para [27]; *Campbell v. MGN Ltd* (2004) UKHL 22, [2004] 2 AC 457, at 499 (Baroness Hale); *Stone v. South East Coast Strategic Health Authority* (2006) EWHC 1668 (Admin), (2007) UKHRR 137, at para (31) and [44]; *HRH Prince of Wales v. Associated Newspapers Ltd* [2006] EWCA Civ 1776, [2008] Ch 57, at 115 and 124; *Bluck v. The Information Commissioner* (2007) 98 BMLR 1, at para [13].

18. *HRH Prince of Wales v. Associated Newspapers Ltd* (2006) EWCA Civ 1776, [2008] Ch 57, at 115–17; *McKennitt v. Ash* (2006) EWCA Civ 1714, (2008) (QB) 73; *Lord Browne of Madingley v. Associated Newspapers* [2007] EWCA Civ 295, [2007] 3 WLR 289, at 301; see also Baroness Hale's comments in *Campbell v. MGN Ltd* (2004) UKHL 22, [2004] 2 AC 457, at pp. 500–1.

19. [2006] EWCA Civ 1714, [2008] (QB) 73, at para (15) per Buxton LJ. This was cited and emphasised in *Lord Browne of Madingley v. Associated Newspapers* (2007) EWCA Civ 295, (2007) 3 WLR 289, at 300.

20. Ibid, at [23].

21.   Toulson, R. G. and Phipps, C. M. (2006) *Confidentiality* (2nd edn), Sweet and Maxwell, p. 23 and see pp. 24–6.
22.   In *Re C (A Minor) (Wardship: Medical Treatment) (No 2)* [1990] Fam 39; *Re Z (A Minor) (Identification: Restrictions on Publication)* (1997) Fam 1.
23.   Loughrey, J. (2003) 'Medical Information, Confidentiality and a Child's Right to Privacy' *Legal Studies* 23(3) 510, at pp. 515–18.
24.   Jackson, E. (2006) *Medical Law: Text, Cases and Materials,* Oxford University Press, pp. 321–2 and see Toulson, R. G. and Phipps, C. M. (2006) *Confidentiality* (2nd edn), Sweet and Maxwell, who seem to argue that the scope of the duty of confidentiality is set by the doctor's professional judgement about whether the disclosure is required in the best interests of the patient: at paras 11-003 and 11-042-11-043.
25.   Kennedy, I. and Grubb, A. (2000) *Medical Law* (3rd edn), Butterworths, p. 1079.
26.   In *Re C (A Minor) (Wardship: Medical Treatment) (No 2)* [1990] Fam 39, at 48–9 and 55; *Re Z (A Minor) (Identification: Restrictions on Publication)* [1997] Fam 1, at 25.
27.   See, for example, *Re B (A Child) (Disclosure)* [2004] EWHC 411 (Fam), [2004] 2 FLR 142, at 177 (4-year-old child) and *A Local Authority v. W, L, W, T and R (by the Children's Guardian)* [2005] EWHC 1564 (Fam), [2006] 1 FLR 1 (two children aged three years and six months); *Re Roddy (A Child) (Identification: Restriction on Publication)* [2003] EWHC 2927 (Fam), [2004]2 FLR 949 (child aged three); *Murray v. Big Pictures (UK) Ltd* [2008] EWCA Civ 446, [2008] FLR (forthcoming).
28.   See Fenwick, H. (2004) 'Clashing Rights, the Welfare of the Child and the Human Rights Act' 67 *Modern Law Review* 889, at p. 920.
29.   *R (Axon) v. Secretary of State for Health (Family Planning Association Intervening)* [2006] EWHC 37 (Admin), [2006] QB 539, at 561 and 566–7. See also *Re Roddy (A Child) (Identification: Restriction on Publication)* [2003] EWHC 2927 (Fam), [2004] 2 FLR 949, although this case concerned a child's right to disclose, rather than withhold, information.
30.   See A. Hall, 'Children's Rights, Parents' Wishes and the State: the Medical Treatment of Children' [2006] *Fam Law* 317; J. Bridgeman, 'Young People and Sexual Health: Whose Rights? Whose Responsibilities?' (2006) 14 *Medical Law Review* 418; R. Taylor, 'Reversing the Retreat from Gillick? R (Axon) v. Secretary of State for Health' [2007] *CFLQ* 81.
31.   Kennedy, I. (1991) 'The Doctor, the Pill and the 15-Year-Old Girl' in *Treat Me Right: Essays in Medical Law and Ethics,* Oxford University Press, pp. 111–17.
32.   Ibid.
33.   Ibid, especially at p. 113.
34.   Fortin, J. (2003) *Children's Rights and the Developing Law* (2nd edn), Butterworths, pp. 6, 76–7, 591; Fortin, J. (2006)'Children's Rights – Substance or Spin' *Fam Law* 759.
35.   *E (by her Litigation Friend the Official Solicitor) v. Channel Four; News International Ltd and St Helen's Borough Council* [2005] EWHC 1144 (Fam), [2005] 2 FLR 913, at para [76].

36. *Gillick* v. *West Norfolk and Wisbech Area Health Authority and Department of Health and Social Security* [1986] AC 112, at 189.
37. *R (Axon)* v. *Secretary of State for Health (Family Planning Association Intervening)* [2006] EWHC 37 (Admin), [2006] QB 539, at 570.
38. Montgomery, J. (2002) *Health Care Law* (2nd edn), Oxford University Press, p. 309.
39. *R (Axon)* v. *Secretary of State for Health (Family Planning Association intervening)* [2006] EWHC 37 (Admin), [2006] QB 539, at 562–5 and at 582–3. See R. Taylor, 'Reversing the Retreat from Gillick? R (Axon) v. Secretary of State for Health)' [2007] *CFLQ* 81, at pp. 85–6.
40. See the significance attached to the fact that disclosure would underline therapy in *Campbell* v. *MGN Ltd* [2004] UKHL 22, [2004] 2 AC 457, at 465, 484 (Lord Hope), 505 (Lord Carswell).
41. Daniels, D. and Jenkins, P. (2000) *Therapy with Children: Children's Rights, Confidentiality and the Law*, Sage Publishing, pp. 39–42. See also case studies at p. 73 and pp. 111–12.
42. [2004] EWHC 2085 (Fam) (unreported) 3 September 2004.
43. Ibid, at para [17].
44. *Re B (Disclosure to Other Parties)* [2001] 2 FLR 1017, at 1022.
45. Ibid, at 1044.
46. Ibid, at 1045.
47. Ibid, at 1045–6.
48. ChildLine, 'Why Do Children and Young People Run Away, or Become Homeless?' http://www.childline.org.uk/Whydochildrenandyoungpeopler unaway,orbecomehomeless.asp (last visited 30 January 2008). The GMC Guidance recommends that where a child under 13 is engaging in sexual activity this should normally be disclosed to 'appropriate people or agencies': General Medical Council, 0–18 years: *Guidance for All Doctors* (GMC, 2007), at paras. 65 and 67.
49. Faced with the same factual scenario, doctors' assessments of whether a teenager is competent can vary widely, so some might find a child competent while others would not: Bartholomew, T. and Carvalho, T. (2007) 'Medical Practitioners' Competence and Confidentiality Decisions with a Minor: An Anorexia Nervosa Case Study' *Psychology, Health and Medicine* 12: 495. Interestingly, the research indicates that some doctors who assess a child as non-competent would, nevertheless, respect confidentiality: ibid, at 502.
50. *R (Axon)* v. *Secretary of State for Health. (Family Planning Association Intervening)* [2006] EWHC 37 (Admin), [2006] QB 539, at 562–4.
51. Article 12(1) provides that: 'States parties shall assure to the child who is capable of forming his or her own views the right to express those views freely in all matters affecting the child, the views of the child being given due weight in accordance with the age and maturity of the child.' Children may also possess this right under article 8: see *R (B)* v. *Crown Court at Stafford* [2006] EWHC 1645 (Admin), [2007]1 WLR 1524, at 1531.
52. [2004] UKHL 22, [2004]2 AC 457, at 465 (Lord Nicholls).
53. Ibid, at 482–3 (Lord Hope).

54. Ibid, at 483.
55. Ibid, at 481 (Lord Hope); at 496 and 499 (Baroness Hale).
56. See *McKennitt* v. *Ash* [2006] EWCA Civ 1714, [2008] QB 73, at 81–2; *HRH Prince of Wales* v. *Associated Newspapers Ltd* [2006] EWCA Civ 1776, [2008] Ch 57, at 118; *Murray* v. *Big Pictures (UK) Ltd* [2008] EWCA Civ 446, [2008] FLR (forthcoming), at 413–14 and 422.
57. Alderson, P. and Montgomery, J. (1996) *Health Care Choices: Making Decisions with Children*, IPPR, p. 64.
58. See text to n. 5 above.
59. *Campbell* v. *MGN Ltd* [2004] UKHL 22, [2004] 2 AC 457, at 484 (Lord Hope), at 496 (Baroness Hale); Fenwick, H. and Phillipson, G. (2006) *Media Freedom Under the Human Rights Act*, Oxford University Press, p. 746.
60. *Murray* v. *Express Newspapers* [2007] EWHC 1908 (Ch), [2008]1 FLR 704, at para [23]. There appear to be no difficulties in applying it to older children: see *Leeds City Council* v. *Channel Four Television Corporation* [2007] 1 FLR 678, at 686 (surreptitious filming of children aged 13–16).
61. *Murray* v. *Express Newspapers* [2007] EWHC 1908 (Ch), [2008] 1 FLR 704; *Murray* v. *Big Pictures (UK) Ltd* [2008] EWCA Civ 446 [2008] FLR (forthcoming).
62. [2007] EWHC 1908 (Ch), [2008] 1 FLR 704, at paras [15] and [17].
63. [2008] EWCA Civ 446, [2008] FLR (forthcoming), at 406–7 and 425.
64. Ibid, at 415–16, although the court also made reference to the parent's reasonable expectations of privacy for the child, rather than the child's: at 424.
65. [2007] EWHC 1908 (Ch), [2008] 1 FLR 704, at para. [23]; [2008] EWCA Civ 446, [2008] FLR (forthcoming), at 416–17 and see 422.
66. [2007] EWHC 1908 (Ch), [2008] 1 FLR 704, at paras. [15]–[17] and [23].
67. *Re H-S (Minors) (Public Interest: Protection of Identity)* [1994] 1 WLR 1141; *Re Z (A Minor) (Identification: Restrictions on Publication)* [1997] Fam 1; *Richmond upon Thames London Borough Council* v. *H* [2001] 1 FCR 541, at 20; *Clayton* v. *Clayton* [2006] EWCA Civ 878, [2006] Fam 83, at 105–6 and 123–4.
68. Such an approach has been criticised as being 'out of consonance with legal and actual reality': Kennedy, I. and Grubb, A. (2000) *Medical Law* (3rd edn), Butterworths, p. 1077; see also Jackson, E. (2006) *Medical Law: Text, Cases and Materials*, Oxford University Press, p. 333 and Toulson, R. G. and Phipps, C. M. (2006) *Confidentiality* (2nd edn) Sweet and Maxwell, 11-043.
69. The courts have adopted this approach to dismiss claims, although the circumstances were very different: *R (S)* v. *Chief Constable of the South Yorkshire Police; R (Marper)* v. *Chief Constable of the South Yorkshire Police* [2004] UKHL 39, [2004] 1 WLR 2196, at 2210; *R (Wood)* v. *Commissioner of Police of the Metropolis* [2008] EWHC 1105 (Admin), (2008) *The Times*, June 13, at paras [43] and [57].
70. See *Peck* v. *United Kingdom (Application No 44647/98)* [2003] EMLR 287, at 58 and the discussion in Fenwick, H. and Phillipson, G. (2006)

Media Freedom Under the Human Rights Act, Oxford University Press, pp. 755–6.

71. *John v. Associated Newspapers Ltd* [2006] EWHC 1611 (QB), [2006] EMLR 27; *R (Wood) v. Commissioner of Police of the Metropolis* [2008] EWHC 1105 (Admin), (2008) *The Times,* June 13, at para [58].

72. Toulson, R. G. and Phipps, C. M. (2006) *Confidentiality* (2nd edn) Sweet and Maxwell, at para. 3–164; Fenwick, H. and Phillipson, G. (2006) *Media Freedom Under the Human Rights Act,* Oxford University Press, at p. 728; Witzleb, N. (2007) 'Monetary Remedies for Breach of Confidentiality in Privacy Cases' *Legal Studies* 27, 430, pp. 440–1.

73. *Bluck v. The Information Commissioner* (2007) 98 BMLR 1, at para. [15].

74. *Cornelius v. De Taranto* [2001] EWCA Civ 1511, [2002] EMLR 112; *Archer v. Williams* [2003] EWHC 1670 (QB); [2003] EMLR 869; *Campbell v. MGN Ltd* [2004] UKHL 22, [2004] 2 AC 457; *Douglas v. Hello! Ltd* (No 3) [2005] EWCA Civ 595, [2006] QB 125.

75. Toulson, R. G. and Phipps, C. M. (2006) *Confidentiality* (2nd edn) Sweet and Maxwell, at paras 9.028–9.043; Witzleb, N. (2007) 'Monetary Remedies for Breach of Confidentiality in Privacy Cases' *Legal Studies* 27, 430, pp. 437–40, 443–54.

76. (unreported) 16 October 2001.

77. In *Re C (A Minor) (Wardship: Medical Treatment) (No 2)* [1990] Fam 39, at 47–8; *Re B (Disclosure to Other Parties)* [2001]2 FLR 1017, at 1045–6; *Richmond upon Thames London Borough Council v. H* [2001]1 FCR 541, at 557.

78. Although not confidentiality cases, the following illustrate the harm even the very young may suffer where their article 8 rights to privacy are infringed: *Re X, Y (Children)* [2004] EWHC 762 (Fam), [2004] EMLR 607, at para. [93]; *Re S (A Child) (Identification: Restrictions on Publication)* [2004] UKHL 47, [2005]1 AC 593, at 600; *A Local Authority v. W, L, W, T and R (by the Children's Guardian)* [2005] EWHC 1564 (Fam), [2006] 1 FLR 1, at 24–5.

79. For a full discussion of remedies see Toulson, R. G. and Phipps, C. M. (2006) *Confidentiality* (2nd edn) Sweet and Maxwell, Ch 9; Witzleb, N. (2007) 'Monetary Remedies for Breach of Confidentiality in Privacy Cases' *Legal Studies* 27, 430.

80. Toulson, R. G. and Phipps, C. M. (2006) *Confidentiality* (2nd edn) Sweet and Maxwell, Ch 6.

81. General Medical Council, *0–18 years: Guidance for All Doctors* (GMC, 2007), at para. 47.

82. Mason, J. K. and Laurie, G. T. (2006) *Mason and McCall Smith's Law and Medical Ethics* (7th edn), Oxford University Press, p. 264.

83. See, for example, *Lion Laboratories v. Evans* [1985] QB 526; *W v. Egdell* [1990] Ch 359; *Woolgar v. Chief Constable of the Sussex Police* [2000] 1 WLR 25.

84. The Guidance, at paras 49, 59–61.

85. Mason, J. K. and Laurie, G. T. (2006) *Mason and McCall Smith's Law and Medical Ethics* (7th edn), Oxford University Press, p. 271, although at p. 259 they suggest paternalistic disclosures may sometimes be permissible.
86. The Guidance, at para. 49.
87. R. Taylor, 'Reversing the Retreat from *Gillick*? *R (Axon)* v. *Secretary of State for Health*)' [2007] CFLQ 81, at p. 94. See also J. Fortin, 'Accommodating Children's Rights in the Post Human Rights Act Era' [2006] 69 MLR 299, at pp. 319–23.
88. *R (Axon)* v. *Secretary of State for Health (Family Planning Association Intervening)* [2006] EWHC 37 (Admin), [2006] QB 539, at 566–7, 579–80.
89. Ibid, at para [79] citing *Mabon* v. *Mabon* [2005] EWCA Civ 634, [2005] Fam 366, at para [28]. See also Thorpe LJ's comments at para [26].
90. R. Taylor, 'Reversing the Retreat from *Gillick*? *R (Axon)* v. *Secretary of State for Health*)' [2007] CFLQ 81, at p. 96.
91. Toulson, R. G. and Phipps, C. M. (1996) *Confidentiality*, Sweet and Maxwell, para. 11–043.
92. *R (Axon)* v. *Secretary of State for Health (Family Planning Association Intervening)* [2006] EWHC 37 (Admin), [2006] QB 539, at para [62].
93. Ibid, at 561. See also May LJ in *R (B)* v. *Crown Court at Stafford* [2006] EWHC 1645 (Admin), [2007] 1 WLR 1524, at 1530.
94. Ibid, at 561–2.
95. The Guidance, at para. 46. This suggests that non-competent children who can make disclosure decisions should only have their confidentiality overridden on public interest, and not best interest, grounds, but see para. 51 which indicates that the Guidance may not recognise this category of child.
96. The Guidance, at para. 51.
97. In relation to the very young it has been argued that disclosures for the child's treatment do not breach the child's rights: see text to n. 69 above. Disclosures for other reasons must satisfy article 8(2).
98. *Re B (Adoption: Natural Parent)* [2001] UKHL 70, [2002]1 FLR 196, at 205.
99. This is how it was approached in *R (Axon)* v. *Secretary of State for Health (Family Planning Association Intervening)* [2006] EWHC 37 (Admin), [2006] QB 539, at 577–81.
100. He actually stated that the parental right to family life terminated when the child became *Gillick* competent: ibid, at 579–80. With respect, this cannot be right since even adult children and their parents can enjoy family life: *Moustaquim* v. *Belgium* (Application No 12313/86) (1991) 13 EHRR 802. For a more accurate explanation see *Re S (Adult Patient) (Inherent Jurisdiction: Family Life)* [2002] EWHC 2278 (Fam), [2003] 1 FLR 292, at 298 and for discussion see R. Taylor, 'Reversing the Retreat from *Gillick*? *R (Axon)* v. *Secretary of State for Health*)' [2007] CFLQ 81, at pp. 91–2; A. Hall, 'Children's Rights, Parents' Wishes and the State: the Medical Treatment of Children' [2006] *Fam Law* 36, at p. 321; G. Douglas, Case Report [2006] *Fam Law* 258.
101. [2006] EWHC 37 (Admin), [2006] QB 539, at 579–80, relying on *Gillick* v. *West Norfolk and Wisbech Area Health Authority and Department of Health and Social Security* [1986] AC 112, at 185.

102. *R (Axon)* v. *Secretary of State for Health (Family Planning Association Intervening)* [2006] EWHC 37 (Admin), [2006] QB 539, at 579–80. If the decisions of *Re R (A Minor) (Wardship: Consent to Medical Treatment)* [1992] Fam 11 and *Re W (A Minor) (Medical Treatment: Court's Jurisdiction)* [1993] Fam 64 have survived the Human Rights Act 1998, parents can consent to life-saving treatment for refusing competent children and, if so, a right to disclosure may exist in such circumstances.

103. *TP and KM* v. *United Kingdom* [2001] 2 FLR 549, at para [80].

104. *Re S (A Child) (Identification: Restrictions on Publication)* [2003] EWCA Civ 963, [2004] Fam 43, at 58–9 (Hale LJ); *Clayton* v. *Clayton* [2006] EWCA Civ 878, [2006] Fam 83, at 101, 117 and 124.

105. See *Re X (A Child) (Injunctions Restraining Publication)* [2001] 1 FCR 541, at 546.

106. For example, J. Herring, 'The Human Rights Act and the Welfare Principle in Family Law – Conflicting or Complementary?' [1999] *CFLQ* 223, at p. 231; Choudhry, S. and Fenwick, H. (2005) 'Taking the Rights of Parents and Children Seriously: Confronting the Welfare Principle under the Human Rights Act' *Oxford Journal of Legal Studies* **25**, 453.

107. *Yousef* v. *The Netherlands* (Application No 33711/96) [2003] 1 FLR 210, at para [73]; *Kearns* v. *France* (Application No 35991/04) [2008]1 FLR 888, at para [79].

108. *Johansen* v. *Norway* (Application No 17383/90) (1997) 23 EHRR 33, at [64]; *Elsholz* v. *Germany* (Application No 25735/94) (2002) 34 EHRR 58, at para [50]; *Hoppe* v. *Germany* (Application No 28422/95) [2003] 1 FLR 384, at para [49].

109. *Johansen* v. *Norway* (Application No 17383/90) (1997) 23 EHRR 33; *Elsholz* v. *Germany* (Application No 25735/94) (2002) 34 EHRR 58, at para [50].

110. *Re S (A Child) (Identification: Restrictions on Publication)* [2003] EWCA Civ 963, [2004] Fam 43, at 59 and [2004] UKHL 47, [2005]1 AC 593, at 609.

111. Fenwick, H. (2004) 'Clashing Rights, the Welfare of the Child and the Human Rights Act', *MLR*, **67**, 889, pp. 917 and 923–4.

112. For a similar approach in another context see J. Herring and R. Taylor, 'Relocating Relocation' [2006] *CFLQ* 517.

113. Fenwick, H. (2004) 'Clashing Rights, the Welfare of the Child and the Human Rights Act' *MLR*, **67**, 889, p. 924.

114. *Ashworth Hospital Authority* v. *MGN Ltd* [2002] UKHL 29, [2002] 1 WLR 2033, at 2051; *R (B)* v. *Crown Court at Stafford* [2006] EWHC 1645 (Admin), [2007]1 WLR 1524, at 1530.

115. *Gillick* v. *West Norfolk and Wisbech Area Health Authority and Department of Health and Social Security* [1986] AC 112, at 170 (Lord Fraser) 184 and 188–9 (Lord Scarman); *R (Axon)* v. *Secretary of State for Health (Family Planning Association intervening)* [2006] EWHC 37 (Admin), [2006] QB 539, at 579–80. The definition of child-centred parental right derives from McCall Smith, A. (1990) 'Is Anything Left of Parental Rights?' in Sunderland, E. and McCall Smith, A. (eds), *Family Rights: Family Law and Medical Advances*, Edinburgh University Press, 4, at p. 9.

116. (1989) 11 EHRR 175, at paras [61] and [69].

117. *R (Axon)* v. *Secretary of State for Health (Family Planning Intervening)* [2006] EWHC 37 (Admin), [2006] QB 539, at 578–9; R. Taylor, 'Reversing the Retreat from *Gillick*? *R (Axon)* v. *Secretary of State for Health*' [2007] *CFLQ* 81, at p. 89. See also A. Hall, 'Children's Rights, Parents' Wishes and the State: the Medical Treatment of Children' [2006] Fam Law 317, at p. 321.

118. (Application No 10929/84) (1989) 11 EHRR 175, at para [72].

119. Ibid, at para [69].

120. R. Taylor, 'Reversing the Retreat from *Gillick*? *R (Axon)* v. *Secretary of State for Health*' [2007] *CFLQ* 81, at p. 89; A. Hall, 'Children's Rights, Parents' Wishes and the State: the Medical Treatment of Children' [2006] Fam Law 317, at pp. 320–1; see also Silber J's comments in *R (Axon)* v. *Secretary of State for Health (Family Planning Association intervening)* [2006] EWHC 37 (Admin), [2006] QB 539, at 575.

121. (1998) 25 EHRR CD 150, at 159. The case involved a mother seeking to permit information about her daughter to be publicised in a documentary. See also *R (S)* v. *Plymouth City Council* [2002] EWCA Civ 388, [2002] 1 WLR 2583, at para [47] where Hale LJ found that the mother of an incompetent adult child had a right to disclosure of his confidential information because her article 8 right to respect for family life gave her a right to be involved in the decision-making process regarding her child. The decision was whether to displace her as nearest relative under the Mental Health Act 1983, a much more direct interference with family life than those discussed herein.

122. (1998) 25 EHRR CD 150, at 162.

123. The interests underpinning a parent-centred right to disclosure could be quite different, and much more weighty: see *TP and KM* v. *United Kingdom* [2001] 2 FLR 549, at para [80]–[81].

124. *Gillick* v. *West Norfolk and Wisbech Area Health Authority and Department of Health and Social Security* [1986] AC 112, at 170 (Lord Fraser), 184–5 and 188–9 (Lord Scarman); *R (Axon)* v. *Secretary of State for Health (Family Planning Association intervening)* [2006] EWHC 37 (Admin), [2006] QB 539, at 579–80.

125. [2004] EWHC 2085 (Fam), (unreported) 3 September 2004.

126. Ibid, at para [67]. There was the briefest of discussions about a mother's article 8 right to privacy where her medical information was at risk of disclosure, and none at all about the child's, although most of the information related to the child.

127. [2005] EWHC 1676 (Fam), [2006] 1 FLR 310.

128. Ibid, at 316.

129. Ibid.

130. *Re S (A Child) (Identification: Restrictions on Publication)* [2004] UKHL 47, [2005] 1 AC 593; *A Local Authority* v. *W, L, W, T and R (by the Children's Guardian)* [2005] EWHC 1564 (Fam), [2006] 1 FLR 1; *Re Webster; Norfolk County Council* v. *Webster* [2006] EWHC 2733 (Fam), [2007] 1 FLR 1146; *Re LM (Reporting Restrictions: Coroner's Inquest)* [2007] EWHC 1902 (Fam), [2008] 1 FLR 1360.

131. *Re S (A Child) (Identification: Restrictions on Publication)* [2004] UKHL 47, [2005] 1 AC 593, at 603; *A Local Authority* v. *W, L, W, T and R (by the Children's Guardian)* [2005] EWHC 1564 (Fam), [2006] 1 FLR 1, at 19; *Re LM (Reporting Restrictions: Coroner's Inquest)* [2007] EWHC 1902 (Fam), [2008] 1 FLR 1360, at para [32].

132. Thus the courts permitted disclosure in *Re S (A Child) (Identification: Restrictions on Publication)* [2004] UKHL 47, [2005] 1 AC 593 and *Re LM (Reporting Restrictions: Coroner's Inquest)* [2007] EWHC 1902 (Fam), [2008] 1 FLR 1360 despite evidence of the risk of real harm to very vulnerable children.

133. *A Local Authority* v. *W, L, W, T and R (by the Children's Guardian)* [2005] EWHC 1564 (Fam), [2006] 1 FLR 1, at 24; *Re Webster; Norfolk County Council* v. *Webster* [2006] EWHC 2733 (Fam), [2007] 1 FLR 1146, at para [113].

134. For example *Hoppe* v. *Germany* (Application No 28422/95) [2003]1 FLR 384, at para [50]–[51]. See also *Re C (Welfare of Child: Immunisation)* [2003] EWHC 1376 (Fam), [2003] 2 FLR 1054, at 1090 and 1093–4.

135. Daniels, D. and Jenkins, P. (2000) *Therapy with Children: Children's Rights, Confidentiality and the Law*, Sage Publishing, pp. 39–42.

136. *In Re C (A Minor) (Wardship: Medical Treatment) (No 2)* [1990] Fam 39, at 47–8.

137. *TP and KM* v. *United Kingdom* [2001] 2 FLR 549, at para [70]; *Elsholz* v. *Germany* (Application No 25735/94) (2002) 34 EHRR 58, at 48; *Hoppe* v. *Germany* (Application No 28422/95) [2003] 1 FLR 384, at paras [48]–[49]. This approach has been adopted domestically: see *Re T (Paternity: Ordering Blood Tests)* [2001] 2 FLR 1190.

138. *R (Axon)* v. *Secretary of State for Health (Family Planning Association intervening)* [2006] EWHC 37 (Admin), [2006] QB 539, at 582–3.

139. Alderson, P. and Montgomery, J. (1996) *Health Care Choices: Making Decisions with Children*, IPPR, p. 64.

140. Bartholomew, T. and Carvalho, T. (2007) 'Medical Practitioners' Competence and Confidentiality Decisions with a Minor: An Anorexia Nervosa Case Study', *Psychology, Health and Medicine*, **12**, 495, p. 506.

Chapter 11

Vulnerability, Autonomy, Capacity and Consent

ROBERT JOHNS

Introduction

This chapter addresses an issue which goes to the heart of ethical social work practice. It raises deep philosophical, legal and moral issues that are played out in decisions which social workers need to make when dealing with vulnerable people:

- What happens when people do not have the ability to make decisions for themselves, or else render themselves vulnerable because of the decisions they make?
- What guidance is there to determine who is defined as vulnerable?
- To what extent can people have autonomy and how can independence be encouraged while keeping people safe?
- What safeguards are there to ensure that people have their wishes respected? Specifically:
  - What happens when people apparently lose the ability to process information and weigh up factors necessary to making decisions for themselves?
  - Can their wishes be overridden?

These are not just academic philosophical questions. Every day, social workers in adult care services confront these issues, for there are a wide range of reasons as to why people may lose the full ability to make decisions for themselves, yet clearly it would be wrong to ride roughshod over people's rights to self-determination. Decisions about whether to agree to go into residential care, about whether to agree to certain forms of medical treatment, about whether to agree to sell one's home and move in with relatives, are all examples of major choices that confront adults, and where it is important to be sure that people understand all the implications of their decisions.

This chapter focuses on adults who might be at risk of harm or abuse. While the questions raised are relevant to work with children, childcare law is clearer in that generally, those with parental responsibility have the right to make decisions for children, and there are more precise rules about consultation with children and their inclusion in decision-making processes. Other chapters in this book set out what these processes are, outlining the case law that clarifies at what point children, as they grow up, can make decisions for themselves.

This chapter starts with some examples of the kinds of cases where social workers need to know what the law says about safeguarding adults, people's capacity to make decisions, and what to do when some people are unable to make decisions yet need to do so. The chapter then presents an overview of the development of law in this area, which starts with the issue of the legal definition of 'vulnerability'. This helps to identify which groups of people should come under the aegis of special laws concerning safeguarding adults. In some cases an adult who might be at risk or in a vulnerable situation might also be subject to specific laws concerning capacity and consent. There then follows a discussion about current law and guidance that seeks to promote the autonomy of the individual, debating the key legislation in this area in England and Wales, the Mental Capacity Act (MCA) 2005. The chapter incorporates key provisions of this Act into further discussion of the case studies, connecting these to core social work principles and concluding with a summary of legislation that authorises social workers and others to make decisions on behalf of people, sometimes despite their objections. Here reference is made to the key legal principle, that of working in the service user's 'best interests' where the service user lacks capacity to make the particular decision for him or herself.

Case studies

● *Case study 1*

Josie and Ben, both in their early 20s, have learning disabilities and since leaving school have attended Cedarwood Grove, a centre that specialises in providing day care and occupational therapy for people who have both learning and physical disabilities. They have announced their intention to live together, and expressed the desire to leave their respective parents' homes and are disappointed when staff at Cedarwood Grove tell them that they cannot help them, and in any case are not sure that this is a good idea.

● Case study 2

Joyce and Charles recently celebrated their 50th wedding anniversary, both being in their seventies. Charles has been diagnosed as having dementia and has periods when he becomes quite unable to remember who people are, but does have occasional periods when he is quite lucid. Their son, Edward, manages the couple's affairs for them, operating their bank account and dealing with all the bills, although Joyce has recently expressed concern about the small amount of money which Edward makes over to them on a weekly basis.

● Case study 3

Sylvia, aged 83, lives alone in her own house. Neighbours have reported several times that she is not looking after herself properly. Her house is in a very poor state of repair and inside there is evidence of uneaten, mouldy food everywhere. She herself is unkempt and dishevelled in appearance, looking emaciated. Her GP arranges for admission to a private residential care home, Windermere Lodge, but after a few days there Sylvia insists that she wants to go home.

Vulnerability

Before addressing these cases, there are some important preliminary questions that need to be posed. What do we mean when we say that someone is vulnerable? Vulnerable to what, when, in what circumstances? What makes someone vulnerable? Is it something inherent about a person that makes them vulnerable or the situation in which they find themselves? It is often assumed that the vulnerable should be protected but who are they and in what ways can vulnerable adults be protected? If people are protected from themselves, surely they then lose their autonomy? How important is independence and can its loss be justified by the greater good of protecting someone and therefore promoting their long-term interests?

These are important questions for social work practice and, of course, for the law – although they are not entirely legal questions. Each of the case examples demonstrates a different form of vulnerability, where there are ethical considerations intrinsically bound up within the legal framework and social work practice principles.

In the first case study, social work practitioners would almost certainly start from principles of empowerment and promoting autonomy, so in that sense they would encourage people to set up home together if that was their wish. When someone becomes an adult (at 18) the law says that people are generally free to choose how and where to live. In short, adults can do what they wish unless either the law says they cannot or their actions would impede other people's rights to autonomy. So what is the problem here? In essence, staff at Cedarwood Grove may be acting from a paternalistic approach of protecting service users because, for whatever reason, they do not believe that these two young adults should set up home together. Clearly the learning disability is driving thinking here, whereas if we start with the agreed principle that adults are entitled to autonomy, then the consideration is not whether these people should be 'allowed' to live together, but what actions workers can take to enable them to do so. In the course of this process workers might want to share with service users some of their reservations and concerns about the important step that they are taking, but there is no legal right to intervene in this process. There may be all sorts of practical considerations but that is another matter. So, where professionals start from the assumption that a person is vulnerable due to their disability, there may be a likelihood of benign, but overbearing use of professional power.

In the second case study, there is a possibility of financial abuse, although it may be that the son's motives are entirely honourable and the allowance carefully calculated. The lack of clarity of the situation hints at some potential vulnerability, not just to the couple themselves who may be at risk from an unscrupulous relative, but, conversely there is the vulnerability of well-meaning carers to unfounded accusations. This case raises the wider issue of addressing fluctuating capacity where someone has intermittent periods when they are unable to look after their own affairs.

In the third case study, Sylvia was vulnerable to self-neglect and as a consequence her life may have been imperilled, and would be again if she returned home. Yet principles of autonomy start with her unequivocal right to decide her own fate. Should this be overridden by compelling her to stay at Windermere Lodge?

In deciding how to respond to each of these case studies, it would clearly be a good starting point to have some kind of definition of vulnerability that would at least clarify to whom or in what circumstances special legislation might apply and in what circumstances people should be protected.

Legal developments

Previously the law has tended to emphasise the concept of a vulnerable adult, that is, a person whose condition or disability was thought to make them more vulnerable to abuse or neglect. Legal provision for the protection of so-called vulnerable adults has developed with roots in common law, tracing its origins back to an age where the monarch had absolute authority, adopting a patriarchal role of protecting vulnerable subjects, exercised through the courts and various other mechanisms. In some cases this led to abuse, where the monarch seized property that rightfully belonged to the child of wealthy deceased parents. *Parens patriae* is a Latin term meaning *parent of the country*. Thus the monarch, acting through the courts, could intervene in cases where parents were unwilling or unable to care for a child, or more generally where an adult needed protection for whatever reason. The concept still has validity: the High Court still deals with some children's cases under its inherent jurisdiction known as 'wardship' derived from *parens patriae* and has a long tradition of protecting the interests of vulnerable adults, although legal commentators regard the concept of *parens patriae* as now less directly relevant to adults who lack capacity due to the introduction of more comprehensive mental health and mental capacity legislation (Bartlett, 2007, p. 23).

Today, however, common law still apparently has a limited role to play. In the past the courts have specifically referred to the common-law doctrine of necessity in order to justify a number of decisions and this came to the fore in the case of *HL* v. *The United Kingdom* (2004) when the use of this doctrine was challenged. This case, usually referred to as the 'Bournewood' case, is worth some attention since it is one of the most important in this area, and one that has had a direct impact on legislation, in part expediting the progression of legislation relating to mental capacity. Under the Mental Health Act 1983, people who lacked capacity to consent, but did not actively resist admission to hospital or treatment, were 'informal' patients and so not subject to the same safeguards as patients detained under an order of that Act. Such 'informal' patients could be kept and treated in hospital, the courts in England and Wales decided, under the common-law doctrine of necessity *(R* v. *Bournewood Community and Mental Health NHS Trust, ex parte L* (1998)). However, the European Court ruled that keeping someone in hospital under common law was incompatible with the European Convention on Human Rights because it was too arbitrary and lacked sufficient safeguards. Hence a new statutory framework was introduced in the form of amendments via the Mental Capacity Act 2005, enabling adults who lack capacity to be deprived of their liberty only where this was deemed to be in their own 'best interests' (this is known as the deprivation of liberty safeguards). This issue is relevant to Case Study 3 discussed further below.

With the introduction of the Mental Capacity Act 2005, the common-law jurisdiction of the courts has been limited in relation to adults who lack capacity. Nevertheless, the High Court has on occasion extended its common law jurisdiction to include the protection of so-called vulnerable adults from abuse, where a person retains capacity to make decisions. One case is particularly worth noting: *Re SA (Vulnerable Adult with Capacity: Marriage)* (2006). SA had a combination of learning disabilities and hearing impairments with no oral communication but retained capacity to make the decisions in question. At the request of the local authority, the court had used its 'wardship' jurisdiction to prevent her from being taken to Pakistan by her parents in order to enter into an arranged, possibly forced, marriage. Once SA attained the age of 18, the local authority's role was diminished, but the fear of marriage without her full consent led to a reference back to the court which had to decide whether it had the authority to carry on preventing SA going to Pakistan. In essence the court decided that it did, claiming the right to decide cases if the court believed that a vulnerable adult who had capacity was prevented from making a decision with genuine consent because of constraint, coercion, or similar reason. Clearly this casts the net quite wide (Dunn et al., 2008), although the court in this case stressed that this was a rare situation and it would be rare that a court would intervene where an adult has capacity to make their own decisions. With judgments deriving from common law interpretations not being written down as part of statute law, the court's role is flexible, which can be both a strength and weakness. The chief merits are adaptability and responsiveness; the cost may be inconsistency and a paternalistic attitude to disabled people who retain capacity to make their own decisions.

Indeed the need for clarification of the law regarding vulnerability has long been recognised, although this became more urgent with the final decision of the European Court in the Bournewood case. Prior to this there had already been pressure from a number of quarters for a more systematic approach based on codified statute law. A number of reports pointed to the need for specific legislation addressing the issue of protection of vulnerable adults. The most important of these were produced by the Law Commission (Law Commission, 1995; Lord Chancellor's Department, 1997). In order to propose legislative reform, it was prudent to start with a definition of the range of people whom the new law should cover:

> A vulnerable adult is someone who is aged 18 years or over who is or may be in need of community care services by reasons of mental health or other disability, age or illness and who is or may be unable to take care of him or herself, or unable to protect him or herself against significant harm or exploitation. (Lord Chancellor, 1997)

This definition was adopted by the protective measures introduced in 2000 by *No Secrets* and *In Safe Hands* (Department of Health and Home Office, 2000; Welsh Assembly, 2000). These documents required local authorities to establish procedures to protect 'vulnerable adults' from physical, sexual, psychological, financial, or discriminatory abuse or neglect. However, in Scotland these procedures have been placed on a statutory footing with a different definition of vulnerability, which talks of 'adults at risk' defined as being 'unable to safeguard their own well-being, property, rights or other interests' and 'at risk of harm, and because they are affected by disability, mental disorder, illness or physical or mental infirmity, are more vulnerable to being harmed than adults who are not so affected' (s.3 (1) Adult Support and Protection (Scotland) Act 2007). There is as yet no specific relevant set of procedures or legislation in Northern Ireland, although an intention to legislate was declared in January 2009 (Northern Ireland Executive, 2009). The differences between the four nations raise some interesting questions for social work practitioners. Does it result in a patchwork of provision for service users and carers? Does it result in differential treatment? Why, for example, in England and Wales are adult protective provisions not on a par with child protection legislation and procedures as set out in the Children Acts of 1989 and 2004 – yet they are in Scotland? Are the differences cultural, political, economic or historical – simply relating to the different ways in which legal systems have developed in the constituent countries of the UK? These are all important topics for reflection and debate.

Mental capacity legislation

There appears to be some consensus concerning the principles upon which mental capacity legislation is founded, mental capacity meaning broadly the ability to make a specific decision for oneself, at the time it needs to be made. Such legislation reflects a specific understanding of autonomy, being generally interpreted to be enabling and empowering individuals to be protected from abuse but also as free as possible from the intrusion of others, whether they are relatives, friends, social workers, advocates or courts. Thus the legislation in Scotland asserts that an adult lacks legal capacity when unable to understand information, or make a decision or act on that information, or communicate or retain the memory of that decision 'by reason of mental disorder or of inability to communicate because of physical disability' (s.1 (6) Adults with Incapacity (Scotland) Act 2000).

The Mental Capacity Act 2005 s.2 (1), which applies to England and Wales, declares that someone lacks capacity if at the 'material time' that person is unable to make a decision because of an 'impairment of, or a disturbance in the functioning of, the mind or brain'. There are five associated principles which are enshrined in s.1 of that Act. These are:

(1) A person must be assumed to have capacity unless it is established that they lack capacity.
(2) A person is not to be treated as unable to make a decision unless all practicable steps to help them to do so have been taken without success.
(3) A person is not to be treated as unable to make a decision merely because they make an unwise decision.
(4) An act done, or decision made, under this Act for or on behalf of a person who lacks capacity must be done, or made, in their best interests.
(5) Before the act is done, or the decision is made, regard must be had to whether the purpose for which it is needed can be as effectively achieved in a way that is less restrictive of the person's rights and freedom of action.

So what does this mean in practice?

Returning to the case studies, there are a number of ways in which the law promotes good practice, meaning practice firmly founded on principles of respect for individuals, including anti-oppressive practice principles, empowerment and fostering well-being and autonomy, consistent with the fundamental belief that 'all persons have a right to well-being, to self-fulfilment and to as much control over their own lives as is consistent with the rights of others' (BASW, 2002).

● Applying mental capacity principles and legislation to Case Study 1: empowering, facilitating, and promoting autonomy

Josie and Ben wish to live together, but are being deterred by lack of support. This lack of support clearly runs contrary to the Mental Capacity Act 2005 principles, unless it can be established that either or both 'lack capacity' (Department for Constitutional Affairs, 2007).

For the purpose of establishing whether someone lacks capacity, the starting point is to determine whether there is 'an impairment of, or a disturbance in the functioning of the mind or brain' (s.2) which may of course be temporary. This will usually involve some kind of medical diagnosis, but note that learning disability of itself does not necessarily mean that someone lacks capacity in accordance with this definition. This is reinforced by the explicit anti-discrimination statutory requirement that lack of capacity cannot be established 'merely' by reference to age, appearance, or 'aspect of behaviour' which 'might lead others to make unjustified assumptions' about capacity (s.2 (3)). The fundamental point to note is that unless someone falls within this s.2 definition, they have an absolute unqualified right to do whatever any adult is legally able to do (subject to the normal rules that govern people's actions, such as the criminal law).

Furthermore, there are two other reasons why the actions of Cedarwood Grove staff in failing to support and encourage the couple may be unlawful. The first reason is that s.1 (3) Mental Capacity Act 2005 requires 'all practicable steps' to be taken to help someone make decisions and only when it is clear that they are unable to do so for reasons defined in s.2 (see above), can their wishes be overridden. The second reason concerns the justification for staff lack of action, specifically their belief that for the couple to live together would be inadvisable. This runs contrary to the s.1 principle which states that lack of capacity is not evidenced simply because someone makes 'an unwise decision' (s.1 (4)).

So in this case study, unless s.2 applies, Josie and Ben are entitled to support to attain their objective, even if others disapprove. Specifically they would be entitled to an assessment of need in accordance with s.47 of the National Health Service and Community Care Act 1990, and through that process they may potentially be eligible for the provision of services in their new home.

Applying mental capacity principles and legislation to Case Study 2: dealing with financial affairs

Joyce is concerned about the money which her son is 'allowing' but she could of course simply cancel this arrangement and revert to the previous arrangement whereby she and her husband managed their own affairs. The dementia is relevant only in so far as it may prevent Charles from managing his own affairs – note his, not the affairs of both of them – but, even so, again the principles insist that he should be enabled to do so to the extent that he can. Also worth noting in this case are the fourth and fifth principles in s.1 of the Mental Capacity Act 2005, namely that the son must, if he does indeed have the power to act on the couple's behalf, act always 'in their best interests' and ought to consider whether he needs to take over affairs to the extent that he has, or as the legislation puts it 'whether the purpose for which it is needed can be as effectively achieved in a way that is less restrictive of the person's rights and freedom of action' (ss.1 (5) and (6)). The concept of acting in someone's best interests is a legal concept and the MCA sets out a checklist of factors for decision makers to consider. Specifically, a social worker might ask why the son has to take over his mother's affairs as well as his father's, and would almost certainly want to encourage an open discussion about this. The assumption would be in this case that financial responsibility had been delegated that was tantamount to a 'power of attorney' arrangement. Such arrangements are common when specific circumstances arise, such as when someone works temporarily abroad and needs someone in the UK to manage their affairs for them. An informal or formal agreement may be drawn up to this end. There is, of course, legally nothing to stop anyone delegating whatever they wish to someone else by agreement as long as they have capacity to make that decision. However for such an arrangement to continue once someone lacks the capacity to make the decisions in question, as may be the case for Charles, the power of attorney needs to be formalised through a 'Lasting Power of Attorney'.

For a Lasting Power of Attorney to be valid, it must be drawn up in accordance with the stipulations of the Mental Capacity Act 2005 concerning prescribed format, witnessing and registration, with a major requirement being that at the point at which the document is filled in and signed, the person delegating (the donor) must have the capacity to do so. Hence the value of the Lasting Power of Attorney is that the donor anticipates that at some future time they may lose the capacity to manage their affairs, and wish the person acting on their behalf (the donee) to carry on doing so. It is therefore vitally important to nominate someone who is entirely trustworthy and, of course, likely to be around at that time.

Lasting Powers of Attorney are of two kinds: one concerns property and financial affairs, while the other relates to personal welfare matters. In this case, the first kind would clearly be of some value but so also might be the personal welfare power which would enable the attorney (donee) to make decisions about, for example, admission to residential care for Charles if this ever became necessary. There is no reason why the same person cannot have both kinds of Lasting Powers of Attorney, but they cannot deal with all affairs if they only have one kind of power. However, there are some decisions which the attorney cannot make: specifically, they cannot refuse treatment or make decisions about where the donor should live if the donor is subject to provisions of the Mental Health Act 1983 (ss.9–14 Mental Capacity Act 2005). Lasting Power of Attorneys are registered with, and supervised by, the Office of the Public Guardian, an administrative body with responsibilities for adults who have lost capacity (s.58 Mental Capacity Act 2005).

In addition to Lasting Power of Attorney, the Mental Capacity Act 2005 makes provision for Advance Decisions which are, in effect, advance refusals to accept a specified kind of treatment. Advance Decisions can be oral or in writing. Although potentially these can be wide-ranging and would allow someone to refuse any treatment they stipulate, there are in practice some limitations. All Advance Decisions must be made when a person has the capacity to do so, so in this case Charles would have to make such arrangements in one of his periods of lucidity. Any Advance Decision to refuse treatment in a life-threatening situation must be made in writing and witnessed. It must also be specific about the type of treatment being refused and the circumstances in which it applies. The Advance Decision emphatically cannot be used in order to introduce a treatment that would hasten the end of someone's life, but can be used to refuse treatments that might otherwise sustain life. It can be overridden by the provisions to impose treatment in Part 4 of the Mental Health Act 1983. Nor can an Advance Decision try to insist on certain kinds of treatment, or try to secure specific social care services that a person believes they may require in the future. The MCA does allow a person to make an advanced statement setting out their wishes and feelings about the treatment they would wish to receive in the event of future incapacity. However, unlike Advance Decisions, these are not binding but a decision maker must have regard to any such statement when making a best interests decision.

One crucial question remains: what if someone has already lost their 'capacity' so is not in a position to make their wishes known or to agree to a Lasting Power of Attorney? This is the point at which the Court of Protection may be directly involved. The Court was reconstituted by the Mental Capacity Act 2005 (s.45), being a court of the same standing as the High Court, able to conduct hearings, decide cases and set precedents. One of its functions is to make welfare or financial decisions on behalf of people who have lost capacity, acting in their best interests, which may include appointing 'deputies' to make day-to-day decisions on their behalf. All decisions and actions by the Court of Protection and its deputies must conform to the Mental Capacity Act 2005 principles, already outlined in this chapter, concerning capacity and empowerment. It is also worth noting that the Court of Protection has powers to arbitrate where there is a dispute, for example in the following situations:

- where there is an irreconcilable difference of opinion as to whether a person has capacity to make a particular decision for themselves (s.15);
- where there is a dispute about the validity of a Lasting Power of Attorney (ss.22–23);
- where there is a need to act when attorneys or deputies fail to carry out their duties (ss.16–19).

The Office of the Public Guardian implements the Court's decisions and has a number of additional related administrative responsibilities, including the oversight of Court of Protection Visitors who visit people who lack mental capacity when they are under the Court's jurisdiction and monitor the actions of deputies (s.58 Mental Capacity Act 2005).

However, it needs to be noted that fees are payable to the Public Guardian, the Court of Protection and any professional deputy mental capacity related responsibilities, and this may be a real obstacle to the empowerment of adults who lack capacity because most people who lack capacity will be unable to afford these protections.

Applying mental capacity principles and legislation to Case Study 3: protecting people unable to care for themselves, making decisions in people's 'best interests'

Such was the concern about Sylvia not looking after herself properly in a house in a poor state of repair, that admission to a private residential care home was arranged, but she now insists on going home.

Prior to admission, a number of pieces of legislation could have been considered if it were considered necessary to remove Sylvia either for her own health and safety or for the protection of others. In brief these are:

- Removal to hospital under Part 2 of the Mental Health Act 1983. This assumes that she would have been medically diagnosed as mentally disordered, as defined by s.1 of the Mental Health Act 2007, and that she did require admission to hospital as opposed to admission to care.
- Placed on a guardianship order under the Mental Health Act 1983. This would allow the guardian to specify where Sylvia must live and if she tried to leave the home she could be forcibly returned.
- Section 47 of the National Assistance Act 1948 through which a magistrate can order the removal of someone who is 'suffering from grave chronic disease or, being aged, infirm or physically incapacitated' and is 'living in insanitary conditions' and not receiving 'proper care and attention'. However, this power is seldom used and because there appear to be few safeguards it may contravene the European Convention on Human Rights (Law Commission, 2008, para. 4.301).
- In extreme 'life and limb' emergencies, there is a general police power that allows officers to enter and search premises: s.17 (1) Police and Criminal Evidence Act 1984. This may be appropriate where an adult is, for example, lying on the floor and in need of urgent medical attention.
- Section 135(1) of the Mental Health Act 1983 which is also an emergency power and allows a person to be removed to a place of safety for up to 72 hours for the purpose of an assessment under the Mental Health Act 1983.

- A best interests decision under the Mental Capacity Act 2005 assuming that Sylvia lacked capacity to make this decision and that her admission to the care home did not require a deprivation of liberty (unless this had been ordered by the Court of Protection).

Once Sylvia is a resident in a care home, it is legally possible for her to be kept there against her expressed wishes if she lacked capacity and this is deemed to be in her 'best interests' in accordance with the Deprivation of Liberty Safeguards provisions in the Mental Capacity Act 2005 as amended (ss.4A and 4B). These safeguards were introduced by the Mental Health Act 2007 (s.50) to meet the objections of the European Court in the Bournewood Case concerning the use of common-law necessity to detain vulnerable adults in their own interests (see above). They are quite precisely circumscribed, focusing on action solely to protect someone from harm, and being restricted to preventing people leaving hospital or a nursing or care home, albeit homes that are in the statutory, voluntary or private sector. The person who decides whether someone should be so deprived of their liberty, known as the Best Interests Assessor, is a professional with post-qualifying expertise in working with adult service users; many are social workers. A 'deprivation of liberty' is legally different to a restriction of liberty but the differences are hard to spot in practice and will depend on the circumstances of the case. For example, restrictions such as locking the front door of a care home at night is highly unlikely in itself to be seen as a deprivation of liberty but where this was accompanied by the person being adamant that they wished to return home to a situation that was inherently unsafe then this is more likely to be seen as a deprivation of liberty. The Deprivation of Liberty Code of Practice (Ministry of Justice, 2008) has a whole chapter dedicated to distinguishing deprivation of liberty from restrictions.

The Deprivation of Liberty Safeguards procedure has to be initiated by the managing authority, that is the organisation that runs the home or hospital, who requests the supervising authority, an NHS trust (health board in Wales) or local authority, to appoint a Best Interests Assessor to organise the assessments and determine whether someone should be deprived of their liberty. There are six assessment components, at least one of which must be carried out by a second assessor, as the following table makes clear:

Table 11.1 Deprivation of Liberty Safeguards assessment components

Assessment	Purpose – to decide whether:	Outcome	Who decides?
Age	the person is at least 18 years old	If legally an adult, may proceed	A Best Interests Assessor
No refusals	an authorisation to deprive someone of their liberty would conflict with an Advance Decision or a valid decision made by a donee or deputy	If it conflicts, cannot proceed	A Best Interests Assessor
Mental health	someone has a mental disorder as defined by the Mental Health Act 2007 (s.1)	If they do, may proceed, otherwise cannot proceed	An approved doctor who has experience of mental health and has undertaken Deprivation of Liberty Safeguards training
Mental capacity	someone lacks capacity, a decision which must accord with the requirements of the Mental Capacity Act 2005 (ss.1–3)	If they lack capacity, may proceed, otherwise they have absolute right to make own decisions	A doctor approved as a mental health assessor or a Best Interests Assessor
Eligibility	someone should really be subject to detention in hospital under Part 2 of the Mental Health Act 1983 rather than the Deprivation of Liberty Safeguards – or they are subject to a conflicting requirement such as guardianship.	If the powers under the Mental Health Act 1983 are not appropriate, may proceed. This provision is necessary to avoid duplication of legislation	A doctor approved under s.12 of the Mental Health Act 1983 or a Best Interests Assessor who is also an Approved Mental Health Professional (s.114 Mental Health Act 1983)
Best interests	deprivation of liberty is actually occurring; it is in the person's best interests to be deprived of their liberty; it is necessary to prevent harm to them (note: not to other people); it is a proportionate response to the likelihood of harm	Authorisation can only apply where there is deprivation of liberty, must be in the person's best interests, must prevent harm, and Best Interests Assessor must consider less restrictive approaches and advise accordingly	A Best Interests Assessor

On the basis of this assessment, the Best Interests Assessor will report to their supervisory body who issues the authorisation in accordance with their recommendations. The supervisory body cannot issue an authorisation unless it is recommended by the Best Interests Assessor and the length of the order cannot be longer than that recommended, with an absolute maximum of 12 months (Mental Capacity Act 2005, Schedule A1, regulation 42). The supervisory body must also appoint a representative, as advised by the Best Interests Assessor, who will have the duty to keep in contact with a person subject to deprivation, and to represent them in future decision making (Schedule A1 s.139). There is also provision for urgent deprivations of liberty to be issued by the managing authority alone but the same assessments must still be carried out (Schedule A1 Part 5).

Finally, this is an appropriate place to discuss the role of the Independent Mental Capacity Advocate, for it appears that Sylvia has no relatives. The Independent Mental Capacity Advocacy service was established by the Mental Capacity Act 2005 (ss.35–36) in order to promote the empowerment of people who lack capacity. It is a professional advocacy service, offered in each area usually through a service level agreement with local authorities, often organised through specialist independent voluntary organisations. There is a statutory duty laid on NHS bodies and local authorities to involve Independent Mental Capacity Advocates in certain kinds of decisions where service users have no family or friends. For example, an Independent Mental Capacity Advocate must be appointed where a person who lacks capacity (who has no other friends or relatives) is being moved or where someone has to make an important decision about such a person's medical treatment (ss.37–39). They can also be involved in case reviews and cases involving adult protection where their views must be taken into account (Mental Capacity Act 2005 (Independent Mental Capacity Advocates) (Expansion of Role) Regulations 2006). Critically, in this case there is a duty to appoint an advocate where the Supervisory Body realises that there is no representative available (s.39A Mental Capacity Act 2005). In addition the person who is being deprived of their liberty and their representative both have a statutory right of access to an Independent Mental Capacity Advocate (s.39D). Ultimately, either through the representative or through the Independent Mental Capacity Advocate, there is a right to appeal to the Court of Protection if someone believes that they have been wrongly deprived of their liberty.

Conclusion

This chapter outlined the legislative framework relating to mental capacity set within the paradox of promoting people's interests by occasionally taking decisions for them. The justification for this can in some cases be the protection of the adults who are at risk, a task shared by courts with social work, medical and legal practitioners. Legal safeguards insist on a concomitant duty to maximise autonomy, clarifying in this process what is meant by capacity and consent to decision making. The importance of the law in this area cannot be overstated and social work practitioners must become familiar with the key principles enshrined in the Mental Capacity Act 2005 and the *No Secrets/In Safe Hands* guidance. Fortunately the principles of the MCA are broadly consistent with core social work values as made explicit in the various professional Codes of Conduct and, equally fortuitously, they are all embodied in a single Act complemented by comprehensive Codes of Practice in England and Wales. For many years practitioners bemoaned the lack of codified legislation in the important area of mental capacity law but now have the benefit of one Act at least, which incorporates empowerment principles right from its first section. There will still be difficult questions for practitioners about how this legislation interfaces with other related laws such as the Mental Health Act 1983 and the *No Secrets/In Safe Hands* guidance.

References

Bartlett, P. (2007) *Blackstone's Guide to the Mental Capacity Act 2005* (2nd edn), Oxford, Oxford University Press.

BASW (British Association of Social Workers) (2002) *Code of Ethics*, Birmingham, Venture Press.

Department for Constitutional Affairs (2007) *Mental Capacity Act 2005, Code of Practice*, London, Stationery Office.

Department of Health and Home Office (2000) *No Secrets: Guidance on Developing and Implementing Multi-agency Policies and Procedures to Protect Vulnerable Adults from Abuse*, London, Stationery Office.

Dunn, M. C., Clare, I. C. H. and Holland, A. J. (2008) 'To empower or to protect? Constructing the "vulnerable adult" in English law and public policy' *Legal Studies*, **28**(2): 234–53.

Law Commission (1995) *Mental Incapacity: Law Commission Report 231*, London, HMSO.

Law Commission (2008) *Adult Social Care: A Scoping Report*, London, Law Commission.

Lord Chancellor's Department (1997) *Who Decides? Making Decisions on Behalf of 'Mentally Incapacitated' Adults*, London, The Stationery Office.

Ministry of Justice (2008) *Mental Capacity Act 2005: Deprivation of Liberty Safeguards*, Norwich, The Stationery Office.

Northern Ireland Executive (2009) *Legislative Framework for Mental Capacity and Mental Health Legislation In Northern Ireland: A Policy Consultation Document*, NI Department of Health, Social Services and Public Safety.

Welsh Assembly (2000) *In Safe Hands* Cardiff, Welsh Assembly Government.

Cases

HL v. The United Kingdom (2004) 40 EHRR 761.

R v. Bournewood Community and Mental Health NHS Trust, ex parte L (Secretary of State for Health and others intervening) [1998] 3 All ER 289.

Re SA (Vulnerable Adult With Capacity: Marriage) [2006] 1 FLR 867.

Chapter 12

Community Care and the Promotion of Independence

ALISON BRAMMER

Introduction

The concept of community care can be traced back to the introduction of the welfare state post second world war. It is now firmly embedded in practice and the law. This chapter will chart the history and development of contemporary community care policy leading up to the National Health Service and Community Care Act (NHSCCA) 1990 and beyond to the present day. Analysis of the central duty to assess for community care services is located in a discussion of entitlement to services. This is an area of social work practice where the financial constraints operating on local authorities have a very real impact on the experiences of service users. This has been acknowledged in decisions of the courts and in formal guidance and the operation of eligibility criteria. The success of community care is dependent on the availability and commitment of informal carers. Recognition of their contribution and rights to support is integral to care planning and any discussion of community care would be incomplete without consideration of their role. Since implementation of the NHSCCA in 1990 it is possible to detect a growing emphasis on service users' and carers' rights, choice and the promotion of independent living. This is clearly evident in the introduction of direct payments and the personalisation agenda.[1] The law relating to adult social care is complex and can be confusing. It is necessary to navigate through a range of statutes, guidance and case law from 1948 onwards. This area of law is currently under consideration by the Law Commission. In its Scoping Study it notes:

> Adult social care is in urgent need of reform. It remains a complex and confusing patchwork of conflicting statutes enacted over a period of 60 years. The law is also based on outdated and often discriminatory concepts and gives rise to human rights concerns. A number of significant costs are incurred as a direct result of the complexity of

this area of law. Finally, there are concerns about how the law negotiates the tension between local and central planning and decision making. In short it is in need of reform. The overall aim of the project is to provide a clearer and more cohesive framework for adult social care. This would help to ensure that service users, carers, social care staff, health professionals and lawyers are clear about rights to services and which services are available. It will also aim to modernise the law to ensure that it is no longer based on out-dated principles. (Law Commission, 2008)

The prospect of comprehensive reform of the law relating to adult social care is promising, although it may be some years before any recommendations for reform translate into new law and practice. In the meantime social work professionals working in this field need a commitment to anti-discriminatory practice and respect for service users' and carers' rights and wishes when engaging with the law relating to community care. As with most areas of social work practice, community care is not discrete and self-contained. It necessarily links to other areas of law and practice. Recent developments in the law such as the introduction of the Mental Capacity Act 2005, the Mental Health Act 2007 and greater awareness of the risk of abuse to adults who may be in receipt of community care services are highly relevant to practice. It is also important to note that a wide range of adults may benefit from community care services including older people, those with physical or learning disabilities or mental health problems, or a combination of these. The term ' vulnerable adult' is sometimes used collectively to describe people who may benefit from services, although there are some concerns that this term locates problems with the individual rather than the way society perceives them. Furthermore, individuals who may be entitled to assessment for community care services may engage with the law and social work interventions in other ways, for example where there are concerns about care of a child whose parents have learning disabilities the social worker must recognise the duty to assess the parents in addition to what services can be provided for the child (*Re L (Care: Threshold Criteria)* [2007]).

Development of contemporary community care policy

In 1986 the Audit Commission reported increasing demand for community care services and noted the under-provision of actual services (Audit Commission, 1986). Subsequently in 1988 the Griffiths Report, *Community Care: Agenda for Action*, (Griffiths, 1988) laid the foundations for the National Health Service and Community Care Act 1990. It identified multiple responsibility for community care across local and central government, the National Health Service and the voluntary and private sectors and recommended a significant change in practice for social services departments. The role envisaged for local authorities was as lead coordinating agency for community care services through arranging and purchasing services in a mixed economy of care. Provision of services would not be restricted to local authorities; rather provision by the public, private and voluntary sector would increase the range of services available and introduce a real element of choice for service users. In practice local authorities supported the expansion of the private sector as much of their budgets, following the introduction of the Act, had to be spent through commissioning external services (Postle, 2002). The White Paper, *Caring for People: Community Care in the Next Decade and Beyond* (DH, 1989), developed these themes further. It commences with a definition of community care:

> Community care means providing the services and support which people who are affected by problems of ageing, mental illness, mental handicap or physical or sensory disability need to be able to live as independently as possible in their own homes, or in 'homely' settings in the community. (DH, 1989, para. 1.1)

The White Paper included six key objectives for the delivery of community care which remain valid:

- to promote development of domiciliary, day and respite services to enable people to live in their own homes;
- to ensure service providers make practical support for carers a high priority;
- to make proper assessment of need and good care management the cornerstone of high quality care;
- to promote the development of a flourishing independent sector alongside quality public services;
- to clarify the responsibilities of agencies and hold them to account for their performance;
- to secure better value for taxpayers' money by introducing a new funding structure for social care. (DH, 1989, para. 1.11)

In recent years a policy shift can be detected in relation to future provision of community care: this is driven by two key factors. First, recognition of increasing demands placed on the system partly as a result of changing demographics and a consequential shortfall in delivery. Second, the disability movement has argued that people with disabilities have been socially excluded and campaigned for greater recognition of rights to independence and choice.

A change of emphasis to government policy is evident in (among others) the Green Paper, *Independence, Well-being and Choice* (DH, 2005), the White Paper, *Our Health, Our Care, Our Say* (DH, 2006) *Putting People First* (DH, 2007), and a further Green Paper, *The Case for Change: Why England Needs a New Care and Support System* (2008a). The latter recognised, 'a radical rethink of how we deliver and pay for care and support services is needed if England is to have a care and support system that is fit for the 21st century'.

National Health Service and Community Care Act 1990

The legal framework for community care is provided by the National Health Service and Community Care Act 1990. It defines community care services as those services which a local authority may provide or arrange to be provided under pre-existing legislation, namely: Part III National Assistance Act 1948; s.45 of the Health Services and Public Health Act 1968; s.21 and Schedule 8 of the National Health Service Act 1977; and s.117 of the Mental Health Act 1983 (s.46). The 1990 Act did not provide for any new services, rather it provided links to a new route for assessment to services authorised under a variety of other legislation.

The term 'community care' is sometimes used to distinguish services provided to enable people to live independently in their own homes, rather than in residential care. In fact the inclusion of Part III of the National Assistance Act 1948 in the above section means that residential accommodation is properly seen as an aspect of community care provision. It would be within the philosophy of the Act however to expect the emphasis of assessment to focus on provision to support individuals to remain in their own homes with residential accommodation as an option when care needs increase.

If the person being assessed is disabled then services listed in the Chronically Sick and Disabled Persons Act 1970 (CSDPA) are also relevant. The CSDPA authorises the provision of a wide range of services including social work support and advice, recreational facilities, practical assistance, meals and adaptations (among others). A person will be considered to have a disability if they meet the definition in s.29 National Assistance Act 1948, as:

> Blind, deaf or dumb or substantially and permanently handicapped by illness, injury, or congenital deformity or such other disabilities as may be prescribed by the Minister.

The 1948 Act was one of the key pieces of legislation introduced following the Beveridge Report of 1942 which provided the foundations of the welfare state. Much community care law and practice still emanates from that legislation. It is unfortunate that the opportunity to reframe the definition of disability in language which is less discriminatory and oppressive, was not taken when the 1990 Act was drafted.

Assessment

In addition to the definition of community care services, above, the 1990 Act also includes a duty to provide information about services. Perhaps the most important section however is s.47, the duty to assess needs for community care services. Any provision of services must be based on a full and proper assessment (excepting some emergencies). Section 47 provides:

> Where it appears to a local authority that any person for whom they may provide or arrange for the provision of community care services may be in need of any such services, the authority –
> (a) shall carry out an assessment of his needs for those services; and
> (b) having regard to the results of that assessment, shall then decide whether his needs call for the provision by them of any such services. (NHSCCA 1990, s.47)

The requirement to assess is a mandatory duty in relation to a potentially great number of individuals as encompassed in the term 'for whom they may provide'. As the section refers to assessment by the local authority of a person who 'it appears' may require services, there is no need for a request for assessment to be made by the individual. In many instances, the appearance of need may present itself – through referrals by other concerned individuals or by other professional involvement, for example GPs or housing departments. Following assessment there is discretion as to service provision.

Good assessment skills are fundamental in community care and this includes a commitment to carrying out assessment in a non-discriminatory manner. Obviously a matter of good social work practice, it is also required by law. The Race Relations (Amendment) Act 2000 provides: 'It is unlawful for a public authority in carrying out any functions of the authority to do any act which constitutes discrimination.' In addition the Act places a duty on public authorities to promote equality of opportunity and good relations between people of different racial groups. Taken together this means that local authorities must deliver their full range of services, including assessment and provision of support, in a way which is free from discrimination, and must also proactively take steps to prevent discrimination in their area. The duty extends to the provision of culturally sensitive and appropriate services for minority ethnic groups, for example specific dietary needs. It may extend to the employment of staff who reflect the service user's culture and ethnicity, as found by Rai-Atkins et al. (2002) in relation to advocacy services. A similar disability equality duty is introduced by the Disability Discrimination Act 2005.

As local authorities are included as public authorities under the Human Rights Act 1998 it is clear that the processes of assessment and provision of services must be carried out in a way that is compatible with the rights contained in the European Convention on Human Rights. Article 8, the right to respect for private and family life, may be engaged in this process. In *A* v. *East Sussex County Council* (2003) which centred on a dispute about manual handling for two severely disabled sisters, the court commented on the application of art.8 to disabled people:

> The other important concept embraced in the 'physical and psychological integrity' protected by art.8 is the right of the disabled to participate in the life of the community and to have what has been described as 'access to essential economic and social activities and to an appropriate range of recreational and cultural activities'.

This is matched by the positive obligation of the State to take appropriate measures designed to ensure to the greatest extent feasible that a disabled person is not 'so circumscribed and so isolated as to be deprived of the possibility of developing his personality'. The statement clearly illustrates the application of human rights principles to community care practice. A further decision, *R (Bernard)* v. *Enfield LBC* (2003), found that in extreme cases individual human rights may be violated by failure to provide adequate community care services. The need to act compatibly with Convention rights is thus a further driver of good social work practice in this and other areas.

In relation to older people, the Community Care Assessment Directions 2004 have confirmed that there should be a 'single assessment' in which local authorities must consult the person to be assessed, take all reasonable steps to reach agreement with the person and, where appropriate, any carers of that person on the community care services which they are considering providing to meet his needs. The single assessment process was initially introduced in the *National Service Frameworks for Older People* (DH, 2001a) to cut across the health and social care divide and avoid unnecessary duplication of assessments.

Any person who is assessed as in need of services should be provided with a care plan which is reviewed regularly. This important document should include: a record of eligible need and risks; preferences in actual provision; emergency contingency plans; details of the services to be provided; details of direct payments if to be made; contributions of carers; and a schedule for reviews. An individual's preference must be taken into account when determining the type of services to be provided, but it will not be determinative. In R v. *Lancashire County Council, ex parte Ingham* (1995), the court upheld the local authority's decision to provide for an assessed need for 24-hour care in a nursing home rather than in the elderly woman's own home. In practice, local authorities often set a financial 'ceiling' as the maximum amount of care that they will provide to an individual at home. Provided that the alternative way of providing care (usually in a care home) will meet the individual's need, and the decision has been taken following an individual assessment, this is lawful practice even if it doesn't meet the individual's expressed preference.

Financial constraints

Local authorities clearly have to operate within financial constraints and do not have endless funds for community care support or any other functions. Inevitably this leads to rationing of services to those considered to be in greatest need. Any such rationing has to operate fairly. The inherent tension where there is a high level of need and limited resources has been considered by the courts and R v. *Gloucestershire County Council, ex parte Barry* (1997) remains the leading decision in this area. This case confirms that resources could be a relevant factor for councils to take into account when assessing need for all community care services. The case came to court as a judicial review application in 1995, when Gloucestershire County Council, facing funding cuts of £2.5 million, withdrew or cut provision of home care services to 1,500 service users and changed its eligibility criteria. Mr Barry challenged the decision of the authority to withdraw services provided to him under s.2 of the Chronically Sick and Disabled Persons Act 1970 (for assistance with laundry and cleaning), on the basis that, although the authority's funding position might have changed, his needs had not. In the House of Lords' judgment there was recognition of the difficulties faced by local authorities in managing resources to fulfil duties in the complex area of community care. The court held, by a majority, that resources might be taken into account when assessing or reassessing whether an individual is in need of services. The concept of need has to be considered in the context of other relevant factors, including an authority's own resources. Since the *Gloucestershire* decision, it is clear that local authorities are justified in using eligibility criteria as a means of rationing resources. Eligibility criteria must be satisfied by an individual before his needs will be met. Local authorities would not be justified, however, in failing to provide services to an individual with an established need simply because the end of a financial year is looming and resources have run out. Eligibility criteria have to be set so as to anticipate such situations and operate to identify what levels of need will attract services. Eligibility criteria may be reset periodically and resources taken into account when setting new criteria. Any person receiving services under the old criteria would need to be reassessed before any reduction in services.

Since the *Gloucestershire* decision guidance on assessment and eligibility criteria was published by the Department of Health entitled *Fair Access to Care Services?* (DH, 2003b). The objective behind the guidance was to lead to fairer and more consistent eligibility decisions across the country, in response to concerns that a 'postcode lottery' operated in relation to service allocation. The guidance is issued under s.7 (1) of the Local Authority Social Services Act 1970. In consequence, following the decision *R v. London Borough of Islington ex parte Rixon* (1998), councils risk breaching the law if (in the absence of a good reason) they depart from the guidance. Mr Justice Sedley ruled, '… a failure to comply with the statutory policy guidance is unlawful and can be corrected by means of judicial review.'

The guidance identifies four eligibility bands – critical, substantial, moderate and low – which relate to individuals' needs and risks to independence. The bands should include consideration of immediate needs as presented and also longer term risks including needs which are likely to worsen without help, as identified through risk assessments. The guidance emphasises that councils should operate only one set of criteria based on the eligibility bands outlined. Separate criteria relating, for example, to the depth and type of assessment and for specific services should be abolished. The guidance draws a distinction between presenting needs, as those issues that are identified when social care support is sought, and eligible needs as those needs that fall within the council's eligibility criteria. Presenting needs which do not fit into eligibility criteria have been known as 'unmet needs', a term which is implicitly discouraged by the new guidance.

In practice a threshold operates in most authorities so that those with presenting needs falling into the critical or substantial risk to independence bands will be eligible for services whereas those whose needs present a moderate or low risk to independence will not. This practice has been confirmed in a CSCI report in 2009 (CSCI, 2009) which found that 62% of councils in England operated only at the highest bands of 'critical' and 'substantial'. Three councils only provided support to individuals whose needs fell in the critical band. A High Court judgment has confirmed that it is lawful only to fund services to meet 'critical needs' (*R (on the application of Chavda)* v. *Harrow London Borough Council* (2007)). This emphasis on high level risk is difficult to reconcile with the original aims of community care policy founded in prevention and support.

Direct payments

As an alternative to direct provision of services, direct payments may be made in certain circumstances so that individuals can purchase their own non-residential services including equipment (Community Care (Direct Payments) Act 1996). Government policy is clearly to make direct payments available to as many eligible people as possible in order to 'give recipients control over their own life by providing an alternative to social services provided by a local council' (DH, 2003a). A possible disadvantage of direct payments may be greater susceptibility to abuse and lesser regulation of certain services. Payments are made to people assessed as needing services and who appear capable of managing a direct payment themselves or with assistance and are often used by the individual to employ a personal assistant. The service to be purchased must meet the assessed need and the individual must consent to receipt of a direct payment. Rate of payment must be 'equivalent to the reasonable cost of securing the provision of the service concerned' (Health and Social Care Act 2001, (s.57)).

Availability of direct payments was extended to carers entitled to services under carer support legislation. The Health and Social Care Act 2008 further extends availability of direct payments. Due to the requirements for the individual to consent to the payment and be able to manage payments, some individuals who lacked capacity in this respect were excluded. This effectively limited the availability of direct payments to some people with learning disabilities. The 2008 Act allows payment to be made to a 'suitable person' who can receive and manage the payment on behalf of the adult lacking capacity and is consistent with the philosophy of promoting independence and empowerment contained in the Mental Capacity Act 2005.

Direct payments can provide greater control to the individual. Full use of direct payments and their extension to people with learning disabilities was one of the key objectives of *Valuing People: A New Strategy for Learning Disability for the 21st Century* (DH, 2001b), which included four key principles: rights, independence, choice and inclusion. This document has had a major influence on subsequent social care policy, in particular the move towards use of individual budgets and personalisation which have further developed this philosophy.

Regulations in 2003 turned the previous local authority discretion to provide direct payments into a duty to make direct payments to an individual who is assessed as eligible for community care support where that person consents to direct payments as a means of providing that support. Despite the existence of this duty and further government encouragement of the use of direct payments, take-up of this option has been disappointing (Unity Sale and Leason, 2004). Further research discovered a number of barriers to the use of direct payments, including problems with guidance, policy and procedures, professional attitudes, lack of suitable information, assumptions about consent and lack of support which meant that some people with learning disabilities were improperly considered ineligible. As with so many areas of social care the provision of accessible information is vital. Individuals who are not aware of particular services or support are unlikely to be able to take advantage of it or to make informed choices.

Who cares?

The majority of community care support and care is provided by 'informal' carers, the greater proportion of whom are female (Parker, 1990). Informal carers may be family members, friends and neighbours and may be contrasted with formal, paid carers. Adult children frequently become carers of their parents in later life, although it should be noted that in contrast to parents of children under 16, adult children are under no legal obligation to care for their parents (Herring, 2008). A significant number of young carers also provide care, sometimes missing school and other opportunities as a result. Undoubtedly community care as we know it would collapse without the contribution of informal carers. In the 2001 census, some 5.2 million people described themselves as carers of family members, friends or neighbours because of long-term physical or mental ill health, disability or old age.

The cost benefit to the economy of this body of volunteers is huge, estimated at a value of £87 billion annually. There are also benefits to the carer in terms of making a positive contribution to the care of an individual they value. The costs to individual carers, however, should not be underestimated. Caring can impact on the carers' physical and mental health, relationships, employment opportunities and financial position. Carers may themselves have entitlement to community care support for their needs, but may also require support to carry out their caring role. Support for carers was a clear objective of community care policy but it has taken three separate pieces of carer legislation to establish carers' rights to support.

The Carers (Recognition and Services) Act 1995 established the right of carers to request an assessment of their ability to provide and continue to provide care for the person being assessed for community care services. Application extended to people who were providing or intended to provide a substantial amount of care on a regular basis. The limitations of this legislation were that the carer had to request an assessment (and had to know they could make such a request) and could only do so if the person they cared for was being assessed. Carers' needs and wishes are not always synonymous with those of the person they care for. There may be situations where a carer desperately needed help but the person they cared for refused any assessment. Under this Act such a carer could not have requested an assessment. A further practical limitation was that no additional funding was allocated for assessments or services.

Five years later the Carers and Disabled Children Act 2000 extended the earlier legislation by giving carers (providing regular and substantial care) the right to an assessment (on request) whether or not the cared-for person is being assessed (even where the cared for person has refused any assessment). There is an absolute duty to assess but not directly to provide services. The carer's ability to care is assessed and the local authority must consider the assessment, then decide whether the carer has needs in relation to the care provided; whether the local authority could meet those needs; and if so, whether services should be provided. As with other assessments, resources will be relevant. Guidance suggested that 'Practitioners carrying out carer assessments are encouraged to consider flexible and innovative use of services which would help minimise the impact of the caring role on the carer's own life.'

Finally in 2004 the Carers (Equal Opportunities) Act 2004 amended the earlier legislation so that the local authority, when carrying out an assessment of a person's needs for community care, is now obliged to proactively inform the carer of his right to an assessment. The scope of assessment is also addressed. Assessments must include consideration of whether the carer works or wishes to work, is undertaking, or wishes to undertake, education, training or any leisure activity, and these matters should be built into the care plan. This piecemeal development of the law goes some way towards recognising rights for carers but it is arguable that the cost of caring is still very high and the role is insufficiently valued in society.

The future – personalisation

The government is committed to reform of many public services and the way they are delivered, including community care. In the field of community care this reform is often referred to as the 'personalisation agenda' but the terms 'person-centred planning' and 'self-directed support' are also used. The government's vision is articulated in *Putting People First: A Shared Vision and Commitment to the Transformation of Adult Social Care* (DH, 2007). It includes greater emphasis on self-assessment, and flexible personal budgets often in the form of direct payments. The approach is explained further in guidance (DH, 2008b):

> The direction is clear: to make personalisation, including a strategic shift towards early intervention, the cornerstone of public services. In social care, this means every person across the spectrum of need, having choice and control over the shape of his or her support, in the most appropriate setting. For some, exercising choice and control will require a significant level of assistance either through professionals or through independent advocates.

Conclusion

It is evident that community as an area of practice has been dominated by debate around resources and rights. Case law and guidance have attempted to introduce clarity, transparency and fairness into resource allocation through the use of eligibility criteria. Regrettably, adoption of the criteria has not produced consistency across councils and in many areas eligibility for community care services is restricted to individuals at risk. The system has depended on the voluntary contribution of carers whose rights have been recognised incrementally through legislation. The key legislation, the National Health Service and Community Care Act 1990, through just a few sections, signalled a change in direction for local authorities, as assessors and coordinators rather than direct providers of services. The legislation failed to fully reform the law however and practitioners must wade through a mass of statutes to fulfil their role in relation to adult service users.

From this somewhat negative picture a shift in government policy can be detected which is philosophically grounded in a commitment to rights and the independence of those who may require community care services. This shift can be traced in part to *Valuing People* and is evident in the personalisation agenda. Community care practice appears to be in transition and it is a challenging time to work in this field. Over the next few years the transformation in adult social care as envisaged by *Putting People First* will need to become embedded. The drive for this transformation is expressed in a 2009 circular:

> People have higher expectations of what they need to meet their own particular circumstances, wanting greater control over their lives and the risks they take. They want dignity and respect to be at the heart of any interaction, so that they can access high-quality services and support closer to home at the right time, enabling them and their supporters to maintain or improve their well-being and independence rather than relying on intervention at the point of crisis. Social care cannot meet these challenges without radical change in how services are delivered. (DH, 2009)

At the same time the Law Commission is to make recommendations which would provide a clearer and more coherent legal framework for adult social care, with an emphasis on simplification, consistency, transparency and modernisation. Assessment, eligibility and actual provision of services are areas which will be addressed in the review. A single consolidated statute to replace the current mass of legislation may provide the legal clarification to support the emerging policy objectives.

References

Audit Commission (1986) *Making a Reality of Community Care*, London, HMSO.

CSCI (Commission for Social Care Inspection) (2009) *The State of Social Care in England 2007–08*, London, CSCI.

DH (Department of Health) (1989) *Caring for People: Community Care in the Next Decade and Beyond*, London, HMSO.

DH (Department of Health) (2001a) *National Service Frameworks for Older People*, London, HMSO.

DH (Department of Health) (2001b) *Valuing People: A New Strategy for Learning Disability for the 21st Century* (White Paper), London, HMSO.

DH (Department of Health) (2003a) *Direct Payments Guidance: Community Care, Services for Carers and Children's Services (Direct Payments)*, London, HMSO.

DH (Department of Health) (2003b) *Fair Access to Care Services?*, (FACS) (LAC (2003)12), London, HMSO.

DH (Department of Health) (2005) *Independence, Well-being and Choice: Our Vision for the Future of Social Care for Adults in England*, London, HMSO.

DH (Department of Health) (2006) *Our Health, Our Care, Our Say* (White Paper), London, HMSO.

DH (Department of Health) (2007) *Putting People First: A Shared Vision and Commitment to the Transformation of Adult Social Care* (White Paper), London, HMSO.

DH (Department of Health) (2008a) *The Case for Change – Why England Needs a New Care and Support System* (Green Paper), London, HMSO.

DH (Department of Health) (2008b) *Transforming Adult Social Care* (LAC (DH)(2008)1), London, HMSO.

DH (Department of Health) (2009) *Transforming Adult Social Care* (LAC (DH) (2009)1), London, HMSO.

Griffiths, R. (1988) *Community Care: Agenda for Action*, London, HMSO.

Herring, J. (2008) 'Together forever? The rights and responsibilities of adult children and their parents', in Bridgeman, J., Keating, H. and Lind, C. (eds) (2008) *Responsibility, Law and the Family*, Farnham, Ashgate.

Law Commission (2008) *Adult Social Care: A Scoping Report*, London, HMSO.

Parker, G. (1990) *With Due Care and Attention: A Review of Research on Informal Care* (2nd edn), London, Family Policy Studies Centre.

Postle, K. (2002) '"Working between the idea and the reality": Ambiguities and tensions in care managers' work' *British Journal of Social Work*, 32(3): 335–51.

Rai-Atkins, A., Ali Jama, A., Wright, N. et al. (2002) *Best Practice in Mental Health: Advocacy for African, Caribbean and South Asian Communities*, Bristol, The Policy Press and Joseph Rowntree Foundation.

Unity Sale, A. and Leason, K. (2004) 'Is help easily at hand?' *Community Care*, 6 May, pp. 28–31.

Cases

A v. *East Sussex County Council* [2003] EWHC 167 (Admin).

R (Bernard) v. *Enfield LBC* [2003] EWHC 2282 (Admin).

Re L (Care: Threshold Criteria) [2007] 1 FLR 205.

R (on the application of Chavda) v. *Harrow London Borough Council* [2007] All ER (D) 337.

R v. *Gloucestershire County Council, ex parte Barry* [1997] 2 All ER 1.

R v. *Lancashire County Council, ex parte Ingham* (1995) 5 July QBD: CO/774.

R v. *London Borough of Islington ex parte Rixon* [1998] 1 CCLR 119.

Note

1. The personalisation agenda seeks to empower service users and their carers by placing the choice with them as to which services to contract. However, this may lead to a 'hands off' approach to the delivery of services, with less local authority involvement and, potentially, the risk of abuse of vulnerable adults

Index

Printed and bound by CPI Group (UK) Ltd, Croydon, CR0 4YY